D0068783

GERMS & SEEDS ANIMALS

Kevin Reilly, Series Editor

THE ALCHEMY OF HAPPINESS
Abu Hamid Muhammad al-Ghazzali
translated by Claud Field
Revised and annotated by Elton L. Daniel

LIFELINES FROM OUR PAST
A New World History
L. S. Stavrianos

NATIVE AMERICANS BEFORE 1492
The Moundbuilding Centers of the Eastern Woodlands
Lynda Norene Shaffer

BALKAN WORLDS
The First and Last Europe
Traian Stoianovich

Sources
and
Studies
in World
History

Alfred W. Crosby
GERMS &
SEEDS
ANIMALS
Studies in
Ecological History

M.E. Sharpe
Armonk, New York
London, England

Earlier versions of the following chapters in this work appeared in other publications and are included here with permission: Chapter 4 was first published in Kendall E. Bailes (ed.), *Environmental History*, 553–576 (Lanham, MD: University Press of America, 1985); Chapter 5 was first published in the *Journal of World History* (2: 2, 119–133); Chapter 8 was first published in Terence Ranger and Paul Slack (eds.), *Epidemics and Ideas: Essays on the Historical Perception of Pestilence*, 175–201 (New York: Cambridge University Press, 1992); Chapter 10 was first published by the Cabrillo Historical Association, San Diego (January 1993); Chapter 11 was first published in the *American Quarterly* (41: December 1989, 661–669); Chapter 12 was first published in Ben Finney and Eric Jones (eds.), *Interstellar Migration and the Human Experience*, 210–219 (University of California Press, copyright (c) 1985 the Regents of the University of California).

An earlier version of Chapter 1 appeared in an American Historical Association essay (1987); of Chapter 2 in *Texas Quarterly* (XXI, Spring 1978); of Chapter 3 in Herman J. Viola and Carolyn Margolis (eds.), *Seeds of Change: A Quincentennial Commemoration* (Washington, DC: Smithsonian Institution Press, 1991); of Chapter 6 in *William and Mary Quarterly* (XXXIII, April 1976); of Chapter 7 in *American Heritage* (29:6, October/November 1978); of Chapter 9 in *Revue Francaise d'Etudes Americaines* (No. 48–49: April–July 1991.).

Library of Congress Cataloging-in-Publication Data

Crosby, Alfred W.
Germs, seeds, and animals : studies in ecological history / Alfred W. Crosby.
p. cm. — (Sources and studies in world history)
Includes bibliographical references and index.
ISBN 1–56324–249–4 (C). — ISBN 1–56324–250–8 (P)
1. Human ecology—History. 2. Epidemics—History. 3. Europeans—Migrations. 4. Imperialism—History. 5. Human geography. 6. Biogeography.
I. Title. II. Series.
GF50.C77 1993
304.2—dc20 93–19629
CIP

| BM (c) | 10 | 9 | 8 | 7 | 6 | 5 | 4 | 3 | 2 | 1 |
| BM (p) | 10 | 9 | 8 | 7 | 6 | 5 | 4 | 3 | 2 | 1 |

CONTENTS

FOREWORD

World history and ecological history are both ancient subjects that are undergoing a modern renaissance. We may date world history from the cross-cultural concerns of Herodotus and ecological history from Thucycdides' detailed account of the plague at Athens. But both types of history were supplanted by theological and philosophical modes of discourse in subsequent centuries. By the first half of the twentieth century, world history was virtually synonymous with philosophical speculation, and ecological history barely existed at all. Only recently have they reemerged, both as empirical and scientific studies, in the age of social science and microbiology.

That the two should regain a mission and a following in recent decades is a testament to the historical imagination as much as to the power of science. Alfred Crosby almost alone redirected the attention of historians to ecological issues that were important precisely because they were global. In doing so, he answered those who believed that world history had become impossible as a consequence of the postwar proliferation of new historical specialities, including not only ecological history but also new social histories, areas studies, histories of mentalities and popular cultures, and studies of minorities, majorities, and ethnic groups.

In the introduction to this volume, Professor Crosby recounts an intellectual path to ecological history that might stand as a rationale for world history in general. He simply decided to study the most pervasive and important aspects of human experience. By focusing on human universals like death and disease, his studies highlight the epidemic rather than the epiphenomenal.

There is a level of courage in the work of Professor Crosby that may not always be appreciated. He consistently tackles the obvious and the ordinary, that which the common wisdom has deemed already known or of no account. To reexamine Columbus and to see the crucial historical impact of germs and seeds (as he does in this volume), or to explore pidgin and Creole syntax (as he does elsewhere), are daring routes to knowledge that also ennoble the ordinary. Professor Crosby has called our attention to the things under our noses by the force of his words as well as the logic of his argument. In coining some of the most memorable categories of world history—the Columbian exchange, ecological imperialism, neo-Europes—he has enriched our language as well as our inquiries.

Alfred Crosby would never sanction a science that was more democratic than true, and he has no interest in celebrating all he surveys. But in the generosity of his range, his healthy intellectual skepticism, and the tenor of his prose, we might well think of him as the Walt Whitman of world history.

Kevin Reilly

INTRODUCTION:
NERDS VERSUS TWITS

A generation ago the English physicist, civil servant, and novelist C.P. Snow pointed to the deplorable division of the educated classes into "two societies," the followers of the liberal arts and those of the sciences.[1] Little has happened since to narrow the gap between the two: in fact, now we might better call it a chasm. Scientists look upon historians, for instance, as (1) methodologically sloppy, i.e., concerned with matters that defy measurement, and (2) devoted to things that are, well, often entertaining, but somehow, don't you know, beside the real point. The first problem may be incurable, considering the poor quality of the poor twits' data, but at least they could concentrate on something more worthwhile than, for instance, Abraham Lincoln's sense of humor.

A good many historians return the compliment by looking upon scientists as nerds fixated on physical minutia, blind to the most important elements of life, which are attitudinal—that is to say, moral, ethical, aesthetic, and intrinsically unquantifiable. Some historians go so far as to look upon scientists as T.S. Eliot looked upon Sweeney, who says to Doris, probably while crushing out his cigar in the yolk of her breakfast egg,

> Birth, and copulation, and death.
> That's all the facts when you come to brass tacks:
> Birth, copulation, and death.[2]

I have, of course, caricatured both scientists and historians. Few of either group are quite that bigoted. But—and I insist upon this—some are, and the rest, in their secret hearts, conceal elements of these prejudices. I am sure I could get the votes of the majority of scientists and historians on a secret ballot if I offered the former the proposition that historians are twits and the latter the proposition that scientists are nerds.

Where do I stand? As a historian, I am a professional twit and I of course share the standard views of my colleagues. But, frankly, as a human being, I lean toward the nerds. Yes, there is much more to life than birth, copulation, and death—but the history of a species, no matter what else it may be, *never ever fails to be at least these three things.* Therefore, historians might do well to begin with these three, the fundamental elements of the human story. We must pay attention to the struggle to survive diseases and find enough to eat—in order to persist. Let me tell you how I came to this dazzling conclusion.

I decided as a young man to enter the division of the historical profession devoted to the chronicle of the English speakers of North America because I was sure that the story was fascinating enough and the techniques commonly used to analyze it valid enough to provide me with intellectual satisfaction for the rest of my years. A decade or so later I found myself slogging through a mid-career Slough of Despond, unsure that Anglo-American history as commonly conceived was broad enough in its vision to enable historians to comprehend the essentials of even the Anglo-American, much less the full American, story, and convinced that mainstream historiography, with its emphasis on politics, produced in the end not much more than an ever-lengthening list of random events. Teaching and writing that kind of history seemed to me rather like spending three score and ten years studying roulette.

Let me try to illustrate what I mean. Franklin D. Roosevelt had three life-threatening experiences as an adult: double pneumonia, polio, and a cerebral hemorrhage. He survived the first two and went on to become one of the greatest of American presidents. He died from the latter and was not present to grapple with Stalin in the negotiations at the end of World War II. There is no doubt that the outcomes of these three medical crises drastically affected history. So can a roulette ball's choice of which slot to drop into.

It is, I realized then and agree now, important to recognize the importance of the random in history. Otherwise, we may become so confident of ourselves as prophets as to feel empowered to set fire to villages in order to improve the villagers' chances for a happy future. But after we enlighten ourselves about the role of chance and, therefore, about our shortcomings as crystal ball gazers, is it worthwhile to go on to study more and more examples of randomness? Should we not focus on matters of a more deterministic nature, matters that might contain clues of wide application? We cannot deny that cerebral hemorrhages influence history. So do thunderbolts. Now, what about malnutrition?

It was while wallowing in my Slough that I read Bernal Díaz del Castillo's eyewitness account of the Spanish conquest of Mexico. I did so for no more respectable reason than one goes to James Bond movies, that is to say, for the excitement, but I did inadvertently discover that smallpox (now, according to the World Health Organization, extinct) arrived in Mesoamerica with the Europeans and swept across the land, killing myriads of Aztecs and other indigines. Ah, I thought, at last a respectable nominee for the real reason why a few hundred Spaniards were able to attract so many Amerindian allies, to conquer a large and fiercely militaristic society, and then to maintain control over all of Mesoamerica.

I consulted that compendium of universal knowledge, the *Encyclopedia Britannica,* which informed me that *Variola major,* the kind of smallpox that swept Mexico circa 1520, commonly killed 20, 25, and even higher percentages of those it infected. In Mesoamerica that would have been 20, 25, etc. percent of nearly everyone, presuming that this breath-borne infection was new there. When I scanned the original sources on the Spanish conquest of Peru, I found much the same story as in Mexico: smallpox and conquistadores as allies, and Native Americans as victims of accidental biological warfare.

I had come upon something that was at least as predictable as that old deterministic favorite, class warfare. Contact between people among whom smallpox was endemic and people among whom the disease was unknown would always mean deadly epidemics for the latter. Examples of this would be easy to find because smallpox was anything but subtle. It moved fast, made people very sick, sometimes hideously so, and often killed them. Smallpox was a thug: it mugged and murdered and forced its way into the record. My depression lifted. At last I could pursue something I would be sure to find whenever and wherever it was important.

But if smallpox was important, why had so many historians overlooked it? The answer was that I was reading only historians of my kind, historians of purely humanistic training, scholars who had spent their entire lives on only one side of the chasm that divides "the two societies." I poked around the library of Ohio State University, where I was then working, and found *The Ranks of Death: A Medical History of the Conquest of America,* a book written by Percy M. Ashburn, a physician, after a long military career, much of it overseas in lands where communicable disease still dominated the mortality tables.[3] Ashburn's book confirmed, with facts derived from sixteenth-century documents and shored up with the theory and praxis of modern bacteriology and immunology, what I was beginning to think about smallpox and the success of European imperialism in America.

I followed Dr. Ashburn into a trove of accounts of Europe's imperialistic expansion, accounts I was now equipped to read without unconsciously skipping the passages of medical significance. He also led me to a treasury of articles and books on infectious disease which sixteenth-century proto-scientists and twentieth-century scientists had heaped up. (He led me, for instance, to enter the debate about the origins of syphilis—American or no?—a debate yet to be resolved.[4]) I discovered that most glorious of all bibliographical aids, *The Index Medicus,* which in its coverage and detail is enough to make an orthodox historian feel like a child watching someone else's birthday party through a window.

This was for me a new and very satisfying kind of history: epidemiological history. It included randomness—sometimes epidemics hung fire for decades and other times leaped over oceans and deserts as if they did not exist—but in lesser amounts than I was accustomed to enduring. And it engendered new questions. Not, for instance, What was there in Aztec attitudes that rendered them so vulnerable to the invaders? Instead, it gave rise to questions like, Was the Aztecs' chief disadvantage their remoteness from the Old World, that is, their lack of experience, immunologically and socially, with most of the Eastern Hemisphere's diseases? I do not know to this day how to produce answers to the first question that can be usefully tested. I can, however, answer the second question and then test that answer by investigating the histories of other isolated peoples. If remoteness was the crucial factor in the Aztecs' fate, then Polynesians and Siberian tribes should also have suffered dreadful epidemics after contact with mainland peoples. They did.

My venture into epidemiological history quickly carried me to a more general subject: ecological history, the history of all organisms pertinent to human history and their (our) environment. Yes, germs were important, and so, it turned out, were insects, fungi, weeds, crops, and domesticated and wild animals. Humanity turned out to be the purposeful but often drunken ringmaster of a three-ring circus of organisms. Humanity affected the organisms, and they affected humanity.

For instance, let us look at the course of events in Brazil and Angola, both contacted by the Portuguese early in the history of European expansion. Each has developed differently from many other parts of Europe's overseas empires, from, for instance, Canada and New Zealand. Could ecological history supply explanations as to why? The quick answer turned out to be that Brazil and Angola are tropical, and their climates are very different from, say, those of the environs of Montreal and Auckland. True—and obvious—but Brazil and Angola developed differently not only from Canada and New Zealand, but from each other. Their climates were and are similar, but not their flora and fauna. Jaguars are not native to Africa, nor lions to South America. What about the *Anopheles gambiae* mosquito, the world's most efficient transmitter of malaria? It is a lot easier for humans, especially Europeans, to stay alive in coastal Brazil than coastal Angola.

The Eastern Hemisphere's domesticated organisms—wheat, barley, cattle, horses, pigs—were unknown in the Western Hemisphere in 1492, and the Amerindian maize, potatoes, and manioc were unknown in the Eastern Hemisphere. Was there, I wondered, a connection between their post-Columbian exchange and the upsurge of global population in the last few centuries? The answer is not an absolute yes or no, but it is unquestionably true that American foods are staples in the diets of hundreds of millions in the Old World, and Old World staples are consumed in quantity every day by myriads of inhabitants of the New World.

Does the continued exchange of food sources promise new surges of food production or of population growth, or both? The Sherpas of Nepal cultivate large quantities of white potatoes because they grow as well in the Himalayas as in their native Andes. Do the Sherpas know anything about quinoa, the Andean grain that will prosper at altitudes far above the limit of any other rich source of plant protein?

xiv   GERMS, SEEDS, AND ANIMALS

The transoceanic exchange of organisms continues. North America's starlings, house sparrows, kudzu, and tumbleweed are invaders, as are gray squirrels in Great Britain, blue hyacinth in the Limpopo and Mekong rivers, and cane toads and prickly pear in Australia. So are the organisms that killed millions upon millions of North America's chestnut trees in my father's time and its elm trees in mine.

New human infections continue to cross oceans. Fresh strains of influenza disembark in American seaports and airports again and again, and other infections embark from the same ports to other lands. AIDS, it seems, did not drop from the skies, but started somewhere outside of the Western Hemisphere, spread widely in North America, and traveled from thence all over the world. There are other such horrendous surprises in store for us. All brands of humanity take their turn as Aztecs.

We all are sailing swiftly into a biologically anarchic future, rudder flapping to and fro in a following sea. Our sources of wisdom are current science and past history. Scientists are very good at doing what they do, but tend to be locked in the moment in which they collect their data. The data that historians work with are inferior in quality to data of scientists, but not impossibly so, and we historians know how to live with ambiguity and omission. We are, as well, professionally dedicated to seeing events in the perspective of time. We should have a lot to contribute to the discussion of where we have been, where we are going, and whether we should alter course.

But we need to look at history not as only politics or religion or economics, but as biology. How efficient were a given people at negotiating their perpetuation? How efficient were they at staying alive and reproducing? What did most of them die of? What did they eat? The cultivation of a Middle Eastern grass, wheat, has paired with the limitation of births in North America to enable that continent to feed its own people and to produce enormous surpluses of food for export. The cultivation of an American grass, maize, has helped to drive an enormous increase in food production in Egypt, and a population explosion, as well. Egypt, which had fewer than 5 million inhabitants when it was the breadbasket of the ancient Mediterranean world, now has 55 million,[5] and imports food. Surely such facts tell us as much about North America and Egypt and their likely roles in the immediate future as do analyses of Judeo-Christian and Islamic modes of thought.

We humans are, before all else, organisms. It is my assumption, having experienced sickness and health, hunger and satiation, that our intestines' flora (both friendly old tenants and guerrilla raiders) and the quantity and quality of the nourishments that pass through the aforesaid plumbing are very important. I also believe that the record of history includes a great deal on such affairs. The history of bowels is as knowable as that of international relations—perhaps even more so because bowels tend to be more candid than diplomats.

I have written three books on the kind of history described above.[6] In these I have said much but not all of what I have wanted to say on the subject. The rest is contained in articles published here and there over the past score or so of years. At the suggestion of Kevin Reilly and with the guidance of my editor, Michael Weber, I have gathered these together and lightly re-edited them (i.e., eliminated repetitions wherever possible, substituted fresh for dated statistics, and shaded a few ex cathedra pronouncements). I continue to maintain the validity of my hypothesis that more organisms, and especially more organisms of immediate significance to human beings, have traveled from the Old to the New World than vice versa, but agree (though I may not have proclaimed loudly enough) that the exchange has been just that, an exchange. For readers who want to know more about the transoceanic migration of organisms, and particularly about the naturalization of American organisms in Europe and elsewhere in the Eastern Hemisphere, I recommend *Biological Invasions in Europe and the Mediterranean Basin,* edited by F. di Castri, A.J. Hansen, and M. Debussche; *Biogeography of Mediterranean Invasions,* edited by R.H. Groves and F. di Castri; and *Dynamics of Biological Invasions,* by Rob Hengeveld.[7]

I also, in spite of the dictates of traditional and unnatural modesty, recommend the following essays to you. As a twit with friends among the nerds, I insist that that which enables human beings to stay alive and reproduce and that which dispatches us to our eternal reward is worthy of our attention.

Notes

1. C.P. Snow, *The Two Cultures and a Second Look* (Cambridge: Cambridge University Press, 1969).

2. T.S. Eliot, *The Complete Poems and Plays* (San Diego: Harcourt Brace Jovanovich, 1971), 80–81.

3. *Who Was Who,* vol. 1, *1897–1842* (Chicago: Marquis–Who's Who, 1966), 33.

4. The jury is still out after four centuries. For the latest discussion, see Brenda J. Baker and George J. Armelagos, "The Origin and Antiquity of Syphilis," *Current Anthropology* 29 (December 1988): 703–37; Gino Fornaciari et al., "Syphilis in a Renaissance Mummy," *Lancet* 2 (1989): 614; Maciej Henneberg, Renata Henneberg, and Joseph C. Carter, "Health in Colonial Metaponto," *Research and Exploration* (Autumn 1992): 455–58.

5. Thomas M. Whitmore et al., "Long Term Population Change," in *The Earth as Transformed by Human Action,* ed. B. L. Turner et al. (Cambridge: Cambridge University Press, 1993), 31.

6. Alfred W. Crosby, *The Columbian Exchange: Biological and Cultural Consequences of 1492* (Westport, Conn.: Greenwood Press, 1972); *Ecological Imperialism: The Biological Expansion of Europe, 900–1900* (Cambridge: Cambridge University Press, 1986); and *America's Forgotten Pandemic: The Influenza of 1918* (Cambridge: Cambridge University Press, 1989).

7. I want to thank Professor Carolyn Merchant for these references.

GERMS & SEEDS ANIMALS

1 THE COLUMBIAN VOYAGES, THE COLUMBIAN EXCHANGE, AND THEIR HISTORIANS

The five hundredth anniversary of the Columbian discovery of America has come, and with it the obligation to assess existing interpretations of the significance of that voyage and the establishment of permanent links between the Old and New Worlds. The most influential of the several schools of interpretation are, on the one hand, the newest and analytic, and on the other, the classic and bardic. The former is for many recondite and discomforting. The latter, the one most often taught, dramatized, and believed in North America, is for most as comfortable as an old pair of slippers: we learned it in primary school.

The Bardic Interpretation

The bardic version of the Columbian voyages and their consequences was the product of narrative historians, most of them nineteenth-century writers, who did their work when the peoples of the republics of the New World looked upon the Americas as fresh and "without sin," at least as compared to "decadent" Europe. These historians narrated the American past in ways consonant both with the documentary record then available and with the ethnocentrism of their fellow white citizens of the New World, particularly of the United States. Their readers wanted history books to provide a story of "the steps by which a favoring Providence, calling our institutions into being, has conducted the country to its present happiness and glory,"[1] to quote the innocently arrogant George Bancroft, whose ten-volume

History of the United States (1834–76) we no longer read but have never forgotten.

The classic narrative that Bancroft and his successors provided can be summarized as follows: At the end of the fifteenth century, Christopher Columbus discovered America, adding to the world two continents populated sparsely with "savages" and, in Mexico and Peru, with "barbarians" experimenting with protocivilization. Then the conquistadores, few in number but courageous, conquered the Amerindian civilizations, which, for all their temples and gold, were evidently no more than paper tigers. Lesser conquistadores performed similarly, if less profitably, in other places, most of them also in tropical America, as did their Portuguese counterparts in coastal Brazil. British, French, Dutch, and other European soldiers, merchants, and settlers did much the same thing in those parts of the New World not occupied by the Iberians. The history of the New World subsequently became the struggle of European imperialist powers for domination, and Amerindians ceased to be important, except as enemies or allies of whites. African Americans, the other of the two non-European peoples who made major contributions to the development of the modern Americas, were obviously present in large numbers during the colonial period but were almost invisible in American history until the Haitian revolt at the end of the eighteenth century, usually viewed as a nightmarish aberration from the "normal" pattern of colonization in the Americas. The Columbian era, the period of European exploration and colonization, ended in the decades around 1800 with successful revolutions led by whites, usually of good family and education, against the parent-countries. Then came the maturation of independent societies and cultures in the New World, a development paradoxically confirmed and made irreversible by the migration of very large numbers of Europeans to the Americas after the mid-nineteenth century.

This narrative is the version of history that most Americans learn as children. It is also a cautionary tale (or interpretation) for scholars and teachers. The bardic version is as deceptive as it is popular because it is the product of an age that is past, with a characteristically selective view of history. It is as dangerous as it is deceptive because it reinforces Euro-American ethnocentrism and confirms historians and teachers in premises and approaches clearly obsolete in the era of the Columbian quincentennial. On the other hand, this classic interpretation is rational and true to the original sources. That it can be rational as well as deceptive is perhaps a useful lesson for seekers after absolute truth in history.

Rather than make a display of our "superiority" over scholars now dead and buried (thus anticipating the smugness of our own successors), let us praise our forebears. They were skilled practitioners of the historian's craft who did their work well, enabling the present generation of historians to make progress, rather than mere corrections. Men like Spain's Martín Fernández de Navarette and Canada's Henri-Raymond Casgrain drew together the documentary evidence that forms the core of what even revisionists must begin with, and assembled the bare data of who was who and where and when. These scholars performed the laborious work that is preliminary to creative scholarship in any field of history. Among them were creative scholars of the first rank who built a model of the past that reconciled the record as they knew it with the values of their own day and made sense to the literate classes of their time. This is what society pays historians to do.

Two of the best of these bardic historians were New England's William Prescott, historian of the Spanish conquest of Mexico and Peru, and Francis Parkman, the Homer of the struggle of Britain and France for empire in North America. Another was Samuel Eliot Morison, whose 1942 biography of Columbus and two-volume *European Discovery of America* (1971, 1974) are as close to being definitive works as one can expect in this mutable world. These men all liked to approach history through biography; they chose sides and were transparently loyal to their heroes. For all three men, the stuff of history was almost always documents, preferably letters, diaries, and memoirs, and not statistics. Seldom did they turn for help to economics, archaeology, biology, or any of the sciences, which resulted in some startling omissions. Prescott managed to write magnificent books on the conquests of Mexico and Peru and omit all but the bare mention of the conqueror's best ally, smallpox. The information on smallpox was in the original sources but not within the range of what Prescott was equipped to perceive as important.

The books of the bardic historians were usually neatly organized around great white men, a strategy whose validity seemed to be confirmed by contemporary events. Prescott did not worry his sources like a dog with an old shoe to find the *real* reason for the success of Cortés and Pizarro, because he lived in an era when white people seemingly always won their wars with nonwhites. In the Second Opium War,

Queen Victoria's plenipotentiary opined that "twenty-four determined [white] men with revolvers and a sufficient number of cartridges might walk through China from one end to the other."[2] Bardic historians thought in terms of biography, and why not? They were children of the nineteenth century, the golden age of rugged individualism and industrial capitalism. The nineteenth century was also an age of rampant nationalism, and when historians thought in terms of large groups of humans, they thought of the nation-state and not of tribes or cultures or language families. It was an age of unembarrassed elitism and racism, and historians tended to ignore plebeians in particular and non-Europeans in general. (Prescott and Parkman were in part exceptions, paying a full measure of attention to Amerindians, at least insofar as they influenced EuroAmerican destinies.) These historians were not much better equipped intellectually to notice those whom Eric R. Wolf has called the "people without history"[3] than they were to judge the stability of ecosystems. The social sciences and biology were new; ecology was not born until after Prescott and Parkman died, and was still immature when Morison was middle-aged.

The Analytic Interpretation

America's classic historians did not even try to answer many of the questions that concern us at the end of the twentieth century because neither they nor their audiences were asking such questions. There were a few fresh minds, however, who provided new ways of looking at the world, which led to new ways of sorting data and new kinds of inquiries. Among the greatest of these innovators were Charles Darwin, Karl Marx, and Louis Pasteur, celebrants of paradox who emphasized the importance of instability and the immense power of the humble, even the invisible. Travelers and archaeologists, at a different level intellectually but no less influential, kept exploring and digging, turning up evidence of dense pre-Columbian populations in the Americas, of peoples of undeniably high culture. Who could continue to think of the Maya as savages after John L. Stephen's volumes and Frederick Catherwood's prints? After the works of W.E.B. Du Bois and Melville Herskovits, what excuse remained for a historian to claim that there was nothing to learn about Africans or African Americans?

Above all, after the hell-for-leather advance of the Japanese military in the early 1940s and the swift collapse of Europe's overseas empires in the following two decades (as astonishing, in its way, as the collapse of the Amerindian empires four centuries earlier), there could be no more doubt that a great many of the "people without history" must have at least some history. The effect on the historical profession of the experiences of the last half-century has been like that on astronomers of the discovery that the faint smudges seen between the stars of the Milky Way were really distant galaxies.

The obsolescence of old conceptions persuaded historians to take a fresh look at the origins of European imperialism: perhaps elements less dramatic than gold and God and heroes had been involved. Charles Verlinden led the way by tracing the roots of European imperialism to the Mediterranean in the age of the Crusades, where organizational structures and exploitative techniques that would be imposed on America in the sixteenth century were first tried, and where Europeans first learned to like sugar and to raise it for profitable export to their homelands. Verlinden followed the precursors of conquerors like Cortés and the plantation owners of Brazil from the Levant to the islands of the eastern Atlantic. There, in the triangle of the great western ocean that has Iberia, the Azores, and the Canaries as its boundary stones—an expanse that Pierre Chaunu has shrewdly called the "Mediterranean Atlantic"[4]—the sailors of southern and western Europe studied the patterns of oceanic winds and learned to be bluewater sailors and how to sail to America and Asia. In Madeira, white settlers, often led by down-at-the-heels Iberian nobility seeking land and wealth to match their titles, discovered how to make a lot of money raising sugar; in the Canaries they learned how swiftly a fierce aboriginal people, the Guanches, could disappear and how easily they could be replaced with imported labor to raise tropical crops for the European market.

While historians of the Middle Ages and Renaissance were disinterring the roots of European imperialism, the students of the Americas and Amerindians were revolutionizing their disciplines. Archaeology thrust the beginnings of American history back at least fifteen thousand years and populated these millennia and both American continents with myriads of clever and mysterious people. Social scientists devised means, often quantitative, to tap into the history of undocumented peoples. The contribution of demographic historians has been of particular value, providing a structure within which other historians can find niches for their own discoveries. Historians opened themselves to (or, fearing obsolescence, rushed to ransack) geology, climatology, biology, epidemiology, and other fields. As a result, the kind of grain that is poured into the historian's mill today would wear out Leopold von Ranke's grindstones. Historians are scientific not only in the care they take with research and attempts to limit bias, but also in their exploitation of whatever the sciences provide that is pertinent to the study of the human past.

European historians of the *Annales* school, centered in France, have been the most noted practitioners of this new kind of history, but similar advances in technique have been developed in the New World and applied to the study of the Amerindian past and the impact of the Columbian voyages on American history. The Berkeley school, as it is loosely and sometimes inaccurately called, led by geographer Carl Ortwin Sauer, physiologist Sherburne F. Cook, and historians Woodrow Borah and Lesley Byrd Simpson, began as far back as the 1930s to reassess pre-Columbian and Amerindian history. They used many kinds of nondocumentary data—geological and botanical, among others— and re-examined, and many times examined for the first time, the yellowed sheets of tribute, tax, and population records of the Spanish Empire. The Berkeley school has revolutionized American historiography. Not everyone accepts its conclusions, but its questions—rarely asked before except by proponents of *indigenismo*—plot the course of historical research in the immediate pre- and post-Columbian centuries in America.

There has been a renewal of interest in the whole picture—the world—and therefore in global history. The forces that propelled Columbus and the forces that the European discovery and exploitation of America triggered were supranational and supracontinental. Columbian and post-Columbian exchanges of raw materials, manufactured products, and organisms cannot be described or analyzed to the full extent of their significance within any unit smaller than the world. Scholars of worldly sophistication have accepted the challenge: Fernand Braudel, William McNeill, Immanuel Wallerstein, Eric R. Wolf, and others. Their work leads us to lands, cultures, and questions that the bardic historians of Columbus rarely considered. To cite one example, nearly one hundred years before Columbus and other European mariners crossed the great oceans, the Chinese admiral Cheng Ho launched a succession of huge fleets, manned by thousands, around the Malay Peninsula and across the Indian Ocean as far as East Africa.

After this the Chinese ceased their transoceanic voyaging completely. Cheng Ho inspires today's world historians to ask two questions that would never have occurred to Prescott, Parkman, or even Morison: Why did the Chinese stop their voyaging, and, the obvious corollary but not a question asked by Western historians until the present, Why did European voyagers start and never stop?

There are vast expanses of time and territory in the new history of the Americas as yet not even roughly surveyed, and the work of detailed description must be left to the next century. There is no body of received wisdom about the New World, but there is a new model of New World history for our consideration and use. America's classic historians were successful in part because their scope was narrow. They wrote almost exclusively about white heroes in the last five hundred years, while today's analytic historians are concerned with the masses of people of numerous ethnic groups in a much larger time frame. To understand how these peoples fared after they met in 1492, we need to know at least something about the species of plants, animals, and microlife associated with them. To know that, we have to go back further than most of our Victorian ancestors thought there was anything to go back to.

The Old and New Worlds had been separate for millions of years before Columbus, except for periodic reconnections in the far north during Ice Ages. In this immense period the biota of the Old and New Worlds evolved and diverged. As of 1492, there were many similar species, especially in Eurasia and North America, such as deer and elm, but the differences were impressive. Europe had nothing quite like hummingbirds, rattlesnakes, and hickory and pecan trees. Further south the contrasts between Old and New World biota were even more amazing. The biggest mammal in Africa was the elephant; in South America, the cow-sized tapir. The native bioas of the Old and New Worlds were decidedly different, and for most of the previous few million years these biota had not been in competition or even in contact.

The last bout of competition before the arrival of Columbus included the initial migration into America of the Old World's *Homo sapiens* and the spread of that species from the Arctic Sea to Tierra del Fuego, effecting changes as yet only partly understood. After the last Ice Age ended some ten thousand years ago and the continental glaciers melted back, releasing so much water that the land connection between Siberia and Alaska was inundated, the ancestors of the Amerindians were left in complete or nearly complete isolation. They developed autochthonous cultures, domesticated American plants and animals, and adapted to American microlife. In 1492 they were living in an imperfect but sustainable balance with each other and with the other tenants of the New World, macro and micro. This homeostasis no doubt wobbled considerably, even violently, in areas with thick settlements of Amerindian farmers, but in all probability it was more stable then than it has been since.

During the same ten thousand–year period, peoples of the Old World, in adjustment to the biota of their continents, engendered their cultures and domesticated and bred their crops, beasts, and, unintentionally of course, their own set of pesky and sometimes fatal germs. These humans were also elements in a system that varied constantly but was, within broad limits, stable. They even had a modus vivendi with the plague, which had reared up in the fourteenth century and killed approximately one-third of the population of western Eurasia and North Africa. By 1500, however, the European population had recovered its pre–Black Death totals and was growing, despite recurrent waves of plague and other deadly diseases. In 1492 these two systems of homeostasis, one of the Old World and the other of the New, collided.

The Old World peoples had some distinct advantages in the biological competition that followed. Although their crop plants were not superior to those of the Amerindians per se—wheat, rice, and yams were "better" than maize, potatoes, and cassava in some ways and inferior in others—the Old World advantage in domesticated animals was great. It was a matter of the Old World's horses, cattle, pigs, goats, sheep, and other domesticated species versus the New World's llamas, guinea pigs, domesticated fowl, and dogs. This advantage was not permanent, because Amerindians adopted many of the new livestock, most spectacularly horses in the Great Plains and the pampa, where these animals helped the Amerindians to maintain their independence until the last half of the nineteenth century. The greatest influence of Old World plants and animals was probably in making it possible for Old World pastoralists and farmers to live in the American colonies as they had at home or, in most cases, better. Old World livestock, which had evolved in what seemingly had been a rougher league than that of the New World, often outfought, outran, or at least outreproduced American predators. Free of the diseases and pests that had preyed on them at home, the European animals thrived and even went wild, often in amazing numbers, providing mounts, meat, milk, and leather much more cheaply in the New World than in the Old. The most spectacular instances of this were in southern South America. The first Spanish attempt to colonize the pampa failed in the 1530s, and the survivors departed, leaving some livestock behind. When settlers returned in 1580 they found "infinite" herds of horses. In 1587 Hernando Arias left one hundred cattle behind him at Santa Fé de Paraná in Brazil, and when he returned in 1607 he found, according to his testimony, one hundred thousand. These Iberians were speaking colorfully, rather than statistically, but the rapid increase in the number of large animals in South America was indeed enormous, probably unprecedented for tens of millennia. Smaller but comparable explosions in animal populations also took place elsewhere in the New World.

The decisive advantage of the human invaders of America was not their plants or animals—and certainly not their muskets and rifles, which Amerindians eventually obtained in quantity—but their diseases. The aboriginal Americans had their own diseases (several of them, like Chagas's disease and Carrion's disease, were as indigenous to the Americas as hummingbirds and tapirs), but the number of these was insignificant compared to the sum of those that came to the New World from the Old after 1492. There is debate about whether certain diseases did or did not exist in America before 1492. Yellow fever, for example, is probably African, but could have been endemic among American monkeys when Europeans first arrived and perhaps attracted no attention until the first epidemic among humans. There is little disagreement on the following list: smallpox, measles, chicken pox, whooping cough, typhus, typhoid fever, bubonic plague, cholera, scarlet fever, malaria, diphtheria, and influenza.[5] These were the most lethal invaders of the New World in the sixteenth century. Even today the worst immediate threats to the native peoples of remote Amazonia are not the soldiers or road builders per se, but the measles and influenza that they bring with them.

The advantage in bacteriological warfare was (and is) characteristically enjoyed by people from dense areas of settlement moving into sparser areas of settlement: the Russians into Siberia, the Chinese into Mongolia, the British into Australia, for example. The diseases that savaged the Amerindians were infections associated with dense populations of humans, which appeared in the Old World long before the

New. In addition, it is probable that a number of these diseases were produced by the exchange of microlife between humans and domesticated animals. Such maladies as influenza seem to be renewed in their virulency by exchanges between species and possibly first evolved into human pathogens as the result of such exchanges. Old World peoples domesticated more species of animals than Amerindians and lived in close contact with animals—often literally cheek and jowl, hip and thigh—for much longer. From their animals Old World peoples obtained much more protein, fat, leather, fiber, bone, manure, and muscle power than were available to the Amerindians, and more epidemic and endemic disease as well. Old World peoples adjusted to these infections, socially and immunologically, and were relatively resistant to the diseases. As a result, they practiced bacteriological warfare whenever they went to places remote from the dense populations of the Old World. The Valley of Mexico had fifty devastating epidemics between 1519 and 1810, including smallpox, typhus, measles, mumps, and pneumonia. Even the fragmentary record of the Yucatán shows fourteen epidemics. The story of Peru, and of every area in the Americas for which there are any records, is similar.

"Wherever the European has trod," wrote Darwin after his circumnavigation of the globe on the *Beagle*, "death seems to pursue the aboriginal. We may look to the wide extent of the Americas, Polynesia, the Cape of Good Hope, and Australia, and we find the same result."[6] Darwin blamed this largely on infectious disease. The Yanomamö of today's Venezuelan-Brazilian borderlands offer a simple explanation for the phenomenon: "White men cause illness; if the whites had never existed, disease would never have existed either."[7]

The most spectacular killer of Amerindians was smallpox, a disease that existed in medieval and Renaissance Europe but did not rise to the first rank of maladies until the sixteenth century. From that time until the spread of vaccination in the nineteenth century, smallpox was one of the continent's most widespread and deadly diseases, so common that it was considered inevitable among children in areas of dense population. In this period, Europe's most important colonies were established in the New World.

Smallpox appeared in the West Indies at the end of 1518 or beginning of 1519 and spread to Mexico on the heels of Cortés; it swept through Central America, and preceded Pizarro into the realms of the Incas. Witnesses estimated the losses at one-fourth, one-third, or even one-half of the infected populations. Such estimates may seem extravagantly high, but very high death rates among the unimmunized were not uncommon in more recent, well-documented outbreaks. In 1972 a pilgrim returning from Mecca brought smallpox to Yugoslavia, where it had not been known for over a generation. Before public health measures stopped the spread of the disease, 174 people contracted smallpox and 35 died, a mortality rate of 20 percent. Readers who are still skeptical about the killing potential of new infections should turn to accounts of the Black Death in the Old World or to a consideration of the potentialities of AIDS in the 1980s. Imagine the consequences if AIDS were not a venereal but instead a breath-borne disease like smallpox.

Although Euro-Americans dubbed America the "virgin land," it had not been virgin for many millennia, if the title is used to mean free from human occupation. By the time Old World settlers, following the explorers, soldiers, and traders, arrived in numbers in most regions— Venezuela, Alberta, Amazonia—Old World pathogens had so reduced the indigenous population that some special name for the ensuing vacancy was required. Francis Jennings, with chilling appropriateness, replaced the phrase "virgin land" with "widowed land."[8]

The widowed land was more open to exploitation than any large area to which western Europeans had access, certainly more open to occupation than the nearest alternative, the lands of eastern Europe, bloodied for centuries by the *Drang nach Osten*. The success of the invaders of widowed America, particularly of the British in North America, inspired Adam Smith to issue an unintentional prophesy, appropriately dated 1776:

> The colony of a civilized nation which takes possession, either of a waste country, or of one so thinly inhabited, that the natives easily give place to new settlers, advances more rapidly to wealth and greatness than any other human society.[9]

In comparison with Eurasia and Africa, both ineradicably populated with their own peoples, the New World was a tabula rasa. Great fortunes could be made in the Americas by exploiting mineral resources and native biota, such as the beaver with its thick, tough fur. The greatest money-maker in America in the first centuries after Columbus, however, was the plantation, which produced tropical and semitropical crops, most of Old World origin, of a quasi-addictive nature for the European market. The foremost crop was sugar, followed by cocoa and tobacco, and then such useful items as cotton. Lands with soils and climates suitable for these crops existed in large areas of the New World, but the establishment and operation of plantations required the incessant labor of a great many people. Entrepreneurs tried using Amerindians as slaves and serfs in the hot, wet lowlands where such crops often grew best; however, they found that not only were the Amerindians intransigent but, worse, that they wilted and died too fast to be useful as laborers.

The plantation masters turned to their own homelands, using persuasion, propaganda, and even kidnapping to get Europeans across the Atlantic. Even shipments of convicts were acceptable. (An English verb for the transportation of these unfortunates, often Celtic backers of the wrong royal family, was "barbadoing," after the island where tobacco and later sugar promised profit.) But few Europeans could be persuaded or forced to become field workers in the American tropics, especially after the spread of malaria and yellow fever. Most Europeans, even serfs, had some civil rights. They could be dragged off to the hot lands of the New World by the thousands, but not by the millions. Until the end of the eighteenth century, most of the people who crossed the Atlantic from the Old to the New World, and the majority of those who took up the ax and machete and hoe to labor on the plantations, were black—about 10 million. The Atlantic slave trade, the greatest such trade in all history and the source of revolutionary changes in all of the four continents facing the Atlantic, was part of the legacy of Columbus.

The Heirs of Columbus

The bardic historians were relatively unconcerned with the geographic, biological, and demographic effects of the Columbian voyages, but these are the themes of current scholarship. The bulk of the research and analysis on these matters remains to be done, especially on the Columbian influence in Africa and Asia, but I can offer an interim report.

Intellectual Effects

"Among the extraordinary though quite natural circumstances of my life," wrote Columbus's countryman, the mathematician and physician

Girolamo Cardano, in the 1570s, "the first and most unusual is that I was born in this century in which the whole world became known; whereas the ancients were familiar with but a little more than a third part of it."[10] In 1491, the European conception of the universe was much the same as it had been a thousand years and more before. The earth was believed to be at the center of crystalline spheres carrying the sun, moon, and stars, with the surface of the world above water divided into three parts—Europe, Africa, and Asia. Humans lived in all three land areas, but not in the Torrid Zone, which was dreadfully hot and therefore uninhabitable. The evidence that did not fit this model was still small enough in significance and quantity to be ignored or subdued to conformity by sophistry. But when Columbus returned in 1493 he rendered the old model obsolete in a stroke. Few realized this immediately, but the system was obviously overloaded with new data and bursting by the time Cardano wrote.

Columbus introduced Europeans to a fourth part of the world, the Americas, and his successors added the Pacific, an immense ocean of unimaginable breadth beyond America. Columbus and his followers also provided eyewitness testimony that torrid America was full of people. (Europeans had somehow been able to ignore earlier reports of Portuguese sailors that tropical Africa was heavily populated.) In addition, the New World was full of plants and animals about which Aristotle and Pliny had nothing to say—electric eels and camels without humps—and of people who were neither Muslim nor Jew, and certainly not Christian. Carolus Linnaeus papered his rooms and tormented his methodical Scandinavian mind with drawings of exotic American plants, and Alexander Humboldt and Charles Darwin puzzled over their American experiences and based their generalizations in large part thereon. Philosophers and thinkers from Michel de Montaigne to Jean-Jacques Rousseau to Henry David Thoreau pondered and wrote on the meaning of Amerindians and their cultures. The Columbian discoveries galvanized anthropology, the product of Europeans trying to understand non-Europeans, into unprecedented acceleration. Protoanthropologists and anthropologists from Pietro Martire d'Anghiera to Lewis Henry Morgan and Claude Lévi-Strauss struggled to fit Amerindians, with all their variety of languages, technologies, religions, and customs, into "rational" explanations of social behavior and founded school after school of thought in the process.

Simply by making a round trip across an ocean, Columbus multiplied humanity's knowledge about its environment and itself many times over, stimulating a multitude of philosophies, literary movements, and sciences. He felt himself a crusader and painted crosses on his sails, but he promoted skepticism. Girolamo Cardano worried that the geographical discoveries of his century would lead in just that direction, and "certainties will be exchanged for uncertainties."[11] He was right, of course, but to humanity's advantage.

Economic Effects

Ask an economist about the significance of Columbus, and the economist might look for a connection between the great explorer and Europe's quantum leap in wealth, commerce, and productivity in the centuries following his life. One of the most apparent and immediate of American influences on Europe during the first post-Columbian centuries was crudely financial. The gold and silver of the New World that raised the pulse of ambitious *hidalgos* and landless younger sons all over western Europe had much the same effect on the European economy. There is no doubt that American specie made possible trade with the Far East that would have been slight otherwise. The Chinese were interested in trading their silks and porcelain with Europeans if they brought Mexican silver. Even so, the exact effect of American specie on Europe per se is a matter of controversy. The influx of American bullion was surely an important factor in the inflation of the sixteenth and seventeenth centuries, enriching some and impoverishing others and in general subjecting Europe to more chills and fevers than historians have sorted out yet. If indeed prices, and therefore profits, soared faster than wages and traditional fees and rents, and if the decline of interest rates was due to the influx of precious metals from America, then that influx had a great deal to do with the rise of the commercial classes in power and influence and the decline of the old aristocracy, and possibly with the Industrial Revolution.

One of the most important changes in the generations after Columbus was Europe's creation of a world market, with itself as the "entrepôt" and bank. Vital to this new phenomenon was the trade between the New World and Europe, the former supplying raw materials and the latter manufactured goods. The American market for manufactured goods became increasingly important as Euro-American populations grew. For instance, English exports to the Americas and Africa (where manufactured goods were exchanged for slaves for the American colonies) increased tenfold in the eighteenth century. But for the sake of brevity, let us consider the New World colonies exclusively in what was unambiguously their primary role for a very long time, that of supplier of materials for European consumption and processing.

Siberia, like North America, sent its furs to western Europe but alone could never have satisfied the demand, which over centuries was insatiable. The profits of the fur trade could be astonishingly high: Hudson's Bay Company produced an average of 23 percent profit annually for the first fifty years of its existence, a total profit of 1,143 percent on the original investment in a half-century. The islands of the eastern Atlantic, the Indian Ocean, and the East Indian archipelago could and did supply sugar and other tropical products to Europe, but the mass of such goods came from America. In the eighteenth century the most profitable colonies in the world were not African, Asian, or even the burgeoning settlements of North America, but the West Indies, or Sugar Islands, as they were often called. The French colony of Saint-Domingue (Haiti and the Dominican Republic today) employed seven hundred vessels manned by eighty-thousand seamen in its trade in a good year. In 1789 about two-thirds of France's total foreign investments were involved in Saint-Domingue, the greatest of the Sugar Islands. Britain's West Indian colonies provided 20 percent of the homeland's total imports between 1714 and 1773, much of which were re-exported at a profit. A contemporary estimated that an average Englishman driving slaves in the sugar plantations brought twenty times more clear profit to England than he would have had he stayed home.

The American plantations were the reason for the existence of the Atlantic slave trade. The lands of southern Asia supplied their own labor and even had a surplus to export when plantation agriculture spread into Oceania. After the sixteenth century the varying, but in total considerable, profits of the Atlantic trade in black laborers flowed largely to the nations leading the commercial and industrial revolutions: Holland, France, and Britain. Portugal was also a major recipient of slave-trade profits but could not hold on to them; they slipped away to join the main current of wealth streaming to Portugal's northern neighbors.

The world market, unimagined when Columbus sailed, was a hardy infant by the end of the sixteenth century. A century later, the world market was an important factor in the lives of millions of people in every continent but Australia and Antarctica, drawing coffles of slaves out of Africa every year, herding Amerindians up and down the ladders of the Potosí silver mines, and dispatching Cree braves to trap beaver in the Canadian forests, in addition to what it was dictating to Gujaratis and Filipinos on the other side of the world. For the first time human labor, raw materials, manufacturing, and transportation systems spanning scores of degrees of longitude and latitude by sail, wheel, and beast of burden were organized on a world scale. The world economy was created by bankers and statesmen, such as the Fuggers and Colbert, but Columbus and his fellow explorers played vital roles, too. These sailors presented entrepreneurs with access to enough land in enough climates, enough bullion, enough visions of potential profit, to spur them from a walk to a gallop. Once in existence, the world market produced a torrent of wealth that swept round and round the globe to and from Ceylon, the Ottoman Empire, Pernambuco, Massachusetts, Java, Muscovy, and Quebec, and on every passage Europe took its tithe.

A lot of that capital went to building Brobdingnagian manor houses and providing fireworks on ducal birthdays, but much was also invested in roads, canals, bridges, warehouses, and the training of naval, clerical, mechanical, and executive talent. The wealth of the New World was not the only cause of the Industrial Revolution, but it is difficult to see how that mysterious and awesome transformation could have happened when and as rapidly as it did without stimulus from the Americas. The Industrial Revolution left Europeans and their descendants overseas richer and with access to more power than men and women of 1492 ever thought possible. Its effects continue today, as other peoples break loose from old moorings and bobble along in the European wake, heading for an age of either material satisfaction or towering disappointment. Columbus's bequest is a sharp sword, and in this case we cannot be sure whether we hold it by the handle or the blade.

Nutritional Effects

"The greatest service which can be rendered any country is to add a useful plant to its culture,"[12] noted Thomas Jefferson. By this standard, Columbus was the greatest benefactor of all time because by bringing the agricultures of the Old and New Worlds into contact, he added many useful plants to each. He enormously increased the kinds and quantities of food available to humans by giving them access to all the masterpieces of plant and animal breeders everywhere, and not just those of two or three contiguous continents.

In the last five hundred years food crops and domesticated animals have crossed the Atlantic and Pacific in both directions, enabling people to live in numbers in places where they previously had had only slim means to feed themselves. The Argentine pampa, Kansas, and Saskatchewan, too dry in large areas for Amerindian maize and in the latter case too far north, are now breadbaskets, producing not only enough Eurasian wheat for themselves, but much more to export to the world. Eurasia's domesticated animals—cattle, sheep, pigs, goats, and even water buffalo—provide Americans from the Hudson Bay to the Straits of Magellan with the means to do what was only meagerly possible before 1492: to turn grass, which humans cannot eat, into meat and milk. In 1991, according to the Food and Agricultural Organization (FAO) of the United Nations, the New World slaughtered 86 million cattle, 27 million sheep, and 152 million pigs; in 1492 none at all. New World peoples derive all but a fraction of their animal protein, and almost all their wool and leather, from Old World animals.

Conversely, cassava, a root plant of South American origin, provides calories for multitudes of Africans and Asians in areas previously too wet, too dry, or too infertile to support more than sparse populations. Similarly, as the white potato of South America spread across northern Europe, peasants from county Kerry to the Urals found themselves with the means to raise more food in bulk per unit of land than ever before (although ultimately there were dire results in Ireland, where an American pestilence arrived to destroy the American plant in the 1840s). In the Far East the impact of the arrival of the products of Amerindian plant breeders was at least as great as in Europe or Africa. By the late 1930s New World crops amounted to 20 percent of the food produced in China, where approximately one-quarter of the human race lived (and lives now). According to Ping-ti Ho, historian of Chinese demography and agriculture:

> During the last two centuries, when rice culture was gradually approaching its limit, and encountering the law of diminishing returns, the various dry land food crops introduced from America have contributed most to the increase in national food production and have made possible a continual growth of population.[13]

In 1991 Amerindian maize accounted for almost one-fourth of all the grain produced in the world. Not surprisingly, the United States was the world's largest producer, but, perhaps surprisingly, China was the second greatest producer. China also harvested more sweet potatoes than any other nation. Sweet potatoes, a native American plant that does marvelously well under conditions that would discourage most other crops, are an old and dependable famine food for the Chinese. Globally, American root and tuber crops, of which the most important are white and sweet potatoes and cassava, exceeded by any means of measurement all others combined. The world produced 575 million metric tons of root and tuber crops in 1991, of which those of Amerindian domestication amounted to 540 million metric tons. The world's leading producer of white potatoes was the area that used to be the Soviet Union, which forked up six times more potatoes in weight than South America, the home continent of the tuber. Africa produced over 69 million metric tons of cassava, dwarfing the 32 million of South America, where the plant was first cultivated.

The significance of Amerindian crops in the future will increase because all the most important ones were first domesticated in the tropics, where many of them still grow best. The developing nations of the world, where human populations are expanding fastest, are mostly in the tropics and in hot, wet lands nearby. The maize production of the developed world in 1991 was 273 million metric tons, and that of the developing world about 70 million less, but a great deal of the former tonnage went to feed livestock while almost all the latter went directly to feed people. The sweet potato production of the developed societies in the same year was a bit over 2 million metric tons, and that of the developing societies over 124 million. All of the cassava raised in 1991 about which the FAO has statistics (154 million metric tons) was raised in the developing nations. Compare these figures with those for wheat, the traditional staple since the Neolithic Age in temperate Eurasia: 312 million metric tons were produced by the developed nations, and 239 million by the developing ones.

Between 1750 and 1991 the population of the world grew from approximately 750 million to 5.4 billion. (In 1991, the population of the developed world was 1.3 billion; that of the developing world, 4.1 billion). The exchange of crops and domesticated animals between the Old and New Worlds cannot be credited with being the sole cause of this awesome increase, any more than the capital produced by Europe's exploitation of America can be said to be the only cause of the Industrial Revolution, but it is hard to see how the colossal effect could have come about without the Columbian exchange.

Demographic Effects

The impact of the Columbian exchange did not always enhance population growth. Columbus triggered population explosion among some peoples and implosion in others. His effect on the Amerindian population, for example, was annihilating.

Fifty years ago, Alfred Kroeber, then perhaps the premier anthropologist in the United States, estimated the total Amerindian population of 1492 at 8.5 million. He believed that his figure might possibly be a bit low, but it is unlikely that he thought that scholars would ever conservatively estimate the number of fifteenth-century Amerindians at 30 to 50 million, or that others, at least as well informed, would not hesitate to say 100 million. Extraordinary numbers! At that time Europe from the Atlantic to the Urals had only 80 million people, with Spain's population perhaps 7 million.

The mammoth increase in the estimates of fifteenth-century Amerindian populations during the past few decades quite properly arouses skepticism because the data these figures are based on are, by twentieth-century standards, disconcertingly imprecise. These estimates are the end results of careful examination and meticulous analysis of all the sources available (which are, admittedly, doubtful, if taken one at a time, but in total impressive). These include the off-the-cuff guesses of the first Europeans to arrive in a given area, the sober judgments and censuses of colonial administrators and churchmen, travelers' accounts, and whatever other scraps of pertinent information that can be found. All are measured against approximations of the carrying capacity of the environment and the size of the Amerindian population suggested by the density of pre-Columbian artifacts and ruins. These figures are matched against each other and then tested by sophisticated demographic techniques, such as careful extrapolation backward from later and more credible data. At the end, the demographic historians make their estimates. We can and should argue about these estimates, but we should also note that they do not stand in suspicious uniqueness: the sources about Australia, New Zealand, and the Pacific islands also indicate that their aboriginal populations were much larger when Europeans first arrived than two or three generations later.

Skepticism is imperative in this new field, as it is in the field of the demographic history of medieval Europe, but not stubborn adherence to a half-century-old orthodoxy. After all, the New World had one-fourth of the land surface of the globe and was rich in sources of food; Amerindians had many thousands of years to expand their numbers before Columbus arrived. It seems only sensible to begin with the assumption that there were a lot of Americans in 1492.

The traditional underestimations of Amerindian populations were due not so much to Euro-American ethnocentrism, though this may have played a role, as to the steep plunge of New World populations very soon after Old World peoples entered a given region. The germs sickened and killed thousands, setting off cascades of mortality. For instance, decimation of young adults interrupted farming and hunting, and malnutrition and even starvation followed. As elders died, the old customs went with them to the grave, leaving vacuums and bequeathing despair and anomie to the young. Typically, by the time two or three generations had passed after an initial white settlement, the Amerindian population of the given region was so low that it made the offhanded estimates of the first explorers and conquerors seem extravagant. By the time libraries were founded, colleges were opened, and historians were sharpening their pencils, the local Amerindians were often either extinct or few in number. The crucial first step for demographic historians of the Amerindians is to decide how steep their plunge in numbers was.

The population losses were undisputably considerable and swift. The angle of descent that Sherburne F. Cook and Woodrow Borah offer for central Mexico starts at about 25 million Amerindians at the beginning of the 1520s, falls to 11.2 million in 1532, to 4.7 million in 1548, to 2.2 million in 1568, and to a nadir of 852,000 in 1608. Even if the controversial first estimate is ignored, the drop from 1532 to 1608 is more than 90 percent. The drop from the dependable 1568 number to 1608's equally respectable total is over 60 percent. David Noble Cook, after painstaking research and analysis, puts forward an educated guess of 9 million for the population of Amerindian Peru in 1520 and a solid figure of 600,000 for the region of a century later, again a decline of over 90 percent.

Relatively isolated regions like the Yucatán, where the full impact of European invasion was diffused over time, may have suffered smaller declines. But peripheral areas did not necessarily suffer less because of their remoteness or even because of a lower density of population; climate and the amount and kinds of food available must always be taken into consideration. In the cold regions of the far north and south, a crisis, if it struck during the season when vital food resources such as salmon were fleetingly available, could be extremely dangerous. Feverish lowlands, whatever their populations and locations, often lost close to 100 percent of their aboriginal populations. At the beginning of the eighteenth century, John Lawson estimated that smallpox and rum had reduced the Amerindians within two hundred miles of Charleston, South Carolina, by five-sixths in only fifty years. A governor of the colony expressed thanks to God for having sent an "Assyrian Angel" among the Aborigines with "Smallpox &c. to lessen their numbers: so that the *English,* in Comparison with the *Spaniard,* have but little *Indian* Blood to answer for."[14]

The study of Amerindian demographic history is still at an early stage, and even if enriched with scores of careful local studies (the indispensable next step), will never be a precise science. Conclusions will always be accompanied by caveats that the final figures are *probably* accurate, plus or minus 10 or 20 or 30 percent. But careful studies, fashioned by meticulous and mutually critical scholars, are already producing great advances in the understanding of the American past. After all, in a field where within living memory one expert offered 8.5 million for the 1492 population of the New World and others 100 million, studies producing conclusions dependable within even 50 percent either way are encouraging.

Already we can be sure that in 1492 the populations of the various regions of the New World were comparable in density to similar regions of the Old. Columbus's arrival in America was much more like Marco Polo visiting the Far East, with its advanced empires and primitive tribes, than Robinson Crusoe landing on a desert island. Mexico and Peru obviously had millions of people living in complex societies. Other regions had smaller populations and their societies were not as advanced, but no informed person today would think of endorsing George Bancroft's statement that before whites came to what is now the United States, the area was "an unproductive waste . . . its only inhabitants a few scattered tribes of feeble barbarians, destitute of commerce and of political connection."[15]

Assessing the Columbian Exchange

The effects of establishing permanent links between continents that had been separate, and thereby interweaving divergently evolved biota and human cultures, were and are too vast to be measured for many centuries and probably millennia, but already the demographic effects of the Columbian exchange are awesome. Of the three human groups chiefly involved in the linkages between the two worlds—Europeans and Euro-Americans, Africans and African Americans, and Amerindians —the first has benefited most by the obvious standard, population size. According to the demographer Kingsley Davis, about 50 million Europeans migrated to the New World between 1750 and 1930, and the populations of the lands to which most of them went increased 14 times, while that of the rest of the world increased by 2.5 times. In that same 180 years the number of Caucasians on earth increased 5.4 times, Asians only 2.3 times, and black Africans and African Americans less than 2 times. One may justifiably question the definitions of the terms Caucasian, Asian, African, and African American, but problems of differentiation should not prevent noting that Columbus benefited some kinds of people far more than others.

Columbus's legacy to black Africans and their descendants is mixed. An estimated 10 million Africans crossed the Atlantic to the Americas, where they worked and died as chattel, to the incalculable benefit of their captors and owners. The slave trade transformed West African society, turning its commerce about-face from the Saharan border and the Mediterranean societies to the Atlantic and the New World, enriching some peoples and creating powerful states, and decimating others and destroying them as political and cultural entities. A cold reckoning of the number of black Africans and African Americans suggests that there are now more of them in total than there would be if the slave trade had never existed. Even if the multitudes who died in the Middle Passage and in African wars stimulated by the slave trade were added to the millions of Africans who arrived in the New World, the total of people lost to Africa was probably fewer than were added because of the cultivation of Amerindian crops brought to Africa by the slavers. The number of African Americans in 1950 was about 47 million, approximately one-fifth of all the blacks on the planet.

Columbus was the advanced scout of catastrophe for Amerindians.

There were a few happy sequelae—the flowering of equestrian cultures in the American grasslands, for instance—but on balance, the coming of whites and blacks brought disease, followed by intimidation, eviction, alcoholism, decapitation of the ruling classes from the peasant bodies of the advanced Amerindian cultures, and obliteration of many peoples and ways of life. The European invasion of the New World reduced the genetic and cultural pools of the human species, as did, to at least some extent, the advance of Chinese settlers into the Szechuan wilderness and the tropical forests of southeast Asia, and the descent of Incan armies down the eastern slopes of the Andes into the jungles. When strangers meet, the degree of difference between their bacterial florae can make more history than the differences between their customs.

The Amerindian population crash in a given area usually lasted no more than one or two hundred years and was followed by a recovery (if there was to be one at all), slow at first and probably not matching the rate of increase of the rest of humanity until the twentieth century. If the nadir populations for Amerindians of the various regions of the New World were added (nadirs were reached in the Caribbean islands by about 1570; in North America not perhaps until 1930), the sum would be about 4.5 million. Although this is no better an informed guess (how was Amerindian defined by the time these populations bottomed out?), in order of magnitude it is acceptable. If this figure is compared to any of the currently and widely respected estimates of Amerindian population in 1492, even to the lowest, 33 million, the conclusion must be that the major initial effect of the Columbian voyages was the transformation of America into a charnal house. The degree to which we have misunderstood our own history is the distance between this undoubted truth, appalling but now solidly established, and the view expressed by the designers of the 1629 seal of the Massachusetts Bay Colony, on which a figure of an Amerindian, longing for a chance to improve himself, calls out, "COME:OVER:AND: HELP:VS."[16] Samuel Eliot Morison repeated this view of the relationship between the Old and New Worlds three centuries later in the peroration to his magnificent *The European Discovery of America:* "To the people of this New World, pagans expecting short and brutish lives, void of hope for any future, had come the Christian vision of a merciful God and a glorious Heaven."[17] We neither ignore nor reconcile ourselves to the sometimes bloody religions of the Amerindians, nor condemn Morison for anything worse than being immured in his own ethnicity, in saying that his was a very selective view of what was surely the greatest tragedy in the history of the human species.

The classic historians of the United States who specialized in the first centuries after the Columbian voyages provided the stories, often deeply researched, accurate, and superbly written, of a small number of white heroes who usually won their battles or who, like Columbus and the Marquis de Montcalm, were noble in defeat. These scholars echoed and amplified a folk version of American history, a hybrid offspring of successful revolution and romantic nationalism, so scanty in disasters and humiliations and so Whiggish in its optimism and blandness that Nathaniel Hawthorne, looking for materials for his novels, complained of his country: "there is no shadow, no antiquity, no mystery, no picturesque and gloomy wrong, nor anything but a common-place prosperity, in broad and simple daylight. . . ."[18]

The most recent scholarship places beside that plaint a sixteenth- or early seventeenth-century document in the Nahuatl language in which an Aztec matron visits a younger woman in Texcoco to congratulate her on her two sons. The older woman calls the boys "precious jewels and emeralds," as indeed they were at that time, for miscarriages, stillbirths, and deaths of children were common. "Hardly anyone who is born grows up, they just all die off," she says. Her mind strays back to her youth, before the conquest and the new god, when the number of rulers and nobles had been many, the commoners beyond counting, and the slaves as numerous as ants. "But now everywhere our Lord is destroying and reducing the land, and we are coming to an end and disappearing. Why? For what reason?"[19]

American historians, if they will grasp this nettle and accept their responsibility to answer her question, will gain in knowledge of the multiplicity of forces impinging upon humanity in all centuries, most of which their liberal arts educations have not prepared them to perceive. They will also gain a sense of tragedy, at present largely missing from at least North American scholarship and essential to mature consideration of the course of our species through time. There is a lot of work to be done. The study of history, said Marc Bloch, "having grown old in embryo as mere narrative, for long encumbered with legend, and for still longer preoccupied with only the most obvious events . . . is still very young as a rational attempt at analysis."[20]

Notes

1. George Bancroft, *History of the United States, from the Discovery of the American Continent* (Boston: Little, Brown, 1834–76), 1:4.

2. Christopher Hibbert, *The Dragon Awakes: China and the West, 1793–1911* (Harmondsworth: Penguin Books, 1984), 234.

3. Eric R. Wolf, *Europe and the People without History* (Berkeley: University of California Press, 1982).

4. Pierre Chaunu, *European Expansion in the Later Middle Ages,* trans. Katherine Bertram (Amsterdam: North Holland Publishing, 1979), 106.

5. This list, most agree, should be longer, but there is no universal agreement about which diseases should be on it, nor, in all probability, will there ever be. There is no single outstanding authority on the subject, but the reader should consult John W. Verano and Douglas H. Ubelaker, eds., *Disease and Demography in the Americas* (Washington, D.C.: Smithsonian Institution Press, 1992), passim.

6. Charles Darwin, *The Voyage of the Beagle* (Garden City: Doubleday, 1962), 433–34.

7. Donald Joralemon, "New World Depopulation and the Case of Disease," *Journal of Anthropological Research* 38 (Spring 1982): 118.

8. Francis Jennings, *The Invasion of America: Indians, Colonialism and the Cant of Conquest* (Chapel Hill: University of North Carolina Press, 1975), 15–31.

9. Adam Smith, *An Inquiry into the Nature and Causes of the Wealth of Nations* (London: Oxford University Press, 1976), 2:564.

10. Jerome Cardano, *The Book of My Life,* trans. Jean Stoner (London: J. M. Dent and Sons, 1931), 189.

11. Ibid.

12. John P. Foley, ed., *The Jeffersonian Cyclopedia* (New York: Funk and Wagnalls, 1900), 25.

13. Ping-ti Ho, *Studies on the Population of China, 1368–1953* (Cambridge, Mass.: Harvard University Press, 1959), 191–92.

14. B. R. Carroll, ed., *Historical Collections of South Carolina* (New York: Harper and Brothers, 1836), 11:89.

15. Bancroft, *History of the United States,* 1:3–4.

16. Jennings, *The Invasion of America,* 229.

17. Samuel Eliot Morison, *The European Discovery of America: The Southern Voyages, 1492–1616* (New York: Oxford University Press, 1974), 737.

18. Nathaniel Hawthorne, *The Marble Faun* (Boston: Houghton, Mifflin, 1888), 15.

19. Frances Karttunen and James Lockhart, *The Art of Nahuatl Speech: The Bancroft Dialogues* (Los Angeles: UCLA Latin American Center Publications, 1987), 147.

20. Marc Bloch, *The Historian's Craft,* trans. Peter Putnam (New York: Alfred A. Knopf, 1961), 13.

2 ECOLOGICAL IMPERIALISM: THE OVERSEAS MIGRATION OF WESTERN EUROPEANS AS A BIOLOGICAL PHENOMENON

Europeans in North America, especially those with an interest in gardening and botany, are often stricken with fits of homesickness at the sight of certain plants which, like themselves, have somehow strayed thousands of miles eastward across the Atlantic. Vladimir Nabokov, the Russian exile, had such an experience on the mountain slopes of Oregon:

> Do you recognize that clover?
> Dandelions, *l'or du pauvre?*
> (Europe, nonetheless, is over.)

A century earlier the success of European weeds in America inspired Charles Darwin to goad the American botanist, Asa Gray: "Does it not hurt your Yankee pride that we thrash you so confoundly? I am sure Mrs. Gray will stick up for your own weeds. Ask her whether they are not more honest, downright good sort of weeds."[1]

The common dandelion, *l'or du pauvre,* despite its ubiquity and its bright yellow flower, is not at all the most visible of the Old World immigrants in North America. Vladimir Nabokov was a prime example of the most visible kind: the *Homo sapiens* of European origin. Europeans and their descendants, who comprise the majority of human beings in North America and in a number of other lands outside of Europe, are among the most spectacularly successful overseas migrants of all time. How strange it is to find Englishmen, Germans, Frenchmen, Italians, and Spaniards comfortably ensconced in places with names like Wollongong (Australia), Rotorua (New Zealand), and Saskatoon (Canada), where obviously other peoples should dominate, as they must have at one time.

None of the major groupings of humankind is as oddly distributed about the world as European, especially Western European, whites. Almost all the peoples we call Mongoloids live in the single contiguous land mass of Asia. Black Africans are divided among three continents—their homeland and North and South America—but most of them are concentrated in their original latitudes, the tropics, facing each other across one ocean. European whites were all recently concentrated in Europe, but in the last few centuries have burst out, as energetically as if from a burning building, and have created vast settlements of their kind in the South Temperate Zone and North Temperate Zone (excepting Asia, a continent already thoroughly and irreversibly tenanted). In Canada, the United States, Argentina, Uruguay, Australia, and New Zealand they amount to between 75 and nearly 100 percent of the population. The only nations in the temperate zones outside of Asia that do not have enormous majorities of European whites are Chile, with a population of two-thirds mixed Spanish and Indian stock, and South Africa, where blacks outnumber whites six to one. How odd that these two, so many thousands of miles from Europe, should be exceptions in *not* being predominantly pure European.[2]

The Demographic Takeover

Europeans have conquered Canada, the United States, Argentina, Uruguay, Australia, and New Zealand not just militarily, economically, and technologically—as they did India, Nigeria, Mexico, Peru, and other tropical lands, whose native peoples have long since expelled or interbred with and even absorbed the invaders. In the temperate zone lands listed above Europeans conquered and triumphed demographically. These, for the sake of convenience, we will call the Lands of the Demographic Takeover.

There is a long tradition of emphasizing the contrasts between Europeans and North American whites—a tradition honored by such people as Henry James and Frederick Jackson Turner—but the vital question is really why Americans are so European. And why Argentinians, Uruguayans, Australians, and New Zealanders are so European in the obvious genetic sense.

The reasons for the relative failure of the European demographic takeover in the tropics are clear. In tropical Africa, until recently, Europeans died in droves of the fevers; in tropical America they died almost as fast of the same diseases, plus a few native American additions. Furthermore, in neither region did European agricultural techniques, crops, and animals prosper. Europeans did try to found colonies for settlement, rather than merely exploitation, but they failed or achieved only partial success in the hot lands. The Scots left their bones as monument to their short-lived colony at Darien at the turn of the eighteenth century. The English Puritans who skipped Massachusetts Bay Colony to go to Providence Island in the Caribbean Sea did not even achieve a permanent settlement, much less a Commonwealth of God. The Portuguese who went to northeastern Brazil created viable settlements, but only by perching themselves on top of first a population of native Indian laborers and then, when these faded away, a population of laborers imported from Africa. They did achieve a demographic takeover, but only by interbreeding with their servants. The Portuguese in Angola, who helped supply those servants, never had a breath of a chance to achieve a demographic takeover.[3] There was much to repel and little to attract the mass of Europeans to the tropics, and so they stayed home or went to the lands where life was healthier, labor more rewarding, and where white immigrants, by their very numbers, encouraged more immigration.

In the cooler lands, the colonies of the Demographic Takeover, Europeans achieved very rapid population growth by means of immigration, by increased life span, and by maintaining very high birth rates. Rarely has population expanded more rapidly than it did in the eighteenth and nineteenth centuries in these lands. It is these lands, especially the United States, that enabled Europeans and their overseas offspring to expand from something like 18 percent of the human species in 1650 to well over 30 percent in 1900. Today 670 million Europeans live in Europe, and 250 million or so other Europeans— genetically as European as any left behind in the Old World—live in the Lands of the Demographic Takeover, an ocean or so from home.[4] What the Europeans have done with unprecedented success in the past few centuries can accurately be described by a term from apiculture: they have swarmed.[5]

They swarmed to lands that were populated at the time of European arrival by peoples as physically capable of rapid increase as the Europeans, and yet who are now small minorities in their homelands and sometimes no more than relict populations. These population explosions among colonial Europeans of the past few centuries coincided with population crashes among the Aborigines. If overseas Europeans have historically been less fatalistic and grim than their relatives in Europe, it is because they have viewed the histories of their nations very selectively.

Explaining the Takeover

Any respectable theory that attempts to explain the Europeans' demographic triumphs has to provide explanations for at least two phenomena. The first is the decimation and demoralization of the aboriginal populations of Canada, the United States, Argentina, and others. The obliterating defeat of these populations was not simply due to European technological superiority. The Europeans who settled in temperate South Africa seemingly had the same advantages as those who settled in Virginia and New South Wales, and yet how different was their fate. The Bantu-speaking peoples, who now overwhelmingly outnumber the whites in South Africa, were superior to their American, Australian, and New Zealand counterparts in that they possessed iron weapons, but how much more inferior to a musket or a rifle is a stone-pointed spear than an iron-pointed one? The Bantu have prospered demographically not because of their numbers at the time of first contact with whites, which were probably not greater per square mile than those of the Indians east of the Mississippi River. Rather, the Bantu have prospered because they survived military conquest, avoided the conquerors, or became their indispensable servants—and in the long run because they reproduced faster than the whites. In contrast, why did so few of the natives of the Lands of the Demographic Takeover survive the initial century of contact with the invaders?

Second, we must explain the stunning, even awesome success of European agriculture, that is, the European way of manipulating the environment in the Lands of the Demographic Takeover. The difficult progress of the European frontier in the Siberian *taiga* or the Brazilian *sertão* or the South African *veldt* contrasts sharply with its easy, almost fluid advance in North America. Of course, the pioneers of North America would never have characterized their progress as easy: their lives were filled with danger, deprivation, and unremitting labor; but as a group they always succeeded in taming whatever portion of North America they wanted within a few decades and usually a good deal less time. Many individuals among them failed—they were driven mad by blizzards and dust storms, lost their crops to locusts and their flocks to cougars and wolves, or lost their scalps to understandably inhospitable Indians—but as a group they always succeeded—and in terms of human generations, very quickly.

In attempting to explain these two phenomena, let us examine four categories of organisms deeply involved in European expansion: (1) human beings; (2) animals closely associated with human beings—both the desirable animals like horses and cattle and undesirable varmints like rats and mice; (3) pathogens or microorganisms that cause disease in humans; and (4) weeds. Is there a pattern in the histories of these groups that suggests an overall explanation for the phenomenon of the Demographic Takeover or that at least suggests fresh paths of inquiry?

Human Beings

Europe has exported something in excess of 60 million people in the past few hundred years. Great Britain alone exported over 20 million. The great mass of these white emigrants went to the United States, Argentina, Canada, Australia, Uruguay, and New Zealand. (Other areas to absorb comparable quantities of Europeans were Brazil and Russia east of the Urals. These would qualify as Lands of the Demographic Takeover except that large portions of their populations are not European.[6])

In stark contrast, very few Aborigines of the Americas, Australia, or New Zealand ever went to Europe. Those who did often died not long after arrival.[7] The fact that the flow of human migration was almost entirely from Europe to her colonies and not vice versa is not startling, or very enlightening. Europeans controlled overseas migration, and Europe needed to export, not import, labor. But this pattern of one-way migration is significant in that it reappears in other connections.

Animals

The vast expanses of forests, savannahs, and steppes in the Lands of the Demographic Takeover were inundated by animals from the Old

World, chiefly Europe. Horses, cattle, sheep, goats, and pigs have for hundreds of years been among the most numerous of the quadrupeds of these lands, which were completely lacking in these species at the time of first contact with the Europeans. By 1600 enormous feral herds of horses and cattle surged over the pampas of the Río de la Plata (today's Argentina, Uruguay, and southern Brazil) and over the plains of northern Mexico. By the beginning of the seventeenth century packs of Old World dogs gone wild were among the predators of these herds.[8]

In the forested country of British North America, population explosions among imported animals were also spectacular, but only by European standards, not by those of Spanish America. By 1700 pigs were everywhere in tidewater Virginia, and young gentlemen were entertaining themselves by hunting wild horses of the inland counties. In Carolina the herds of cattle were "incredible, being from one to two thousand head in one Man's Possession." In the eighteenth and early nineteenth centuries the advancing European frontier from New England to the Gulf of Mexico was preceded into Indian territory by an avant-garde of semiwild herds of hogs and cattle tended, now and again, by semiwild herdsmen, white and black.[9]

The first English settlers landed in Botany Bay, Australia, in January of 1788 with livestock, most of it from the Cape of Good Hope. The pigs and poultry thrived; the cattle did well enough; the sheep, the future source of the colony's good fortune, died fast. Within a few months two bulls and four cows had strayed away. By 1804 the wild herds they founded numbered from three to five thousand head and were in possession of much of the best land between the settlements and the Blue Mountains. If they had ever found their way through the mountains to the grasslands beyond, the history of Australia in the first decades of the nineteenth century might have been one dominated by cattle rather than sheep. As it is, the colonial government wanted the land the wild bulls so ferociously defended, and considered the growing practice of convicts running away to live off the herds as a threat to the whole colony; so the adult cattle were shot and salted down and the calves captured and tamed. The English settlers imported woolly sheep from Europe and sought out the interior pastures for them. The animals multiplied rapidly, and when Darwin made his visit to New South Wales in 1836, there were about a million sheep there for him to see.[10]

The arrival of Old World livestock probably affected New Zealand more radically than any other of the Lands of the Demographic Take-over. Cattle, horses, goats, pigs and—in this land of few or no large predators—even the usually timid sheep went wild. In New Zealand, herds of feral farm animals were practicing the ways of their remote ancestors as late as the 1940s and no doubt still run free. Most of the sheep, though, stayed under human control, and within a decade of Great Britain's annexation of New Zealand in 1840, her new acquisition was home to a quarter-million sheep. In 1989 New Zealand had over 55 million sheep, about twenty times more sheep than people.[11]

In the Lands of the Demographic Takeover the European pioneers were accompanied and often preceded by their domesticated animals, walking sources of food, leather, fiber, power, and wealth, and these animals often adapted more rapidly to the new surroundings and repro-duced much more rapidly than their masters. To a certain extent, the success of Europeans as colonists was automatic as soon as they put their tough, fast, fertile, and intelligent animals ashore. The latter were sources of capital that sought out their own sustenance, improvised their own protection against the weather, fought their own battles against predators and, if their masters were smart enough to allow calves, colts, and lambs to accumulate, could and often did show the world the amazing possibilities of compound interest.

The honeybee is the one insect of worldwide importance that human beings have domesticated, if we may use the word in a broad sense. Many species of bees and other insects produce honey, but the one that does so in greatest quantity and that is easiest to control is a native of the Mediterranean area and the Middle East, the honey bee *(Apis mellifera)*. The European may have taken this sweet and short-tempered servant to every colony he ever established, from Arctic to Antarctic Circle, and the honeybee has always been one of the first immigrants to set off on its own. Sometimes the advance of the bee frontier could be very rapid: the first hive in Tasmania swarmed sixteen times in the summer of 1832.[12]

Thomas Jefferson tells us that the Indians of North America called the honey bees "English flies," and St. John de Crèvecoeur, his con-temporary, wrote that "the Indians look upon them with an evil eye, and consider their progress into the interior of the continent as an omen of the white man's approach: thus, as they discover the bees, the news of the event, passing from mouth to mouth, spreads sadness and conster-nation on all sides."[13]

Domesticated creatures that traveled from the Lands of the Demographic Takeover to Europe are few. Australian Aborigines and New Zealand Maoris had a few tame dogs, unimpressive by Old World standards and unwanted by the whites. Europe happily accepted the American Indians' turkeys and guinea pigs, but had no need for their dogs, llamas, and alpacas. Again the explanation is simple: Europeans, who controlled the passage of large animals across the oceans, had no need to reverse the process.

It is interesting and perhaps significant, though, that the exchange was just as one-sided for varmints, the small mammals whose migrations Europeans often tried to stop. The American or Australian or New Zealand equivalents of rats have not become established in Europe, but Old World varmints, especially rats, have colonized right alongside the Europeans in the temperate zones. Rats of assorted sizes, some of them almost surely European immigrants, were tormenting Spanish Americans by at least the end of the sixteenth century. European rats established a beachhead in Jamestown, Virginia, as early as 1609, when they almost starved out the colonists by eating their food stores. In Buenos Aires the increase in rats kept pace with that of cattle, according to an early nineteenth-century witness. European rats proved as aggressive as the Europeans in New Zealand, where they completely replaced the local rats in North Island as early as the 1840s. Those poor creatures are probably completely extinct today or exist only in tiny relict populations.[14]

The European rabbits are not usually thought of as varmints, but where there are neither diseases nor predators to hold down their numbers they can become the worst of pests. In 1859 a few members of the species *Orytolagus cuniculus* (the scientific name for all the Peter Rabbits of literature) were released in southeast Australia. Despite massive efforts to stop them, they reproduced—true to their reputation—and spread rapidly all the way across Australia's southern half to the Indian Ocean. In 1950 the rabbit population of Australia was estimated at 500 million, and they were outcompeting the nation's most important domesticated animals, sheep, for the grasses and herbs. They have been brought under control, but only by means of artificially fomenting an epidemic of myxomatosis, a lethal American rabbit disease. The story of rabbits and myxomatosis in New Zealand is similar.[15]

Europe, in return for her varmints, has received muskrats and gray squirrels and little else from America, and less from Australia or New

Zealand, and we might well wonder if muskrats and squirrels really qualify as varmints.[16] As with other classes of organisms, the exchange has been largely a one-way street.

Pathogens

None of Europe's emigrants were as immediately and colossally successful as its pathogens, the microorganisms that make human beings ill, cripple them, and kill them. Whenever and wherever Europeans crossed the oceans to settle outside of the Old World, the pathogens they carried created prodigious epidemics of smallpox, measles, influenza, and a number of other diseases. These pathogens, unlike the Europeans themselves or most of their domesticated animals, did at least as well in the tropics as in the temperate Lands of the Demographic Takeover. Epidemics devastated Mexico, Peru, Brazil, Hawaii, and Tahiti soon after the Europeans made the first contact with aboriginal populations. Some of these populations were able to escape demographic defeat because their initial numbers were so large that a small fraction was still sufficient to maintain occupation of, if not title to, the land, and also because the mass of Europeans were never attracted to the tropical lands, even if they were partially vacated. In the Lands of the Demographic Takeover the aboriginal populations were too sparse to rebound from the onslaught of disease or were inundated by European immigrants before they could recover.

The first strike force of the white immigrants to the Lands of the Demographic Takeover were epidemics. A few examples from scores of possible examples follow. Smallpox first arrived in the Río de la Plata region in 1558 or 1560 and killed, according to one chronicler possibly more interested in effect than accuracy, "more than a hundred thousand Indians" of the heavy riverine population there. An epidemic of plague or typhus decimated the Indians of the New England coast immediately before the founding of Plymouth. Smallpox or something similar struck the Aborigines of Australia's Botany Bay in 1789, killed half, and rolled on into the interior. Some unidentified disease or diseases spread through the Maori tribes of the North Island of New Zealand in the 1790s, killing so many in a number of villages that the survivors were not able to bury the dead.[17] After a series of such lethal and rapidly moving epidemics came the slow, unspectacular but thorough cripplers and killers like venereal disease and tuberculosis. In conjunction with the large numbers of white settlers, these diseases were enough to smother aboriginal chances of recovery. First the blitz-krieg, then the mopping up.

The greatest of the killers in these lands was probably smallpox. The exception is New Zealand, the last of these lands to attract perma-nent European settlers. Europeans came to New Zealand after the spread of vaccination in Europe and so were poor carriers. As of the 1850s, smallpox still had not come ashore, and by that time two-thirds of the Maori had been vaccinated.[18] The tardy arrival of smallpox in these islands may have much to do with the fact that the Maori today com-prise a larger percentage (9 percent) of their country's population than that of any other aboriginal people in any European colony or former European colony in either temperate zone, save only South Africa.

American Indians bore the full brunt of smallpox, and its mark is on their history and folklore. The Kiowa of the southern plains of the United States have a legend in which a Kiowa man meets Smallpox on the plain, riding a horse. The man asks, "Where do you come from and what do you do and why are you here?" Smallpox answers, "I am one with the white men—they are my people as the Kiowas are yours. Sometimes I travel ahead of them and sometimes behind. But I am always their companion and you will find me in their camps and their houses." "What can you do?" the Kiowa asks. "I bring death," Small-pox replies. "My breath causes children to wither like young plants in spring snow. I bring destruction. No matter how beautiful a woman is, once she has looked at me she becomes as ugly as death. And to men I bring not death alone, but the destruction of their children and the blighting of their wives. The strongest of warriors go down before me. No people who have looked on me will ever be the same."[19]

Europeans received little in return for the barrage of diseases they directed overseas. Australia and New Zealand provided no new strains of pathogens to Europe—or none that attracted attention. And of America's native diseases, none had any real influence on the Old World—with the possible exception of venereal syphilis, which almost certainly existed in the New World before 1492 and probably did not occur in its present form in the Old World.[20]

Weeds

Weeds are rarely history makers, for they are not as spectacular in their effects as pathogens. But they, too, influence our lives and migrate over the world despite human wishes. As such, like varmints and germs, they are better indicators of certain realities than human beings or domesticated animals.

The term *weed* in modern botanical usage refers to any type of plant which—because of especially large numbers of seeds produced per plant, or especially effective means of distributing those seeds, or especially tough roots and rhizomes from which new plants can grow, or especially tough seeds that survive the alimentary canals of animals to be planted with their droppings—spreads rapidly and outcompetes others on disturbed, bare soil. Weeds are plants that tempt the botanist to use such anthropomorphic words as "aggressive" and "opportunistic."

Many of the most successful weeds in the well-watered regions of the Lands of the Demographic Takeover are of European or Eurasian origin. French and Dutch and English farmers brought with them to North America their worst enemies, weeds, "to exhaust the land, hinder and damnify the Crop."[21] By the last third of the seventeenth century at least twenty different types were widespread enough in New England to attract the attention of the English visitor, John Josselyn, who identified couch grass, dandelion, nettles, mallowes, knot grass, shepherd's purse, sow thistle, clot burr, and others. One of the most aggressive was plantain, which the Indians called "English-Man's Foot."[22]

European weeds rolled west with the pioneers, in some cases spreading almost explosively. As of 1823, corn chamomile and maywood had spread up to but not across the Muskingum River in Ohio. Eight years later they had crossed the river.[23] The most prodigiously imperialistic of the weeds in the eastern half of the United States and Canada were probably Kentucky bluegrass and white clover. They spread so fast after the entrance of Europeans into a given area that there is some suspicion that they may have been present in pre-Columbian America, although the earliest European accounts do not mention them. Probably brought to the Appalachian area by the French, these two kinds of weeds preceded the English settlers there and kept up with the movement westward until reaching the plains across the Mississippi.[24]

Old World plants set up business on their own on the Pacific coast of North America just as soon as the Spaniards and Russians did. The climate of coastal southern California is much the same as that of the Mediterranean, and the Spaniards who came to California in the eighteenth century brought their own Mediterranean weeds with them via Mexico: wild oats, fennel, wild radishes. These plants, plus those brought in later by the Forty-niners, muscled their way to dominance in the coastal grasslands. These immigrant weeds followed Old World horses, cattle, and sheep into California's interior prairies and took over there as well.[25]

The region of Argentina and Uruguay was as radically altered in its flora as in its fauna by the coming of the Europeans. The ancient Indian practice, taken up immediately by the whites, of burning off the old grass of the pampa every year, as well as the trampling and cropping to the ground of indigenous grasses and forbs by the thousands of imported quadrupeds who also changed the nature of the soil with their droppings, opened the whole countryside to European plants. In the 1780s, Félix de Azara observed that the pampa, already radically altered, was changing as he watched. European weeds sprang up around every cabin, grew up along roads, and pressed into the open steppe. Today only a quarter of the plants growing wild in the pampa are native, and in the well-watered eastern portions, the "natural" ground cover consists almost entirely of Old World grasses and clovers.[26]

The invaders were not, of course, always desirable. When Darwin visited Uruguay in 1832, he found large expanses, perhaps as much as hundreds of square miles, monopolized by the immigrant wild artichoke and transformed into a prickly wilderness fit neither for humanity nor its animals.[27]

The onslaught of foreign and specifically European plants on Australia began abruptly in 1778 because the first expedition that sailed from Britain to Botany Bay carried some livestock and considerable quantities of seed. By May of 1803 over two hundred foreign plants, most of them European, had been purposely introduced and planted in New South Wales, undoubtedly along with a number of weeds.[28] Even today so-called "clean seed" characteristically contains some weed seeds, and this was much more so two hundred years ago. By and large, Australia's north has been too tropical and her interior too hot and dry for European weeds and grasses, but much of her southern coasts and Tasmania have been hospitable indeed to Europe's willful flora.

Thus, many—often a majority—of the most aggressive plants in the temperate humid regions of North America, South America, Australia, and New Zealand are of European origin. It may be true that in every broad expanse of the world today where there are dense populations, with whites in the majority, there are also dense populations of European weeds. Thirty-five of eighty-nine weeds listed in 1953 as common in the state of New York are European. Approximately 60 percent of Canada's worst weeds are introductions from Europe. Most of New Zealand's weeds are from the same source, as are many, perhaps most, of the weeds of Australia's well-watered southern coasts. Most of the European plants that Josselyn listed as naturalized in New England in the seventeenth century are growing wild today in Argentina and Uruguay, and are among the most widespread and troublesome of all weeds in those countries.[29]

In return for this largesse of pestiferous plants, the Lands of the Demographic Takeover have provided Europe with only a few equivalents. The Canadian waterweed jammed Britain's nineteenth century waterways, and North America's horseweed and burnweed have spread in Europe's empty lots, and South America's flowered galinsoga has thrived in her gardens. But the migratory flow of a whole group of organisms between Europe and the Lands of the Demographic Takeover has been almost entirely in one direction.[30] Englishman's Foot still marches in seven-league jackboots across every European colony of settlement, but very few American or Australian or New Zealand invaders stride the wastelands and unkempt backyards of Europe.

Conclusion

European and Old World human beings, domesticated animals, varmints, pathogens, and weeds all accomplished demographic takeovers of their own in the temperate, well-watered regions of North and South America, Australia, and New Zealand. They crossed oceans and Europeanized vast territories, often in informal cooperation with each other—the farmer and his animals destroying native plant cover, making way for imported grasses and forbs, many of which proved more nourishing to domesticated animals than the native equivalents; Old World pathogens, sometimes carried by Old World varmints, wiping out vast numbers of Aborigines, opening the way for the advance of the European frontier, exposing more and more native peoples to more and more pathogens. The classic example of symbiosis between European colonists, their animals, and plants comes from New Zealand. Red clover, a good forage for sheep, could not seed itself and did not spread without being annually sown until the Europeans imported the bumblebee. Then the plant and insect spread widely, the first providing the second with food, the second carrying pollen from blossom to blossom for the first, and the sheep eating the clover and compensating human beings for their effort with mutton and wool.[31]

There have been few such stories of the success in Europe of organisms from the Lands of the Demographic Takeover, despite the obvious fact that for every ship that went from Europe to those lands, another traveled in the opposite direction.

The demographic triumph of Europeans in the temperate colonies is one part of a biological and ecological takeover that could not have been accomplished by human beings alone, gunpowder notwithstanding. We must at least try to analyze the impact and success of often mutually supportive plants, animals, and microlife, which in their entirety can be accurately described as aggressive and opportunistic, an ecosystem simplified by ocean crossings and honed by thousands of years of competition in the unique environment created by the Old World Neolithic Revolution.

The human invaders and their descendants have consulted their egos, rather than ecologists, for explanations of their triumphs. But the human victims, the Aborigines of the Lands of the Demographic Takeover, knew better, knew they were only one of the many categories being displaced and replaced; they knew they were victims of something more irresistible and awesome than the spread of capitalism or Christianity. One Maori, at the nadir of the history of his race, expressed this when he said, "As the clover killed off the fern, and the European dog the Maori dog—as the Maori rat was destroyed by the Pakeha [European] rat—so our people, also, will be gradually supplanted and exterminated by the Europeans."[32] The future was not so grim as he prophesied, but we must admire his grasp of the complexity and magnitude of the threat looming over his people and over the ecosystem of which they were a part.

Notes

1. Page Stegner, ed., *The Portable Nabokov* (New York: Viking, 1968), 527; Francis Darwin, ed., *Life and Letters of Charles Darwin* (London: Murray, 1887), 2: 391.

2. *The World Almanac and Book of Facts 1993* (New York: Pharos Books, 1992), passim.

3. Philip D. Curtin, "Epidemiology and the Slave Trade," *Political Science Quarterly* 83 (June 1968): 190–216 passim; John Prebble, *The Darien Disaster* (New York: Holt, Rinehart and Winston, 1968), 296, 300; Charles M. Andrews, *The Colonial Period of American History* (New Haven: Yale University Press, 1934), vol. 1, n. 497; Gilberto Freyre, *The Masters and the Slaves,* trans. Samuel Putnam (New York: Knopf, 1946), passim; Donald L. Wiedner, *A History of Africa South of the Sahara* (New York: Vintage Books, 1964), 49–51; Stuart B. Schwartz, "Indian Labor and New World Plantations: European Demands and Indian Responses in Northeastern Brazil," *American Historical Review* 83 (February 1978): 43–79 passim.

4. Marcel R. Reinhard, *Histoire de la population mondiale de 1700 à 1948* (n.p.: Editions Domat-Montchrestien, n.d.), 339–411, 428–31; G.F. McCleary, *Peopling the British Commonwealth* (London: Farber and Farber, n.d.), 83, 94, 109–10; R. R. Palmer and Joel Colton, *A History of the Modern World* (New York: Knopf, 1965), 560; *World Almanac and Book of Facts, 1978* (New York: Newspaper Enterprise Association, 1978), 34, 439, 497, 513, 590.

5. Charles Darwin, *The Voyage of the Beagle* (Garden City, N.Y.: Doubleday Anchor Books, 1962), 433–34.

6. William Woodruff, *Impact of Western Man* (New York: St. Martin's, 1967), 106–8.

7. Carolyn T. Foreman, *Indians Abroad* (Norman: University of Oklahoma Press, 1943), passim.

8. Alfred W. Crosby, *The Columbian Exchange: Biological and Cultural Consequences of 1492* (Westport, Conn.: Greenwood, 1972), 82–88; Alexander Gillespie, *Gleanings and Remarks Collected during Many Months of Residence at Buenos Aires* (Leeds: B. DeWhirst, 1818), 136; Oscar Schmieder, "Alteration of the Argentine Pampa in the Colonial Period," *University of California Publications in Geography* 2 (September 27, 1927): n. 311.

9. Robert Beverley, *History and Present State of Virginia* (Chapel Hill: University of North Carolina Press, 1947), 153, 312, 318; John Lawson, *A New Voyage to Carolina* (Chester, VT: Readex Microprint Corp., 1966), 4; Frank L. Owsley, "The Pattern of Migration and Settlement of the Southern Frontier," *Journal of Southern History* 11 (May 1945): 147–75.

10. Commonwealth of Australia, *Historical Records of Australia* (Sydney: Library Committee of the Commonwealth Parliament, 1914), ser. 1, vol. 1, 550; vol. 7, 379–80; vol. 8, 150–51; vol. 9, 349, 714, 831; vol. 10, 92, 280, 682; vol. 20, 839.

11. Andrew H. Clark, *The Invasion of New Zealand by People, Plants, and Animals* (New Brunswick, N.J.: Rutgers University Press, 1949), 190; *The World Almanac and Book of Facts 1993* (New York: Pharos Books, 1992), 783.

12. Remy Chauvin, *Traité de biologie de l'abeille* (Paris: Masson et Cie, 1968), 1:38–39; James Backhouse, *A Narrative of a Visit to the Australian Colonies* (London: Hamilton, Adams and Co., 1834), 23.

13. Merrill D. Peterson, ed., *The Portable Thomas Jefferson* (New York: Viking, 1975), 111; Michel-Guillaume St. Jean de Crèvecoeur, *Journey into Northern Pennsylvania and the State of New York,* trans. Clarissa S. Bostelmann (Ann Arbor: University of Michigan Press, 1964), 166.

14. Bernabé Cobo, *Obras* (Madrid: Atlas Ediciones, 1964), 1:350–51; Edward Arber, ed., *Travels and Works of Captain John Smith* (New York: Burt Franklin, n.d.), 2:xcv; K.A. Wodzicki, *Introduced Mammals of New Zealand* (Wellington: Department of Scientific and Industrial Research, 1950), 89–92.

15. Frank Fenner and F. N. Ratcliffe, *Myxomatosis* (Cambridge: Cambridge University Press, 1965), 9, 11, 17, 22–23; Frank Fenner, "The Rabbit Plague," *Scientific American* 190 (February 1954): 30–35; Wodzicki, *Introduced Mammals*, 107–41.

16. Charles S. Elton, *The Ecology of Invasions* (Trowbridge and London: English Language Book Society, 1972), 24–25, 28, 73, 123.

17. Juan López de Velasco, *Geografía y descripción universal de las Indias* (Madrid: Establecimiento Topográfico de Fortanet, 1894), 552; Oscar Schmieder, "The Pampa—A Natural and Culturally Induced Grassland?" *University of California Publications in Geography* (September 27, 1927): 266; Sherburne F. Cook, "The Significance of Disease in the Extinction of the New England Indians," *Human Biology* 14 (September 1975): 486–91; J. H. L. Cumpston, *The History of Smallpox in Australia, 1788–1908* (Melbourne: Albert J. Mullet, Government Printer, 1914), 147–49; Harrison M. Wright, *New Zealand, 1769–1840* (Cambridge: Harvard University Press, 1959), 62. For further discussion of this topic, see Crosby, *The Columbian Exchange,* chaps. 1 and 2; Crosby, *Ecological Imperialism: The Biological Expansion of Europe, 900–1900* (Cambridge: Cambridge University Press, 1986); and Henry F. Dobyns, *Native American Demography: A Critical Bibliography* (Bloomington: Indiana University Press/Newberry Library, 1976).

18. Arthur C. Thomson, *The Story of New Zealand* (London: Murray, 1859), 1:212.

19. Alice Marriott and Carol K. Rachlin, *American Indian Mythology* (New York: New American Library, 1968), 174–75.

20. Crosby, *The Columbian Exchange,* 122–64, passim.

21. Jared Eliot, "The Tilling of the Land, 1760," in *Agriculture in the United States: A Documentary History,* ed. Wayne D. Rasmussen (New York: Random House, 1975), 1:192.

22. John Josselyn, *New England's Rarities Discovered* (London: G. Widdowes at the Green Dragon in St. Paul's Church-yard, 1672), 85, 86; Edmund Berkeley and Dorothy S. Berkeley, eds., *The Reverend John Clayton* (Charlottesville: University of Virginia Press, 1965), 24.

23. Lewis D. de Shweinitz, "Remarks on the Plants of Europe Which Have Become Naturalized in a More or Less Degree, in the United States," *Annals Lyceum of Natural History of New York* 3 (1832): 1828–1836, 155.

24. Lyman Carrier and Katherine S. Bort, "The History of Kentucky Bluegrass and White Clover in the United States," *Journal of the American Society of Agronomy* 8 (1916): 255–56; Robert W. Schery, "The Migration of a Plant: Kentucky Bluegrass Followed Settlers to the New World," *Natural History* 74 (December 1965): 43–44; G.W. Dunbar, "Henry Clay on Kentucky Bluegrass," *Agricultural History* 51 (July 1977): 522.

25. Edgar Anderson, *Plants, Man, and Life* (Berkeley and Los Angeles: University of California Press, 1967), 12–15; Elna S. Bakker, *An Island Called California* (Berkeley and Los Angeles: University of California Press, 1971), 150–52;

R.W. Allard, "Genetic Systems Associated with Colonizing Ability in Predominantly Self-Pollinated Species," in *The Genetics of Colonizing Species,* ed. H.G. Baker and G. Ledyard Stebbins (New York: Academic Press, 1965), 50; M.W. Talbot, H.M. Biswell, and A.L. Hormay, "Fluctuations in the Annual Vegetation of California," *Ecology* 20 (July 1939): 396–97.

26. Félix de Azara, *Descripción e historia del Paraguay y del Río de la Plata* (Madrid: Imprenta de Sánchez, 1847), 1:57–58; Schmieder, "Alteration of the Argentine Pampa," 310–11.

27. Darwin, *Voyage of the Beagle,* 119–20.

28. *Historical Records of Australia,* ser. 1, vol. 4, 234–41.

29. Edward Salisbury, *Weeds and Aliens* (London: Collins, 1961), 87; Ángel Julio Cabrera, *Manual de la flora de los alrededores de Buenos Aires* (Buenos Aires: Editorial Acme S.A., 1953), passim.

30. Elton, *The Ecology of Invasions,* 115; Hugo Ilitis, "The Story of Wild Garlic," *Scientific Monthly* 68 (February 1949): 122–24.

31. Otto E. Plath, *Bumblebees and Their Ways* (New York: Macmillan, 1934), 115.

32. James Bonwick, *The Last of the Tasmanians* (New York: Johnson Reprint Co., 1970), 380.

3 THE BIOLOGICAL METAMORPHOSIS OF THE AMERICAS

Chimalpahin Cuauhlehuanitzin, one of our best sources of information on Mexico in the years immediately before and after the Spanish conquest, was an Indian historian whom the invaders trained in the reading and writing of the Roman alphabet in the sixteenth century. His writings (in Nahuatl) inform us that the year 13-Flint before the invasion was a grim one in the Valley of Mexico. There was sickness, hunger, and an eclipse of the sun; an eruption of some sort between the volcanoes lztaccíhuatl and Popocatépetl; "and many ferocious beasts devoured the children." But 13-Flint, Chimalpahin makes clear, was an exception in what was an era of triumph for the Aztecs. They, who within recorded memory had been wanderers from the savage north, now exacted tributes of food, gold, quetzal feathers, and human hearts from vassal states all the way from the remote dry lands from which they had emerged to the rain forests of the south and east. The stiff-necked Tarascos, at the cost of perennial war, retained their independence, as did—precariously—the anciently civilized Mayas, and there were a few others who survived in the chinks of the Aztec Empire. Otherwise, central Mexico lay under the hegemony of the Aztecs.

Lord Ahuitzotl, who was ruler of the Aztecs in 13-Flint, used the legions and wealth under his command to improve and adorn his capital, the incomparable Tenochtitlán. He built a new aqueduct to bring fresh water to its scores of thousands of inhabitants. He rebuilt and reconsecrated the gigantic temple to the Aztec tribal deities, Huitzilopochtli and Tezcatlipoca. He did not—how could he have?—see in the strange events of 13-Flint portents of the end of his empire and of his world.

A decade later, in 10-Rabbit, his nephew Motecuhzoma Xocoyotzin, known to us as Montezuma, succeeded him as leader of the Aztecs. Montezuma's subjects numbered in the millions, and, so far as he or they knew, the empire had no equal in power and riches under the sky. Montezuma made plans to rebuild the great temple once more, higher and more extravagantly than any of his predecessors.

Reports drifted in from the eastern coast of pale, hairy visitors in boats "like towers or small mountains." There were only a few of them, and invaders traditionally came from the north, as had the Aztecs themselves, not from the east and never from the sea. Gods, however, might come from the sea.

The Onslaught

In the year 1-Reed the visitors came to invade and to stay forever. The invaders proved to be humans, not gods, but they were incomprehensibly alien and powerful. They had light skin and much hair on their lips and chins; some of them had yellow hair. They dressed in metal and brought weapons of metal. They had huge animals allied with them. The invaders had at their sides dogs bigger and fiercer than any seen before: "The color of their eyes is a burning yellow; their eyes flash fire and shoot off sparks." They had, also, man-animals that ran faster than any man and were more powerful than any creature the Aztecs had ever known. Then these creatures split, and the Aztecs saw that the invaders had "deer to carry them on their backs wherever they wish to go. These deer, our lord, are as tall as the roof of a house."

Most hideous of all the invaders' allies was a pestilence, a *hueyzahuatl,* that swept all the land immediately after the Aztecs, quickened by atrocities, turned on the invaders, killing half of them as they fought their way out of Tenochtitlán. The pestilence spared the invaders but was a thing of agony, disfigurement, and death for the peoples of Mexico. There was no defense against it nor cure for it. Bernardino de Sahagún learned how it struck in the month of Tepeilhuitl and

> spread over the people as great destruction. Some it quite covered on all parts—their faces, their heads, their breasts, and so on. There was a great havoc. Very many died of it. They could not walk; they only lay in their resting places and beds. They could not move; they could not stir; they could not change position, nor lie on one side; nor face down,

nor on their backs. And if they stirred, much did they cry out. Great was its destruction. Covered, mantled with pustules, very many people died of them.

One-third, one-half—no one knows how many—of the Aztecs and the other peoples of Mexico died.

Then the invaders and their human allies, the Aztecs' former vassals and enemies, diminished by the epidemic but emboldened by the presence of the invaders, fought their way down the causeways and across Lake Texcoco into Tenochtitlán. Seventy-five days later, on the day 1-Serpent of the year 3-House, the siege of Tenochtitlán ended. Aztec poets expressed the grief of those who, somehow, had survived:

> Weep my people:
> know that with these disasters
> we have lost the Mexica nation.
> The water has turned bitter,
> our food is bitter.

The invaders' chief, Hernán Cortés, ordered that stones from the temple of which Lord Ahuitzotl had been so proud should be gathered up, and that a Christian cathedral should be made of them in the center of what had become, by his victory, Mexico City. The vanquished learned that the ominous year 13-Flint was more properly designated as the year 1492 of a deity both more imperialistic and more merciful than Huitzilopochtli or Tezcatlipoca, and that Tenochtitlán had fallen in the year 1521, not 3-House.

The fall of Tenochtitlán in the year 3-House was the worst discrete event in the Aztecs' history. Worse, however, was this: 3-House was the beginning of the most tragic century of their history. Their civilization suffered massive amputations and survived at the root only by accepting alien graftings in the branch, as the conquistadores and the friars replaced their ancient noble and priestly classes. There were advantages that came with the defeat: an alphabet, a more supple instrument for expression than their own logo-syllabic system of writing; the true arch to replace the corbel; tools with an iron edge that did not shatter like an obsidian edge when it struck the rock hidden in the leaves. But the magnitude of the change, good and bad, was almost greater than the mind could encompass or the heart endure. The metamorphosis was more than political or religious or intellectual or technological; it was biological. The biota of Mexico—its *life*—and, in time, that of the entire Western Hemisphere changed.

The Change

If Lord Ahuitzotl had returned to Mexico (now New Spain) a hundred years after 13-Flint he would have found much the same as in his lifetime. He would have recognized the profiles of the mountains, all the wild birds, and most of the plants. The basic and holy food of his people was still maize. But he would have been stunned by the sight of plants and creatures he had never seen or dreamed of during his days on earth. Alien plants grew alongside the old plants in Mexico, and its 1592 fauna, in its large animals, was as different from that of 1492 as the native fauna of Zimbabwe is from that of Spain.

The invaders had brought in wheat and other Eurasian and African grains; peach, pear, orange, and lemon trees; chick-peas, grape vines, melons, onions, radishes, and much more. A Spanish nobleman come to America could require his *indios* to furnish his table with the foods of his ancestors. Along with the Old World crops had come Old World weeds. European clover was by now so common that the Aztecs had a word of their own for it. They called it Castilian *ocoxochitl,* naming it after a low native plant that also prefers shade and moisture.

Of all the new sights of 1592—the cathedrals, the fields of wheat, wheeled vehicles, brigantines with sails and lounging sailors on Lake Texcoco where there had once been only canoes and sweating paddlers —nothing could have amazed Ahuitzotl more than the new animals: pigs, sheep, goats, burros, and others. Now there were cattle everywhere, and ranches with more than a hundred thousand each in the north. Now there were thousands upon thousands of horses, and they were available to any European (and, despite the law, the Indian, too) with a few coins or the skill to rope them. The horsemanship of the Mexican *vaquero* was already legendary on both sides of the Atlantic.

During Lord Ahuitzotl's lifetime the best way to move four hundred ears of maize in Mexico was on the bent back of a man, and the fastest means to deliver a message was by a runner. Now the bent man loaded four thousand ears onto a wheeled wagon pulled by a burro, and the messenger vaulted onto a horse and set off at several times the fastest pace of the fastest sprinter.

But Lord Ahuitzotl was an Aztec, an *indio,* and what would have put a catch in his breath a century after 13-Flint was not so much the new animals, for all their number, but his own kind of people, in their meager number. War, brutality, hunger, social and family disarray, loss of farmland to the invading humans and their flocks, and exploitation in general had taken their toll, but disease was the worst enemy. The *hueyzahuatl* of 1520–21, like the fall of Tenochtitlán, may have been the worst of its kind, but, more important, it was the beginning of a series of pestilential onslaughts. The worst of the worst of the times of *cocoliztli* were 1545–48, a time of bleeding from the nose and eyes, and 1576–81, when, again, many bled from the nose and windrows of Indians fell, but few Spaniards. If Lord Ahuitzotl had returned a century after his death, he would have found one for every ten or even twenty *indios* who had lived in his time.

Some of the survivors were *mestizos,* children of European men and Indian women. The mestizo, with his Indian skin and Visigothic eyes, proffering a cup of cocoa, a mixture of *chocolatl* and Old World sugar; the wild Chichimec on his Berber mare; the Zapotec herder with his sheep; the Aztec, perhaps the last of the line of Ahuitzotl, receiving the final rites of the Christian faith as he slipped into the terminal coma of an infection newly arrived from Seville—in so many ways New Spain was *new,* a combination, crossing, and concoction of entities that had never before existed on the same continent.

Explanations

To understand the complexity of that concoction, we have to look far back in the history of our planet, farther back than Europeans of the age of exploration could imagine. They believed that God had created the world a cozy six thousand years earlier, a colossal underestimation that forestalled comprehension of the causes of the differences between biota on opposite sides of the Atlantic. Columbus and his contemporaries had no inkling that 200 million years ago the continents of the earth were parts of one immense world continent in which physical contiguity minimized the development of biological diversity. That is to say, the world's land biota, though it varied from one region or even neighborhood to another, was more homogeneous than at any time since, because true geographic isolation was very rare, except for oceanic islands.

Then slow and unimaginably powerful tectonic forces tore the supercontinent into several, eventually six, masses and shouldered them
to the positions where they were in 1492, where they are today, with a
few centimeters difference. During the interval of more than 150 million years the dinosaurs disappeared, birds appeared, and mammals
advanced from minor status to dominance over most of the terrestrial
globe. In the large Eurasian-African mass, most of the species of mammals that are most widely distributed in the world today originated or
evolved into their present forms. In the other land masses, life evolved
divergently, and thus Australia's biota is very different from Eurasia–
Africa's.

Columbus wrote of the West Indies that the trees were "as different
from ours as day from night, and so the fruits, the herbage." He was so
surprised by the differences in the plants, and animals too, that he even
claimed the rocks were different.

In Africa a few geological eras ago arboreal mammals with binocu-
lar eyesight and prehensile hands and feet moved down from the trees
and out onto the grasslands. The toes of some of them shortened and
the palms of their feet flattened and rose into arches for walking, and
two of their ten fingers developed into thumbs. They developed bigger
and better brains to compensate for the puniness of their teeth and
claws and their slowness in pursuit and flight. They learned how to live
and to hunt in teams, how to make and use tools, how to make clothing, how to control fire, and how to teach their young these skills.
Their numbers increased; they began to migrate, first throughout
Africa–Eurasia and even into the blue shadows of the retreating glaciers, and then to Australia, and across from Siberia to Alaska and the
Western Hemisphere.

That was, for the geologist or paleontologist, barely yesterday, but
for the anthropologist or historian it was a long time ago. The most
recent common ancestor of Native Americans, whose ancestors
crossed from the eastern extreme of Eurasia into America, and of
Europeans, who sailed from the western extreme in 1492, lived tens of
thousands and perhaps even more years ago. The Tainos and Spaniards
who met in the Greater Antilles were products of physical and, more
significantly, cultural evolutions that had been diverging for a very
long time. The Tainos reached out to touch the Spaniards "to ascertain
if they were flesh and bones like themselves." For the Spaniards, the
Tainos were the most exotic people they had ever met, with their hair

not tightly curled like the Africans' "but straight and coarse like horse-hair." Columbus wrote of them that "the whole forehead and head is very broad, more so than any other race that I have ever seen." They did not have the wheel or wheat or rice or iron or bronze. They did have a few trinkets of gold.

The contrasts continued to astonish Native Americans and Europeans after the latter reached the mainland. And no wonder: these two peoples had migrated in opposite directions around the world and for millennia before they met each other. The duration of their period of separation ensured that not only their physical appearance but their cultures had developed divergently. In the crude test of confrontation, one would be likely to have, at least for the short run, material advantages over the other. History makes clear that it was the Europeans who had the edge.

But to exploit their advantages, the Europeans had to get them across the Atlantic. They could no more have successfully invaded the Americas from Europe in the sixteenth century than the Allies could have invaded Normandy from North America in 1944. Large offshore bases were essential in both cases, the British Isles in the latter, the Greater Antilles in the former. The Allies needed the British Isles as a center from which to gather intelligence about the mainland and as a storage, training, and staging area. The conquistadores needed the Antilles for all that and—much more importantly—for the seasoning and propagation of their biological allies.

Except for the Tainos and bats, the only land mammal in the Greater Antilles in 1492 was the *hutia*, a tasty rabbit-sized rodent. There was a profusion of birds and many reptiles, including the large, extravagantly ugly but tasty iguana. The Tainos, whom Columbus noted as "very unskilled with arms" and fit to be servants and even slaves, were numerous, at least three million on Española (Hispaniola) alone, said an eyewitness.

Columbus returned to Española and the Antilles in 1493 with seventeen ships; twelve hundred men; seeds, cuttings, and stones for wheat, chick-peas, melons, onions, radishes, salad greens, grapevines, sugarcane, and fruit trees; and horses, dogs, pigs, cattle, chickens, sheep, and goats. That he also brought weeds, vermin such as rats, and germs is certain: there was no such entity then (or now) as a sack of truly clean seed, an absolutely clean ship, or a horse, pig, or man without microorganisms in its feces, fluids, and breath.

European crops, though they eventually prospered in both Americas, did not thrive in the tropical Antilles; the conquistadores were obliged to substitute the Taino staple, manioc, for wheaten bread. But their livestock did well, some fabulously well, in the Antilles, where the large carnivores were rare, where there were no local equivalents of rinderpest or hoof-and-mouth disease, and where, at first, the quantity of nourishment was immense and its quality splendid. Most of the imported animals prospered, most notably for the purposes of Cortés, Pizarro, and the like, the horses, cattle, and swine. They increased so fast that soon the backcountry of the Antilles swarmed with feral livestock. When the time came for launching invasions of the mainland, good mounts, pack animals, pork, beef, and hides were cheap—free, if you were willing to go get them yourself. Cortés did not invade Mexico with horses emaciated from weeks crossing the Atlantic, but with horses fresh from Cuba. Hernando de Soto traveled amid herds of hundreds of succulent pigs, all probably descendants from the eight Columbus brought from Spain to Española in 1493. The masters of America's first *haciendas* did not begin with bulls too weak to mount cows that were too frail to carry calves to full term, but with healthy beasts selected from the avant-garde herds of the Antilles.

The conquistadores' most powerful ally of all, the smallpox virus, also incubated in the Antilles. Smallpox had been a common affliction in the more densely populated regions of Europe in the Middle Ages, but it was not commonly a killer. Then, around 1500 it added to its ease of transmission a tendency to kill its hosts. It was so common in the cities facing west across the Atlantic that nearly all urban children caught it and were soon dead or immune—either way, no longer media for its propagation. Not for two more decades did chance provide the virus with a way to cross to the Americas. However it came, either by means of a few smallpox scabs in a bale of waste cloth or the serial infection of a few African slaves immunologically virgin of *hidalgos* from rural Castile who decided to gamble their futures in the colonies; it arrived not long before or after Christmas of 1518.

It seared through the Tainos like a fire driven through dry brush by the wind they called *hurakan*. Their number had been falling precipitously since the 1490s, and now came the worst single blow of all. Bartolomé de las Casas recorded that the smallpox left no more than one thousand alive on Española "of that immensity of people that was on this island and which we have seen with our own eyes."

Within thirty years of Columbus's first landfall in the West Indies those islands contained all that the conquistadores needed for the successful invasion of the mainland: considerable numbers of their ambitious selves, livestock in cheap abundance, and at least one highly infectious and deadly disease to which almost every adult invader was immune and for which Native Americans were kindling. This team of invaders conquered the Aztecs within two years of first penetrating their empire. In the following decade, the same team, pushing south from the Spanish settlements in Central America, achieved an equally dramatic conquest of the Inca Empire. There were no more such magnificent conquests because there were no more such empires in the Western Hemisphere; but whenever the Spaniards—de Soto, Coronado, Valdivia—made their spectacular *entradas* into unknown lands, and wherever they founded permanent settlements—Buenos Aires, Guatemala City, Florida's Saint Augustine—their successes were as much due to their biological allies as to their abilities. The feats of the conquistadores seem to us, four and five centuries later, superhuman precisely because they were just that—the triumphs of teams that included more than humans.

The Companions of the Conquistadores

The reputations of the conquistadores and their Portuguese, French, Dutch, British, and Russian equivalents need no more burnishing than historians have already afforded them, but the other large creatures of the invading team have been relatively neglected. In the long run, such species as chickens, sheep, and goats were crucially important, particularly for the Native Americans, but let us focus on the imported organisms that were most important in the short run, particularly to the invaders: pigs, cattle, horses, and pathogens.

First, the noble swine who accompanied the conquistadores were not the pampered, paunchy Neros of our barnyards, but the lean, fast, tusked boars and sows of medieval Europe. They were intolerant of direct sunlight and high temperatures, but there were shade and wallows in plenty in the American tropics. More food was immediately available for these omnivorous beasts in the areas first settled by Europeans in the Americas than for any other immigrant animal. In the Antilles they rooted the Tainos' manioc tubers and sweet potatoes out of the ground, stole their guavas and pineapples, gobbled lizards and baby birds—everything went down their maws. Within a few years of their debarkation in Española they were running wild there in numbers *infinitos*. Swine explosions of commensurate magnitude took place in the other islands of the Greater Antilles.

Pigs adapted similarly everywhere in continental America. In New England they thrived on the shellfish they rooted out of the tidal flats; in Virginia they did "swarm like Vermaine upon the Earth." In the open pampas the sun was hostile, but they adapted and went wild along the watercourses; and in Brazil, according to a visitor in 1601, "they beginne to have great multitudes, and heere [pork] is the best flesh of all." Much of the meat in the first European colonists' diet, from Nova Scotia to Patagonia, was American green turtle or venison or other game, but after that it was usually pork—plentiful, tasty, nourishing, cheap in the market, and free to the hunter.

Cattle do not have the swine's sensitivity to sunlight and heat, but neither are they as good at crawling under logs, nor are they omnivorous. In other words, cattle were not as ready to seize the opportunity for independence in so wide a variety of American environments as pigs. Jungles, for instance, are not to their liking, and they often require a period of several generations to adapt to hot, wet grasslands. On the other hand, they were agile, swift, and formidably equipped for survival. They were more like their Pleistocene ancestors or Texas longhorns than upholstered Guernseys and Holsteins.

The Spanish cattle took to the meadows and savannas of the Antilles like Adam and Eve returning to Eden. The cows were soon dropping calves two and three times a year, and the first American bulls were massively bigger than those back in Spain, a report confirmed by modern archaeology. In 1518 Alonzo de Zuazo informed his king that thirty or forty strays would grow to three or four hundred in as little as three or four years. Feral cattle were roaming the hinterlands of Española by the 1520s and, soon after, the other Antilles. When the Europeans set them loose in the grasslands of northern Mexico and the pampa, the cattle propagated into scores upon scores of millions.

Columbus brought horses, essential to almost every European endeavor in the Americas, across the Atlantic in 1493. Many of these large animals, awkward to care for and difficult to feed properly on shipboard, died during the crossings, and the West Indian environment was not ideal for them; but by 1501 there were twenty or thirty on Española and two years later no fewer than sixty or seventy. Horses, good ones, were available when the conquistadores set off for the mainland. They were slow in adapting to the tropical lowlands of the continents but achieved a population explosion when they reached the temperate grasslands of the Western Hemisphere.

At the end of the sixteenth century the horses roaming free in Durango were beyond possibility of counting. Taken to New Mexico and California, beyond the great deserts, by Spanish explorers and settlers, they inspired the covetousness of the northern Indians, who rustled them and traded some to Indians further north. That process repeated itself until horses reached Alberta by the mid-eighteenth century. When the Aztecs first saw horses they called them deer; the Mayas called them tapirs; and Indians to the west of the Great Lakes called them moose. Mounted upon these wonderful animals, the Indians moved on to the plains to live off the buffalo and became light cavalry nonpareil. They were the last Native Americans north of Mexico to wage war against the invaders from the eastern ocean.

On the pampas, the Mexican drama of the horse was matched and surpassed. As in North America, Indians swung up onto their backs and moved into the grasslands to live off the herds of wild quadrupeds, which here were not indigenous buffalo but exotic horses and cattle. Native American resistance on the pampas would not be broken until the nineteenth century, at approximately the same time as the Great Plains Indians were defeated. The differences between the new kings of the great grasslands of the Americas—*vaqueros*, gauchos, cowboys —were not discernible at more than a few hundred meters, nor were the differences between their lightly tamed mounts.

The impact of the animals the Europeans brought with them to the Americas transformed whole ecosystems. For example, cattle and horses were so numerous on the pampas early in the seventeenth century that there were reports that they were destroying the ground cover. That is quite plausible, considering their density and the fact that, in time, Eurasian and North African grasses and forbs took over much of the pampas, a usurpation that could have taken place only along with the destruction of the native flora. Similar usurpations took place in Mexico and Texas in the first post-Columbian centuries.

The first Euro-Americans paid little attention to the impact of the smaller creatures they brought with them, but it may have been as great as that of the larger animals, even as great as that of the close-cropping sheep and goats. Old World rats swarmed in and around European colonies from Quebec to Patagonia, decimating the native small animals and minor flora and enhancing the importation and spread of disease. Imported domestic cats and dogs threw off their allegiances to humanity and went wild everywhere the environment allowed, living off whatever creatures they could pounce upon or drag down. Nothing, however, that crossed from the Eastern to the Western Hemisphere made as much difference in the first any other post-Columbian century as disease.

Native Americans are not native to the Americas, if by the adjective you mean in possession of a pedigree that goes back forever in association with a particular geographical region. Tapirs qualify as native Americans, but Indians are descendants of immigrants from Asia who crossed through the Arctic into the Western Hemisphere a phylogenetically short time ago. Human beings are not native to the Americas, nor are their direct ancestors and near relatives, the chimps, gorillas, and such.

This has not only zoological but great historical importance because it means there could have been no microorganisms or parasites adapted and predisposed to preying on humans when those clever bipeds came down through the glaciers into America. These immigrants were not free of infections, of course. They brought some infections with them, but not those informally known as the "crowd diseases." The proto-Indians were hunters and gatherers and traveled and lived in small bands, not crowds. The microorganisms of diseases like smallpox or measles disappear in small populations of hosts. These viruses need animal hosts to circulate among while not circulating among humans; they quickly die outside living bodies, and they race through small populations either killing or producing permanent immunity as they go. That is, they swiftly burn up all their fuel and disappear like a forest fire that has run out of trees. As for the germs of long-lasting infections like tuberculosis or syphilis, the proto-Indians could have and doubtlessly did bring some in that category with them, but perhaps not as many as you might think. The proto-Indians came as nomads through the climatically hostile Arctic, where the chronically ill could not have lasted for long: they either died or were, for the sake of the band, left behind to perish.

To put it in a nutshell, a medical officer in Alaska at the end of the Pleistocene epoch would have given most of these Asian immigrants a clean bill of health. They were entering a Western Hemisphere free of specifically human infections, but not a totally wholesome Eden. A few American microorganisms and parasites managed in the brief interval (i.e., thousands, but not millions of years) between the first entry of humans into the Americas and the appearance of Christopher Columbus in the West Indies to adapt to living in and off the newcomers. Chagas's disease, for instance, is natively American. But most of what were in 1492 and have since been the leading causes of morbidity and mortality among the world's communicable diseases were not present in the Western Hemisphere.

The world's leading infections were the by-products of the rise of agricultural and pastoral peoples in not the Western but the Eastern Hemisphere, where humans began living in dense, often sedentary, and usually unhygienic concentrations before even the most advanced American Indians. Many Eurasians and Africans lived, as well, in close proximity with their livestock, exchanged infections with their herds, and, one might almost say, cultivated pathogens and parasites.

There is much debate about which historically important infectious diseases were present in the Eastern but *not* in the Western Hemisphere at the beginning of 1492. A truly definitive list may never be made, but most paleopathologists, epidemiologists, and scholars who have perused the early records of Europe's first American empires agree that the list should probably include smallpox, measles, chicken pox, whooping cough, typhus, typhoid fever, bubonic plague, cholera, scarlet fever, malaria, yellow fever, diphtheria, and influenza. The list should probably be longer, but this one is long enough to indicate what devastation the arrival of Europeans could visit upon an immunologically naive population.

The densest populations of the Eastern Hemisphere from China and Java to western Europe and Africa (the natives of the last two never long out of contact with America after 1492) were also the sickest, especially the city dwellers. They caught all the endemic or commonly epidemic infections long before advancing to adulthood, hence the name given to many historically significant infections, the "childhood diseases." Those who survived had efficiently adapted to their environments, and they often had long and productive lives. Children who died were quickly replaced by means of what was, over the years and by the standards of the developed nations of the twentieth century, a high birth rate.

When the Europeans and Africans carried their diseases to America, "virgin soil epidemics" followed, infecting the great majorities of all populations at risk and killing adults as often as children. These epidemics were as effective in breaking resistance to the invaders as the air raids on civilian targets were intended to be in World War II, but were not. That is to say, they slaughtered great numbers, especially in the centers of population where the leadership elites lived; they paralyzed normal economic, religious, and political functions; and they terrorized the survivors. We cannot be sure when the first post-Columbian virgin soil epidemic detonated in America. The decline of the Antillean Tainos in the first quarter-century after 1492 seems to have been steeper than can be attributed to Spanish brutality. The swarms of pigs certainly provided a medium for an influenza epidemic, but the early chroniclers did not mention one, and whether anything as explosive as an influenza epidemic could have escaped their attention is doubtful. The fact is that the record does not mention any unambiguously epidemic infection until the end of 1518 or the very beginning of 1519.

The Spaniards in Española, where that infection struck first, identified the disease as smallpox. Bartolomé de las Casas said it was from Castile. It rarely affected the Europeans but devastated the Indians, killing one-third to one-half, a death rate not far out of line with what the population at risk in European ports—that is, the children—suffered. The affliction quickly spread throughout the Antilles, reaching Cuba just late enough for the Cortés expedition to the Mexican mainland to embark without it. In the next year a following expedition to Mexico included a man who carried smallpox. He infected the household in Cempoala where he was quartered, and the infection "spread from one Indian to another, and they, being so numerous and eating and sleeping together, quickly infected the whole country."

This, America's first recorded pandemic, spread far beyond the Antilles and Mexico. It rolled ahead of the Europeans and reached the lands of the advanced peoples of South America before the conquistadores' invasion of the fabulous Inca Empire. It slaughtered the Inca's subjects, killed the Inca himself, disrupted the succession, and set off a civil war. The people whom Pizarro conquered were the survivors of one of the worst periods of their history. How much further south and east the smallpox spread we can only guess, but if fire spreads in tinder, then why would this infection have stopped at the far boundaries of the Inca Empire?

To the north of Mexico the record on the subject is blank, but again we must grant that there was little reason for disease not to have spread. A decade after the fall of the Inca Empire, a veteran of Pizarro's invasion of Peru, Hernando de Soto, led an expedition on a long maraud through what is now the southeastern part of the United States in search of other Tenochtitláns and Cuzcos. He found hierarchical societies, village complexes, dense populations, pyramid temples, but nothing as attractively lootable as Mexico or Peru. He also found evidence of the passage of epidemic disease. In Cofachiqui, somewhere in present-day Georgia, he came upon recently emptied villages and large funereal houses filled with the drying cadavers of people who had perished in an epidemic. What he saw in Georgia may have, should have, reminded him of what he had seen in Peru.

Onslaughts of the new diseases swept over the Native American peoples throughout the sixteenth century and for all the generations since. It may be that we distort reality if we try to count epidemics, plucking them up out of the surmounting tide of infection, but for the sake of getting some idea of the dimensions of the flood, let us take the chance. About fifty epidemics swept through the Valley of Mexico between 1519 and 1810. Peru underwent twenty between the arrival of the Spaniards and 1720, Brazil perhaps forty of smallpox alone between 1560 and 1840.

The epidemiology of England's beginnings in America was similar to Iberia's. When Sir Francis Drake raided Saint Augustine in the 1580s, he brought an epidemic with him. The local Florida Indians "died verie fast and said amongest themselves, it was the Inglisshe God that made them die so faste." Another (conceivably the same) epidemic swept the coastal tribes of Carolina and Virginia before the end of that decade; "the like by report of the oldest men in the country never happened before, time out of mind." The Pilgrim settlement to the north at Plymouth was preceded by an epidemic that began in 1616 and, said contemporary sources, killed 90 percent of the coastal Indians.

The Onslaught Continues

The material effect of these tidal waves of infection is one that we can at least crudely apprehend even at a distance of many years. The psychological effect—that is to say, the interpretations the invaders and the invaded placed on these epidemics—is not as apparent to people like ourselves, who blame infections on germs, not on the supernatural.

Consider for a moment a statement made by an early nineteenth-century clergyman on the precipitous decrease of New England Indians since the first coming of the English: "Must we not ascribe it to the sovereign pleasure of the Most High, who divides to the nations their inheritance: who putteth down one and raiseth up another?" Both invaders and the invaded may have found this idea plausible.

And on and on to the present day. Alaska's and Canada's most remote Eskimos and Indians and South America's last tribes of hunter-gatherers and horticulturists have been decimated by tuberculosis, measles, and influenza within living memory. In 1990 the Yanomamö of the borderland of Brazil and Venezuela were decreasing rapidly under the attack not only or even primarily of the encroaching gold miners, but of malaria, influenza, measles, and chicken pox. The best ally of the invaders continues to be disease.

An avalanche of exotic organisms from the Eastern Hemisphere has been pouring onto the shores of the Americas for five hundred years. It continues, altering the ecosystems in all parts of the Western Hemisphere and the fates of Americans of every ethnicity and generation. The more recent immigrant organisms have often, like the wheat and peach trees that arrived in the sixteenth century, had positive effects. The Far East's soybean, for instance, has become a major crop and source of nourishment in the Americas since World War II, but the nastiest newcomers, like the Japanese beetle and Dutch elm disease, are the ones that get the most attention. Kudzu, a vine introduced from the Far East about a hundred years ago, was a decorous sort of a plant until the 1930s; since then it has been spreading cancerously through the Gulf and southern Atlantic states. The notorious "killer bees," aggressive African bees first released in Brazil in 1957, have spread in spite of every effort to hold them back and in the early 1990s are advancing into the United States. Flying Asian cockroaches, newly arrived, infest Florida. Significant and infamous above all recent imports is the AIDS virus, which probably first appeared in the Western Hemisphere in the 1970s. By sea and by air, by mammoth container ship and by jet aircraft, by diplomatic pouch and by impromptu encounter, the homogenizing process accelerates.

Native Americans often object to the name "New World," a European term for the lands of the Western Hemisphere. They point out that those lands were familiar to them long before Christopher Columbus was born, and their argument is one the rest of us owe respectful consideration. But we all are justified in the use of the title for the Americas since 1492. Until Columbus found his way across the Atlantic, the biota of the two sets of continents on either side were markedly different, the products of what, through time, had usually been divergent evolution. Since then the biota of both, most undeniably of the Americas, have in significant part been the product of revolution, that is, the abrupt addition and explosive propagation of exotic species from the lands on the other side of the waters that Columbus crossed in 1492. The great Genovese navigated, administered, crusaded, enslaved, but above all he mixed, mingled, jumbled, and homogenized the biota of our planet.

4 THE BRITISH EMPIRE AS A PRODUCT OF CONTINENTAL DRIFT

Demographically, the eighteenth and nineteenth centuries are among the most amazing of all centuries. The number of people in the world soared, with, for most of the period, the white populations of the British colonies of settlement—Canada, including New France; the thirteen colonies, which became the United States of America; Australia; and New Zealand—leading the way, swollen by vast migrations from Europe and by amazing rates of natural increase. Rates of natural increase (the excess by births over deaths) as high as 2 or 3 percent and even higher, extremely rare in the Old World, were the rule for scores of years in the Neo-Britains across the great oceans from the British Isles.[1]

These population explosions had negative counterparts in population crashes among the indigenes of the Neo-Britains. The native people decreased as fast as or, often, faster than the whites increased, until at the end of the nineteenth century when whites and indigenes as well commonly believed the latter were literally dying out. The words "vanishing race" became a normal way of referring to American Indians, as did equivalently dismal appellations for Australian Aborigines and New Zealand Maori.[2]

This actual replacement of one race by another is something rare. Tweedledum has always conquered Tweedledee and been conquered in return—Napoleon marches to Berlin and then Bismark follows his footsteps back to Paris—but this phenomenon of runaway immigrant increase and precipitous indigine decrease on a large scale and in several widely separated locations around the world was unprecedented in recorded history.

At the turn of the nineteenth century the Reverend Thomas Malthus interpreted the surge in the number of whites in the northern colonies of British America—"a rapidity of increase probably without parallel in history"—as the measure of just how fast all humans would reproduce if, God forbid, they all had enough to eat. As for the decline of Indian numbers, he chalked that up to liquor, infanticide, war, mistreatment of women, imported epidemics, and, of course, hunger and the threat of hunger.[3]

A generation later Charles Darwin pronounced the general success of colonial whites—specifically the success of those in the United States—as "the results of natural selection; for the more energetic, restless and courageous men from all parts of Europe have emigrated during the last ten or twelve generations to that great country, and have there succeeded best." He blamed the decline of the indigenes on disease primarily, and on famine, violence, and other factors triggered by contact with the Europeans. But why, he wondered, had not the tribes of ancient Europe succumbed similarly in the presence of the imperialistic Greeks and Romans?[4]

Social Darwinists, armchair theorists and popularizers who in the last half of that great biologist's century simplified his mighty generalities and applied them to society (something he did only rarely and offhandedly, as above), found no mystery in the advance of the colonial whites and the ebb of the indigenes: racial superiority on the part of the former and inferiority on that of the latter.

The racist explanation seems to have come particularly easily to the Social Darwinists who claimed Anglo-Saxon genes; and some of them were as sure of their future as of the past. John Fisk, in the late Victorian decades one of the most respected and popular historians and lecturers in both Great Britain and his homeland, the United States, traced the lines of Anglo-Saxon triumph on the graph of the past, extended them into the future, and was rendered silly by what he thought he saw. If Anglo-Saxons had so easily conquered North America, Australia, and New Zealand militarily and, more important, demographically, then why would the process not go on and on, to the vast enrichment of all the world? Who could doubt, for instance, that Africa would in two or three centuries be "a mighty nation of English descent"? By 1980, he predicted, the United States would have 600 million people, Australia and New Zealand 150 million, and much of the rest of the world would be populated by legions of ferociously fertile Anglo-Saxons.

"The day is at hand when four-fifths of the human race will trace its pedigree to English forefathers."[5]

Fisk was an inaccurate prophet not because of ignorance of history but because of his naive interpretation of that history. The success of European imperialism nearly everywhere and, in addition, the magnitude of the British demographic victories in North America and Australasia seemed too enormous to be merely a matter of guns versus spears, especially after the indigenes got their own guns, as they often did. There had to be something more profound involved, something, perhaps, having to do with Laws of Nature. What could it be?

His answer to that question was racist, but can we let that persuade us to pass over the question itself? Is it not still worth asking, worth speculating about? Doesn't ignoring it leave a silence in which the only sound is the mumbling echo of old *rathskeller* talk about master races?

Let us ask the question about the white takeover in the Neo-Britains again, but this time in terms more scientific and less self-serving than those used by Fisk and company a hundred years ago. Did European colonists in North America, Australia, and New Zealand ally themselves, probably by chance, with some natural condition that worked in their favor and against the indigenous peoples?

The Biogeographical Advantage

This condition was, if it existed at all, no doubt one of many factors, but let us consider just one—geographical location—and see where that consideration takes us. The British Isles lie within sight of continental Europe, the western extreme of Eurasia, the largest single piece of land on the globe, which is connected or nearly connected with Africa, the second largest piece, at Gibraltar and the Sinai Peninsula, and separated elsewhere by easily navigated seas. This world island of Eurasia–Africa, known to most as the Old World, contains humanity's original homeland somewhere within its tropics, probably Africa. It contains, as well, all the early centers of dense human population and civilization, except those of Meso- and Andean America.

The Neo-Britains of North America and Australasia are remote from the Old World and separated from it by major oceans. These lands were never home to *Homo sapiens*'s ancestors or close relatives, the anthropoid apes. In fact, they are quite different from Great Britain, specifically, and the Old World, generally, in their fauna and in their flora, as well.

North America and Western Europe have the fewest differences, but these are significant. Oak, ash, elm, beech, birch, maple, poplar, willow, linden, and holly are much the same on both sides of the North Atlantic, but the Europeans who came to America had never seen hickory or pecan before, nor many of the American pines, because Western Europe has very few pines. Many of the animals were familiar —deers, foxes, wolves, black bears—but Europeans found wapiti, gray squirrels, and opossoms and humming birds startlingly new.[6] Many species and certainly genera are shared between the two areas, but there are enough contrasts to persuade botanists and zoologists to classify the two as separate biological realms.[7]

The floras and faunas of Australia and New Zealand differ wildly from those of Britain, Europe, and the Old World. Australian plants and animals are distinctive, almost unique on this planet, as a comparison of what is perhaps the Old World's most widespread browser, the deer, and Australia's, the kangaroo, suggests. Australia's fauna is dominated by marsupials; the Old World's and America's by placental mammals. New Zealand has stunningly distinctive flora and fauna: the fact that the latter was dominated not by any kind of mammals at all but by giant birds when the humans first arrived is a measure of that country's uniqueness.[8]

The Neo-Britains are so different because they are so remote from most of the other lands of the world—so remote, in fact, that they were the last habitable areas to be settled by humanity, excepting certain islands. Humans reached America and Australia only when, during the Ice Age, the heaping up of much of the world's water in the form of continental glaciers lowered the oceans, and hunters and gatherers were able, by short boat trips or on foot, to escape Eurasia–Africa and enter the lesser continents. This took place between ten thousand and fifty thousand years ago, very recently in terms of the time that the genus *Homo* has lived on this planet. The continental glaciers melted back to approximately their present locations and the oceans rose again some ten thousand years ago, isolating the Stone Age pioneers from further significant contact with Eurasia–Africa before humanity built its first cities, cultivated its first crops, and tamed its first animals, excepting man's oldest friend, the dog.[9]

The story of the first people to reach New Zealand is different from that of the first pioneers to America and Australia, but in general outline similar. The first New Zealanders, the Maori, were one branch of that family of agriculturalists called Polynesians, whose ancestors had set off island-hopping into the Pacific vastness from the Asian mainland five or so millennia ago. The Maori arrived in New Zealand only a thousand years ago, bringing with them a few other cultigens and one domesticated animal, the dog. (They also brought the Polynesian rat, if the reader wishes to call that animal domesticated.) Sporadic contact with other Polynesian islanders, weeks and weeks away by canoe, continued for a few hundred years, and then ceased. Thereafter, the most important single influence on the Maori, as on all the forms of life living in New Zealand, was the hermetic remoteness of their homeland.[10]

The Europeans, starting a few centuries ago, changed oceanic navigation from an art—the level at which the Polynesians had left it—to a science, and changed the oceans from barriers into canals. This Eurasian people brought the Neo-Britains into the biological mainstream of this planet almost as effectively as if the white mariners had attached cables and towed them to the shoal waters of the Old World. Many organisms from the latter gained access to the Neo-Britains for the first time. Neo-Britons, themselves, enjoyed population booms, as we have seen. So did other exotic species, and their histories may help to illuminate the reasons for the immigrant humans' success.

What the Europeans Brought with Them

Old World cultigens went ashore with the first European settlers to the Neo-Britains. There, after what the settlers felt was a period of adjustment that was long and difficult but which the Portuguese in Brazil and Angola, for instance, would have called sweetly brief, European crops —wheat, oats, peas, turnips, peaches, cherries, flax, and so forth— sprouted, came to fruit and seed, sprang up again the following spring, sometimes spontaneously, and created a plenty. North American whites shifted from European grains to maize for their staple for a couple of centuries, and that Indian plant also played a vital role in feeding Australia's early white pioneers, but by and large the diets of the Neo-Britons differed from those of the old Britons more in being superior in quality and quantity than in kind.[11]

Within a decade or so of first settlement, most of Britain's North American colonies were producing surpluses of Old World foodstuffs —New York, Pennsylvania, and New Jersey were nicknamed the Bread Colonies—and exporting them to every market in the Atlantic Basin permitted them by British mercantilism and to a number of forbidden ones. The southern mainland settlements did the same—rice, in fact, became South Carolina's chief export—but are better and more properly remembered for their enormous exports of such nonfoods as tobacco, indigo, and, in the nineteenth century, cotton.

Most of the Australian and New Zealand settlements also produced food surpluses soon after their founding, but the distance between them and their chief markets in Europe tended to restrict their exports to sheep's wool, a product resistant to spoilage and of high value relative to its bulk, until the invention of refrigerator ships toward the end of the nineteenth century. But in the last hundred years, mutton, beef, wheat, honey, and so on—an avalanche of foodstuffs of Old World origin—have streamed from Australasia to Europe and the world.

Wheat provides a good example of the "Europeanization" of agriculture in the Neo-Britains. The Neo-Britons cultivated it from their earliest years in their new homes, and where these settlers spread into regions similar to eastern Europe's steppes—the Great Plains of the United States and Canada, the fertile country inland of Australia's Great Dividing and Darling Ranges, and the Canterbury Plain of New Zealand—wheat became the chief crop. In our century wheat has become the most important food in the world's export trade, and the Neo-Britains provide more than half the world's exported wheat.[12]

The story of Eurasian domesticated animals in Britain's colonies indicates even more clearly than does that of her cultigens the special affinity of many Old World life forms for the new environments. European animals grew to full size more rapidly, became bigger and brawnier, and reproduced more often than at home. They provided unquestionable proof of their liking for the colonies by successfully casting off human guidance and protection, by going wild in multitudes, and often initiating the Europeanization of the local ecosystems before the immigrant frontiersmen and women even arrived.

Pigs went ashore in the Gulf of Mexico area of what is now the United States with Hernando de Soto in the 1540s and, unlike their masters, prospered and founded families. These Spanish swine are probably the earliest American ancestors of the feral razorback hogs of the southeastern United States. English swine also disembarked on the east coast with the early white settlers, also went feral, and soon joined their Spanish cousins in the woods.[13]

By the early eighteenth century, Spanish cattle, ancestors of the famous Texas longhorns, were grazing in wild multitudes in the northern reaches of Mexico, a region that was to become the southern reaches of the United States a bit more than a hundred years later; and a cattle frontier of wild or, at most, semidomesticated cattle was moving into Indian territory from the east coast colonies. One Briton observed droves of cattle on the South Carolina and Georgia frontier "under the auspices of cowpen keepers, which move (like unto the ancient patriarch or the modern Bedowin in Arabia) from forest to forest as the grass wears out or the planters approach."[14]

Mustangs run away or rustled from Mexico were moving north into the grasslands of the future United States long before the English crossed the Appalachians, and by the middle of the eighteenth century had reached present-day Canada. Horses came from the east, as well; within less than a century of the founding of Jamestown horses running wild in Virginia's frontier counties were in sufficient number for that colony's young gentlemen to hunt them for fun. (It was, however, for the "pleasure of the hunt" alone because the animals were so fast and the pursuit so long that "when they are taken, 'tis odds but their grease is melted or else being old, they are so sullen that they can't be tamed."[15])

The first corner of Australia to be settled by Europeans, New South Wales, is half a world away from Virginia, but swine, cattle, and horses did about as well in the former as in the latter. Swine, come ashore with the white settlers, were soon fending for themselves in the bush, where they reproduced into multitudes of thousands and tens of thousands, flowing across the coastal plain to and through the mountains. Some of them became as lean and fast as their American cousins, and were also called razorbacks.[16] Within a few months of the settlers' arrival in 1788, two bulls and four cows (of South African rather than Eurasian origin) strayed off, and by 1804 the feral herds (or "mobs," to be properly Australasian) numbered three to five thousand head. Imported cattle went feral again and again in Australia: in 1836, for instance, the explorer Thomas Mitchell came upon cattle trails "resembling roads" near the Murrumbridgee River, "and at length the welcome sight of the cattle themselves delighted our longing eyes, not to mention our stomachs. . . ." Wild horses (they are called Brumbies, not mustangs, down under) prospered and propagated as extravagantly in Australia as in North America. They became "a very weed among animals" in the nineteenth century, and as late as 1967 still existed in the tens of thousands.[17]

The story of European livestock in New Zealand is complicated in detail, but simple in general terms. Seemingly every animal the Europeans brought that could adapt to a warm-to-cool damp climate went feral, particularly mammals. Pigs, brought first by Captain Cook, swarmed there long before British annexation in 1840. The islands' rough terrain and dense forests hindered the formation of herds ("mobs") of cattle and horses as large as those of America and Australia, but, for all of that, no European colony, with the possible exception of those on small islands, was ever so Europeanized in its fauna, especially in its mammalia, as was New Zealand. Even sheep, which usually are able to find some carnivore to eat them or some cliff to walk off, successfully went wild. New Zealand was and is so suitable for sheep that today she has sixty million of them, as compared with not much over three million people.[18]

The most spectacularly and immediately successful of all the Old World's emigrants to the Neo-Britains were pathogens, the microlife that cause disease and death. Maladies that had come to ancient and medieval Britain one at a time over the centuries from the more densely populated Mediterranean Europe and Middle East arrived in the Americas and Oceania in a rush of a few decades, creating a series of pandemics probably unprecedented in Neo-British history, about which more later.

Of course, the triumph of Old World organisms was not total. Many failed to obtain so much as a toehold, and others no more than that, and there are few examples of invaders totally replacing native species. Immigrants did drive the passenger pigeon and the Tasmanian human into extinction, but the invaders' victory was much more often no more than getting ashore and spreading widely. They often drove the native life forms back into the odd corners of the environment, but the majority of local species survived and, in some cases, such as that of the striped skunk of North America, even prospered under the new regime. The eucalyptus still rules in Australia and generations of grass-loving shepherds have not been able to eradicate the New Zealand bush. Even so, we must recognize that the success of the invaders, from humans to

rabbits to houseflies, has been astonishing, and requires more explanation than a reference to mere chance.

The immigrant life forms often found few strong indigenous rivals
for the eco-niches they coveted in the Neo-Britains. The horse, to cite
an obvious example, found no competitors for its specific niche whatsoever. Pigs found only weak rivals for the food supply of the mast and
roots of vast forests of the Neo-Britains, and reproduced for many
generations before their numbers began to press on the carrying capacity of those environments.

In the Neo-Britains, many immigrant life forms found few predators, parasites, or diseases. It is a naturalist's rule of thumb that organisms usually flourish best away from their points of origin, given a
salubrious climate, because the life forms, macro and micro, of their
new homes have had a shorter time to adapt to feeding on, upon, and in
them, and therefore do so less effectively than equivalents had in the
old homes.[19]

Neo-British examples of this rule of thumb are many. For instance,
Spanish longhorns, descendent of animals who for millennia had survived the appetites and hunting skills of carnivores at least equal and
often superior to American flesh eaters, found the latter no great challenge and rapidly and hugely increased in numbers. In Australia the most
troublesome predator when the whites came was the dingo, a dog that the
Aborigines probably had brought with them from the islands to the
north and northwest. This canine has killed multitudes of sheep and
cattle and other livestock, but is no rival to the wolf. Captain Watkin
Tench of the first white settlement described the dingo, which stands
about two feet high at the shoulder, as resembling "the fox dog of
England."[20] It is not surprising that on the nineteenth-century Australian frontier, single shepherds successfully cared for mobs of thousands of animals wandering over vast spreads of grassland.

New Zealand had no lions, tigers, wolves, coyotes, or dingos when
the whites arrived with their livestock—in fact, it had no predators at
all, according to the standards of the continents. Europeans have unintentionally created predators by importing dogs and cats and allowing
them to go wild, but have come up with only one native one, and then
only by exercise of imagination. The large New Zealand parrot, the
kea, is supposed by some to swoop down on sheep, fix itself in the
fleece at a spot the poor animal cannot defend, and then peck and tear
the creature to death. Most experts doubt that this ever happened more

than a very few times, and then only with disabled sheep; even the most credulous must agree that a flock of the fiercest keas cannot compare with a pack of ravening Eurasian wolves.[21]

A low incidence of pests, parasites, and disease was crucial to the success of Old World organisms in the Neo-Britains. North America's first wheat belt was flourishing along the Delaware River in the eighteenth century before the Hessian fly, one of wheat's old pests, followed the grain across the Atlantic and began to spread.[22] Rabies, an ancient disease of dogs, cats, bats, and wild rodents in the Old World, also did not reach America until the mid-eighteenth century, and has never established itself in Australasia.[23] Rinderpest, long established in Eurasia, slaughtered millions of domestic and wild ungulates in southern Africa and, indirectly, thousands of humans dependent upon them when it arrived there in the late nineteenth century, but has never gained a foothold in the Neo-Britains.[24] Foot-and-mouth disease, an established scourge in most major livestock-producing countries, has appeared a number of times in the Neo-Britains, but has always been eradicated.[25]

The cycle of population explosion of immigrant organisms in the Neo-Britains and of the tardy arrival of their parasites is still going on. Soybeans, a Far Eastern cultigen, first arrived in North America generations ago, but was not cultivated in quantity until the twentieth century. As late as 1922, United States production amounted to only 4 million bushels, but has soared since, especially after World War II. In 1991 the United States produced 54 million metric tons, far more than any other nation.[26]

This "soybean explosion" in North America was, among other things, the product of the absence of several of the plant's ancient Far Eastern parasites, specifically the soybean cyst nematode. It did finally appear in North America in 1954 and has, despite quarantines and the ministrations of agricultural scientists and the chemical industry, spread widely since.[27]

Immigrant Europeans, as well as immigrant plants and animals, had population explosions in the Neo-Britains, and for many of the same reasons. The lack of man eaters in the Neo-Britains was not important because for many thousands of years *Homo sapiens* have been the eaters, not the eaten, in all climes and locations. The fact that most of the white settlers in the Neo-Britains were young adults, a group that characteristically has a lower death rate and higher birth rate than children and the old, is important. The improvement of diet that these settlers often enjoyed after arrival in their new homes surely helped lengthen lives and produce quantities of healthy mothers and babies. The general improvement of future prospects for the immigrants, who, being humans, could to some extent adjust their birth rates in accordance with those prospects, may also have boosted the population increase.[28]

Germs

The sparseness of population in the Neo-Britains and the distances both between settlements, and between them and the Old World, slowed the spread of disease. In many cases epidemics of infectious disease burned themselves out for lack of fresh fuel. Smallpox, for instance, never became an endemic disease in colonial North America nor in Australia until long after the arrival of the colonists simply because of the shortage of victims.[29]

Smallpox was not native to New Zealand, Australia, or America, nor to any other lands outside of Eurasia–Africa; nor were, in all probability, many other of humanity's dangerous infections: measles, whooping cough, chicken pox, bubonic plague, malaria, diphtheria, amoebic dysentery, influenza, and a variety of helminthic infestations.[30]

The second wave of humans to the Neo-Britains, the Europeans, often suffered initial periods of high mortality caused by malnutrition and exposure, but then prospered and multiplied. In Virginia the troubled initial period lasted for a generation. That colony and the other southern mainland colonies in North America, all of them tropical in the summers and only briefly cold in the winters, suffered chronically from warm climate fevers and parasites; even so, the natural increase of the white populations was considerable.[31]

The colonies to the north of Virginia profited from the same stream of immigration and high birth rate as did the southern settlements, and in addition had a very low death rate. It was these colonies, growing at a rate that doubled their populations every thirty years or less (even after subtracting the number of fresh immigrants from Europe) that so impressed Malthus with humanity's maximum capacity for reproduction. The Yankees vaguely credited much of their good fortune to their climate, praising "the very wholesomeness of the Aire, altering, digesting and drying up the cold and crude humours of the Body," and recommended "all cold complections to take Physick in New England; for a sup of New-England's aire is better than a whole draught of old England's Ale."[32]

In 1790, after two years in Australia, Governor Arthur Phillips reported that "a finer and more healthy climate is not to be found in any part of the world." Of the 1,030 people who had disembarked with him, many suffering from scurvy and half of them convicts from Britain's malnourished lower classes, only seventy-two had died, "and by the surgeon's returns, it appears that twenty-six of those died from disorders of long standing, and which it is more than probable would have carried them off much sooner in England."[33]

Thirty odd years later, Peter Cunningham, in a book written to persuade British emigrants to go to New South Wales rather than to North America, noted that yellow fever and malaria had, albeit tardily, arrived in the latter region, but that Australia had neither, "nor indeed *any* fever but the *rum* fever—while measles, hooping cough, smallpox, and all your similar European pests are alike strangers to our soil— the most common and fatal disease being dysentery, which is seldom productive of danger to any but the imprudent and intemperate." He exaggerated in calling the European pests strangers—several, like tuberculosis, had established permanent beachheads, and others, like smallpox, had made visits—but we must give Cunningham his proper due: few of the Old World's infectious diseases had yet come to stay. Australia was a very healthy place for white people.[34]

New Zealand was the healthiest of all colonies for Britons: so said Arthur S. Thompson, M.D., surgeon, 58th Regiment, in 1850, and he produced the statistics to prove it. In Great Britain the number of deaths annually from all diseases per thousand British soldiers was 14; in New Zealand, 8.25. The data pertaining to lung diseases, including tuberculosis, one of the century's most prevalent killers in Europe, were even more lopsidedly in favor of the colony. The yearly mortality rate per thousand soldiers in Britain suffering with "pectoral complaints" was 148; in New Zealand 60. Dr. Thompson recommended the North Island, where he was stationed, as a convalescence center for Europeans fallen ill elsewhere in the empire. He also noted the paradox that New Zealand, so salubrious for whites, was becoming increasingly unhealthy for its native race, the Maori.[35]

The European explorers and very first settlers in the Neo-Britains almost always remarked on the glowing good health of the indigenes, but the whites who followed had an entirely different story to tell. For example, at the beginning of the eighteenth century John Lawson, a traveler in Carolina, British North America, called the Indians of that region "a People very apt to catch any Distemper they are afflicted withal. . . ." A century later, Thomas Malthus, musing over the case of all American Indians, concluded that "The diseases to which man is subject to in the savage state, though fewer in number, are more violent and fatal then those which prevail in civilised society."[36] The soybean cyst nematode caught up with soybeans in America in the 1950s. The human diseases of the Old World caught up with the first wave of *Homo sapiens* to the Neo-Britains when the second wave, the Europeans, arrived and settled.

The deadliest of all the imported diseases of the Neo-Britains—or, at least the most spectacular—was smallpox. It made the first of its many recorded sweeps through North America in the 1630s, but had probably made sorties north from Spanish Mexico during the previous century. Wherever it broke out, it hit the Indians much harder than the whites, to the great advantage of the latter. Examples are legion. Increase Mather cites one in his description of the year 1633 in New England:

> The Indians began to be quarrelsome touching the Bounds of the Land which they had sold to the English, but God ended the Controversy by sending Smallpox amongst the Indians of Saugust who were before that time exceedingly numerous. Whole Towns of them were swept away, in some not so much as one soul escaped Destruction.[37]

This disease, or something very much like it, ravaged the Aborigines of New South Wales in 1789, just a bit more than a year after the initial British settlement there and at a time when the Aborigines were beginning actively to resist the invasion. In May the new settlers made a chilling discovery: the corpses of two of their own people in the bush, one with four spears in him. But the expected sequels of accelerating violence did not follow. Within a month an epidemic of a pustular disease struck the indigenes, halving their number and raging far into the interior.[38]

Smallpox was an extremely effective pathogen in eliminating native resistance, but by no means the only or indispensable exterminator. By the time that disease came ashore in New Zealand, at least two-thirds of the Maori had been vaccinated against it, yet this did not save them from steep population decline. Like the indigenes of other Neo-Britains, they underwent devastating sieges of dysenteric diseases, measles, pneumonia, influenza, whooping cough, and so forth. Venereal disease, which so often became chronic among the conquered peoples of the European empires, killed some Maori and destroyed the reproductive powers of more, vastly diminishing their capability of recovering demographically.[39]

Tuberculosis was, above all, the enemy of the Maori. Dr. Arthur S. Thompson stated flatly in the mid-nineteenth century, by which time the Maori had probably plunged halfway to utter extinction, that scrofula, tuberculosis of the lymph nodes and skin, was the chief threat to the Maori, predisposing children to "marasmus, fevers and bowel complaints," and adults to "consumption [pulmonary tuberculosis], spinal diseases, ulcers, and various other maladies." He called scrofula "the curse of the New Zealand race."[40]

Disease made indigene resistance to the new order of things in America and Australasia useless. In 1906, Uaui Pomare, then a Maori health officer, despairing of the future of his people, told them they must take up the ways of the Europeans, of the *Pakeha,* or accept extinction:

> Was not this way uttered by the mouth of a dying chief many generations ago:
> *Kei muri i te awa kapara he tangata ke, mana te ao, he ma*
> ("Shadowed behind the tattooed face, a stranger stands, he who owns the earth and he is white.")[41]

Conclusions

Today European whites amount to 70, 80, 90 percent and even higher of the populations of the Neo-Britains, and the indigenes are small minorities in their ancient homelands. Many forces were involved in producing this remarkable phenomenon, not the least of which was the superiority of the Europeans in economic and political organization and, above all, in technology relative to the indigenes. Of greater importance, however, was the ecological advantage of the European invaders over the indigenes. The whites' Demographic Takeover was but one part of the general success of Old World immigrant organisms.

The phenomenon can best be understood if one views the Old World onslaught as a whole—not, for instance, as Englishmen versus Algonkins on the east coast of North America, but as Englishmen plus smallpox, cattle, horses, wheat, and so forth versus Algonkins. The latter were probably capable of pushing the first white colonists into the sea—certainly of making their lives so dangerous and unprofitable as to discourage further waves of immigrants from Europe—but the Indians had no allies to match smallpox and the rest.

We must extend the theories of the Social Darwinists to include explanations for the triumphs of European plants and animals, as well as European people, and, à la Comte de Buffon, talk about some sort of *general* Old World superiority; or we must ask again what were the natural conditions that so favored the invaders as to tempt the Social Darwinists to extravagant speculation a century ago.

The chief advantages of the invaders fall neatly into two groups. First, the Neo-Britains or, at least, large parts of them, have climates roughly similar to that of the British Isles and Western Europe. Wladimir Koppen, the famed geographer and climatologist, places the British Isles, northwestern Europe, and most of the most heavily populated parts of the Neo-Britains in what he calls the Humid Temperate category. All these areas lie approximately the same distance from the equator, some to the north and some to the south, and the effects of what differences there are in their latitudes are moderated by benign currents and winds. For instance, Australia may be one-third in the tropics and in large part a desert continent, but the average annual temperature and rainfall of its southern coastal regions are much like Britain's or no more different than, say, Mediterranean Europe's. Organisms that will "work" in the British Isles will, generally speaking, do the same in large parts of the areas of South and Western Australia that face poleward, and in New South Wales, Victoria, and Tasmania.[42]

Second, the floras, faunas, and peoples of the Neo-Britains that were in part or whole displaced by the invading Old World organisms were peculiarly vulnerable to such displacement because of the vagaries of evolution. Geological theorists attribute these vagaries to a phenomenon they, with a stoney indifference to nuance, call Continental Drift. Two hundred million years ago, all the continents, that is, all the land masses with granitic bases, were parts of one giant continent called Pangaea, or lay near its shores. At that time the climates, floras, and faunas of the areas of that vast slab destined to become the British Isles and the Neo-Britains were more alike than at any time since. Then Pangaea began to split along lines of tectonic activity, into which the oceans advanced. For the scores upon scores of millions of years since, the pieces of Pangaea have drifted independently (occasional collisions like that of India and Asia need not concern us) and life forms on each have evolved independently and divergently, one piece producing elk (wapiti) and humming birds, another kangaroos, another kiwis, another the genus *Homo* and the ancestors of our cattle, sheep, measles viruses, and so on.[43]

The section that produced humans, cattle, and measles is the chipped core of Pangaea, Eurasia–Africa, the largest contiguous piece of land in the world. There the number of species is greatest, therefore the competition between them fiercest, and the winners, in one way and another, obviously among the world's toughest competitors. More important for our purposes, the old core of Pangaea is the homeland of humanity and of most of our civilizations. Old World plants, animals and micro life, which had evolved symbiotically with the genus *Homo* and with practitioners of the Old World cultures, were better adapted to living with humans, in general, and with Neo-British colonists, in particular, than the life forms of America or Australasia. In turn, the human immigrants from the Old World were better adapted in many ways—culturally, for certain, and also by immunological experience— to live with the other immigrant life forms than were the indigenous humans, the descendants of the first human pioneers to reach these lands.

The Demographic Takeover by Europeans in North America, Australia, and New Zealand was one aspect of a large-scale successful invasion by a number of species, only one of which, despite the theories of John Fisk et al., was *Homo Britannicus*. In fact, it was not necessary for Britons to participate at all. The first people from temperate Eurasia,* whatever their race or culture, who crossed the oceans to the Neo-Britains in large enough numbers, along with their symbiotic macro- and micro-life, to create the ecologist's equivalent of the atomic physicists' "critical mass" were likely, perhaps even certain, to triumph demographically.

---

*The tip of South Africa also lies in a temperate zone, but is so far from the centers of Old World civilization that its native people lacked many of the ingredients of that civilization.

The bulk of eastern China has a climate similar to that of Western Europe and the Neo-Britains, and the plants, animals, and micro-organisms of the Yangzi and Yellow river valleys have lived symbiotically with civilized humans for much longer than those of the Thames and Humber valleys. It is an accident of history that New England, New South Wales, and New Zealand are not New Kiangsu, New Chekiang, and New Fukien, and that some Asian counterpart of John Fisk did not explain the demographic miracles of the colonial Chinese by inventing a theory about the genetic superiority of the eastern Chinese subdivision of the Chinese division of the Mongoloid people of the human race.

Notes

1. Colin McEvedy and Richard Jones, *Atlas of World Population History* (Harmondsworth: Penguin Books, 1978), 348–49; J. Potter, "The Growth of Population in America, 1700–1860," in *Population in History: Essays in Historical Demography,* ed. C.V. Glass and D.E.C. Eversley (London: Edward Arnold, 1965), 631–38; Daniel Smith, "The Demographic History of Colonial New England," *Journal of Economic History* 32 (March 1972): 165–83; A.H. McLintock, ed., *An Encyclopedia of New Zealand* (Wellington: R.E. Owen, Government Printer, 1966), 2:823; M.F. Lloyd Prichard, *An Economic History of New Zealand to 1939* (Auckland: Collins, 1970), 97, 142, 144; W.D. Borrie, *Population Trends and Policies: A Study of Australian and World Demography* (Sydney: Australasian Publishing Co., 1948), 37–40.

2. *Encyclopedia of New Zealand* 2:431, 455; C.D. Rowley, *The Destruction of Aboriginal Society* (Harmondsworth: Penguin Books, 1972), 383; William M. Denevan, ed., *The Native Population of the Americas in 1492* (Madison: University of Wisconsin Press, 1976), 2–4.

3. Thomas R. Malthus, *First Essay on Population* (New York: Sentry Press, 1965), 105–7, 126–27; *An Essay on Population by the Rev. T. R. Malthus,* 7th ed. (London: J. M. Dent and Sons, n.d.), 1:26–43; 2:74. Malthus was demonstrably influenced by Benjamin Franklin's 1751 essay, "Observations Concerning the Increase of Mankind, Peopling of Countries, &c.," Leonard W. Labaree, ed., *The Papers of Benjamin Franklin* (New Haven: Yale University Press, 1961), 4:225–34, in which the American predicted that there would be more Englishmen on the western than the eastern side of the Atlantic in a century's time.

4. Charles Darwin, *The Voyage of the Beagle* (Garden City: Anchor Books, 1962), 433–34; Darwin, *The Origin of the Species and the Descent of Man* (New York: Modern Library, n.d.), 508, 542–43.

5. John Fisk, *Political Ideas Viewed from the Standpoint of Universal History* (New York: Harper and Brothers, 1903), 141, 143, 145, 152.

6. Carl O. Sauer, "The Settlement of the Humid East," in *Climate and Man: Yearbook of Agriculture, 1941* (Washington, D.C.: United States Department of Agriculture, 1941), 159.

7. Phillip J. Darlington, *Zoogeography: The Geographical Distribution of Animals* (New York: John Wiley and Sons, 1957), 427, 472–73; Ronald Good, *The Geography of Flowering Plants* (New York: John Wiley and Sons, 1964), 30–31.

8. Maurice Burton, *Systematic Dictionary of Mammals of the World* (New York: Thomas Y. Crowell Co., 1962), 36–37; Graeme R. Stevens, *New Zealand Adrift: The Theory of Continental Drift in a New Zealand Setting* (Wellington: A.H. & A.W. Reed, 1980), 244–69.

9. Jesse D. Jennings, *Prehistory of North America* (New York: McGraw-Hill, 1974), 47–70; A. G. Thorne, "The Arrival and Adaptation of Australian Aborigines," *Ecological Biogeography of Australia*, ed. Allen Reast (The Hague: Dr. W. Junk Publishers, 1981), Vol. 3, Part 6, 1751–60.

10. P.S. Bellwood, "The Peopling of the Pacific," *Scientific American* 243 (November 1980): 178–79.

11. Percy W. Bidwell and John I. Falconer, *History of Agriculture in the Northern United States, 1620–1860* (Washington, D.C.: Carnegie Institution of Washington, 1925), 9–17, 42–45; Sauer, "The Settlement of the Humid East," 157–66; Edgars Dunsdorfs, *The Australian Wheat-Growing Industry* (Melbourne: The University Press, 1956), 47.

12. Dunsdorfs, *The Australian Wheat-Growing Industry*, 114, 115, 167, 185–86; *The World Almanac of Facts* (1981), 217; C. Warren Thornthwaite, "Climate and Settlement of the Great Plains," in *Climate and Man: Year Book of Agriculture, 1941* (Washington, D.C.: United States Department of Agriculture, 1941), 177–87; Wilfred Malenbaum, *The World's Wheat Economy, 1885–1939* (Cambridge: Harvard University Press, 1953), 127–53, 227; Food and Agricultural Organization of the United Nations, *World Grain Statistics, 1965* (Rome: Food and Agricultural Organization of the United Nations, 1966), 13.

13. Bidwell and Falconer, *History of Agriculture in the Northern United States*, 18, 31; Carl O. Sauer, *Sixteenth Century North America* (Berkeley: University of Caliornia Press, 1969), 301; Robert Beverley, *The History of Virginia in Four Parts* (Richmond: J.W. Randolph, 1855), 262.

14. J. Frank Dobie, "The First Cattle in Texas and the Southwestern Progenitors of the Longhorns," *Southwestern Historical Quarterly* 42 (January 1939): 171–97; Frank L. Owsley, "The Pattern of Migration and Settlement on the Southern Frontier," *Journal of Southern History* 11 (May 1945): 151.

15. Robert M. Denhardt, *The Horse of the Americas* (Norman: University of Oklahoma Press, 1975), 92; Beverley, *The History of Virginia*, 257–58.

16. Eric C. Rolls, *They All Ran Wild: The Story of Pests on the Land in Australia* (Sydney: Angus and Robertson, 1969), 336–37.

17. Rolls, *They All Ran Wild*, 348–52; Commonwealth of Australia, *Historical Records of Australia*, Series 1 (Sydney: Library Committee of the Commonwealth Parliament, 1914–1925), 1:550; 7:379–80; 8:150–51; 9:349, 714, 831; 10:92, 280, 682; Thomas L. Mitchell, *Expeditions into the Interior of Eastern Australia* (London: T. and W. Bone, 1834), 1:306.

18. *The World Almanac and Book of Facts, 1993* (New York: Pharos Books, 1992), 783; *Encyclopedia of New Zealand*, 2:280–90; R.A. Wodzicki, *Introduced Mammals of New Zealand* (Wellington: Department of Scientific and Industrial Research, 1950), passim; Andrew H. Clark, *The Invasion of New Zealand by*

People, Plants and Animals (New Brunswick: Rutgers University Press, 1949), 190.

19. Edgar Anderson, *Man and Life* (Berkeley: University of California Press, 1967), 187.

20. Watkin Tench, *Sydney's First Four Years* (Sydney: Angus and Robertson, 1961), 49.

21. *Encyclopedia of New Zealand*, 2:212–13.

22. Bidwell and Falconer, *History of Agriculture in the Northern United States*, 93, 95–96; E.L. Jones, "Creative Disruption in American Agriculture, 1620–1830," *Agricultural History* 48 (October 1974): 523.

23. *The Merk Veterinary Manual* (Rahway, N.J.: Merk and Co., 1972), 232; Folke Henschen, *The History and Geography of Diseases*, trans. Joan Tate (New York: Delacorte Press, 1966), 41. For arrival of rabies elsewhere, see Darwin, *Voyage of the Beagle*, 354–55.

24. *Merk Veterinary Manual*, 263; Helge Rekshus, *Ecology Control and Economic Development in East African History: The Case of Tanganyika, 1850–1950* (London: Heinemann, 1977), 1–32.

25. United States Department of Agriculture, *Animal Diseases: Yearbook of Agriculture, 1956* (Washington, D.C.: Government Printing Office, 1956), 186.

26. Allan Smith and Sidney J. Circle, eds., *Soybeans: Chemistry and Technology* (Westport, Conn.: Avi Publishing Co., 1978), 1:1; *Food and Agricultural Organization Yearbook: Production 1991* (Rome: Food and Agricultural Organization of the United Nations, 1991), 107; Folke Dovring, "Soybeans," *Scientific American* 230 (February 1974): 14–20; Harry Fornari, *Bread upon the Waters: A History of United States Grain Exports* (Nashville: Aurora Publishers, 1972), 46.

27. Klare S. Markley, ed., *Soybeans and Soybean Products* (New York: Interscience Publishers, 1950), 1:50; Cynthia Westcott, *Plant Disease Handbook* (Princeton: D. Van Nostrand Co., 1960), 258; Bob Coffman, "Soybean Cyst Nematode Invades Corn Belt," *Farm Journal* 100 (November 1976): 46.

28. Benjamin Franklin credited the population explosion among Neo-Britons in North America to this latter factor. See his "Observations Concerning the Increase of Mankind," in Labaree, ed., *The Papers of Benjamin Franklin*, 4:227–34.

29. John Duffy, *Epidemics in Colonial America* (Baton Rouge: Louisiana State University Press, 1971), 103, 107; Cumpston, *History of Smallpox in Australia*, 7.

30. Woodrow Borah, after decades of work on the subject of the demography and diseases of the Americas, judges the above maladies to be non-American in origin. They are almost certainly non-Australasian, as well. See William M. Denevan, ed., *The Native Population of the Americas in 1492*, 5. For the latest discussion on this, see John W. Verano and Douglas H. Ubelaker, eds., *Disease and Demography in the Americas* (Washington, D.C.: Smithsonian Institution Press, 1992), passim.

31. Edmund S. Morgan, *American Slavery, American Freedom: The Ordeal of Colonial Virginia* (New York: W. W. Norton, 1975), 158–79, 405–10; Duffy, *Epidemics in Colonial America*, 138–63, 204–27.

32. Smith, "Demographic History of Colonial New England," *Journal of Economic History* 32 (March 1972): 165–83; Kenneth A. Lockridge, "The Population of Dedham, Massachusetts, 1636–1736," *Economic History Review*, 2d Series, 19

(August 1966): 326–28; Edmund Morgan, ed., *The Founding of Massachusetts: Historians and Documents* (Indianapolis: Bobbs Merrill, 1964), 144–45.

33. *Historical Records of Australia,* Series 1, Vol. 1, 144.

34. Peter Cunningham, *Two Years in New South Wales* (London: Henry Colburn, 1828) 1:7.

35. A.S. Thomson, "Observations of the Influence of the North Island of New Zealand in the Production and Prevention of Disease among Emigrants from Great Britain and Ireland," *Irish University Press Series of British Parliamentary Papers: Colonies; New Zealand* 7:51–55; and also in the above, "Observations on the Climate of the North Island of New Zealand," 10:290–97.

36. John Lawson, *A New Voyage to Carolina* (Chester, VT: Readex Microprint Corp., 1966), 10; Malthus, *An Essay on Population,* 30.

37. John Duffy, "Smallpox and the Indians in the American Colonies," *Bulletin of the History of Medicine* 25 (July–August 1951): 327.

38. *Historical Records of Australia,* Series 1, Vol. 1, 47–48; Cumpston, *History of Smallpox in Australia,* 164–73.

39. D. Ian Pool, *The Maori Population of New Zealand, 1769–1971* (Auckland: Auckland University Press, 1977), 93–97, 106–44.

40. Ibid., 115; Arthur S. Thomson, *The Story of New Zealand, Past and Present—Savage and Civilized* (London: John Murray, 1859), 1:212, 214–19.

41. *Encyclopedia of New Zealand,* 2:431.

42. Edward B. Espenshade, Jr., and Joel L. Morrison, eds., *Goode's World Atlas* (Chicago: Rand McNally, 1974), 12–15; Glenn T. Trewartha, *An Introduction to Climate* (New York: McGraw-Hill, 1968), 394–95.

43. *Continents Adrift and Continents Aground* (San Francisco: W.H. Freeman, 1976), 34–35, 126–27, 176, 178; Stevens, *New Zealand Adrift,* 1–182.

5 INFECTIOUS DISEASE AND THE DEMOGRAPHY OF THE ATLANTIC PEOPLES

I want to present a new version of the history of the peoples of the Atlantic basin based on a new reading of the documents and data of their story during the last half-millennium. I am not the first to propose such a version[1] (being a member of the second generation to have taken it up), but it is new to most people outside the ranks of Americanists, anthropologists, and a few varieties of historians. This version has only begun to appear in college textbooks, and it is still absent from high school textbooks as far as I know. One of the chief reasons for the slowness of its advance into popular perception is that it focuses not on politics and war, which many still think of as *real* history, but on demography and epidemiology, which many would prefer not to think about at all. It focuses on deadly disease, and on how most of us who are now living in the Americas are doing so because our ancestors were either attracted or dragged across the Atlantic to fill vacancies opened up by disease. This is not a particularly ennobling story, and a lot of people believe history should ennoble or be forgotten.

1492

Let me begin with what some will consider a startling premise. I believe that in 1492, population densities in the areas occupied by the advanced peoples of the Old and New Worlds (Europe, Persia, India, China, Mesoamerica, Peru, and so forth) were not very different from each other. For instance, it seems likely that the density of settlement in the central Valley of Mexico was not far less than that in the Yangzi

Valley. Such areas were more numerous and several of them more extensive in the eastern than in the western hemisphere, but these were, I suggest, roughly similar in density of inhabitants. I grant that the number of people per square kilometer in the American grasslands was lower than in the Old World grasslands because Amerindians had no crop as well adapted to steppe climate as the Old World's wheat, barley, millet, or sorghum, and no domesticated herbivore of size except the llama (and that in only one part of the continent). On the other hand, the population densities in the hot, wet lands of the Americas were, according to our best knowledge about the character and geographical distribution of diseases and crops in pre-Columbian times, probably equal to those of similar lands in southern Asia and greater than those in Africa. Old World peoples did have a great advantage over peoples of the New World in livestock and its meat, milk, fiber, skins, and fertilizing manure. But the great advantage of Amerindians over Eurasians and Africans was in suffering from a smaller number of infectious diseases.[2]

There is an obvious and undeniable contrast in the duration of occupation between Old World peoples and Amerindians circa 1492. The Eastern Hemisphere was the original home of *Homo sapiens*, and the Western Hemisphere was, comparatively speaking, a new residence for the species. Eurasians and Africans had all the time they needed and more to produce dense populations, but what about Amerindians, who had only inhabited their continents for as few as eleven thousand years, according to some archeologists? To answer that question, let me dig up and adapt to my purposes an old demographic chestnut. It is a statistical fact that if an Amerindian Adam and an Amerindian Eve had initiated human procreation in the New World only eleven thousand years ago and if the number of their descendants had increased by only 1 percent annually—an easy assumption to accept (at first), considering the amounts of space and food available to them—then the Amerindian population in 1492 would have been a sphere of living flesh thousands of light years in diameter, expanding at many times the speed of light.[3] Ergo, the sharp difference in the durations of human occupation between the Old and New Worlds has no real significance demographically.

The burden of evidence rests more heavily on those who state (often on the basis of tradition rather than data) that there were only a few million Native Americans in 1492 than on those who state (usually after much research and analysis of original sources) that there were tens of millions of people in the New World when Columbus arrived. I doubt that there were any large areas in the New World suitable in soil fertility, climate, flora, and fauna for dense populations that were not already thoroughly occupied in 1492.[4]

After 1492

If the preceding statement is true, then it leads us to a paradox. How could post-Columbian migration from the Old World to the New have been as enormous and swift as it was if the New World were as heavily populated as I claim? Transatlantic migration leaped from zero migrants with zero significance to immense numbers and immense significance in what was, by any standard but that of the recent past, a very short time indeed. The *Völkerwanderung,* the *Drang nach Osten,* the Bantu advance south into Khoisan Africa, the Chinese advance into the Yangzi Valley and beyond—these were driftings that took many centuries; they must be contrasted against rather than compared with the vaultings of the Atlantic since 1492.

The efficiency of the three-masted sailing vessel of Renaissance Europe, then the steamship, and finally the airplane help to explain the size and speed of transatlantic migration, but these astonishing machines only explain how, not why, the post-Columbian millions made the trip. After all, the machines also provided fast transportation to India and China, where fortunes and empires were to be made, but only thousands, not millions, of migrants embarked from the Atlantic world for Asia. The abruptness and magnitude of the transatlantic transfer of population to the New World were the products of a phenomenon more complicated than innovation in transportation technology.

Today North Americans of all ancestries are apt to think of colonization as the seizure of land and the elimination and displacement of the incumbent population by invaders. But that is not the way conquest has usually worked. It was not, for instance, what William the Conqueror had in mind when he and his Normans took over England in 1066. Land is worthless without laborers, who are as essential to a conquest as the land's flora and fauna. Most of the conquistadores and their early successors in America were not trying to propagate an ideology or a religion or their particular subspecies of *Homo sapiens* so much as they were trying to rise economically and socially in the traditional way, through the acquisition of lands with families of laborers to work them.

The first European colonists, Portuguese as well as Spanish, did not want Amerindians to die. They wanted them to be producers, customers, tribute payers, serfs, peasants, peons, and servants. Columbus's original plan for Española (modern-day Haiti and the Dominican Republic) was not that it should become a colony of settlement, but that Europeans should establish trading "factories" there, such as those his fellow Italians had in the Levant and the Portuguese had on the coast of West Africa—small colonies of merchants and their aides organized to carry on trade with and milch the indigenous people. The plans of many of the first Spanish colonists in newly discovered Española were somewhat different, but even more in line with European tradition. They did not want to trade with Amerindians on anything like an equal basis; they wanted to become their lords, supported by the Native Americans with gold, food, and labor. The demand of Spanish rebels in Española in 1499, a demand to which Columbus had to acquiesce, was for *encomiendas*, which were defined not as grants of land, but as grants of rights to the labor and tribute of native communities. If Columbus and the sixteenth-century European colonists had been able to do what they had originally planned, there might have been no greater a proportion of Europeans crossing the Atlantic after 1492 than Normans crossing the English Channel after 1066.[5] But then came the epidemics, which changed the colonists' plans, all American societies, and Europe—indeed, the entire world.

The Epidemics

The arrival of large numbers of Europeans and Africans in a given area of the Americas was always followed by a rapid, even catastrophic, decline in the aboriginal population. The invaders' gross mistreatment of the indigines steepened the decline, but its chief cause was the pathogens the invaders inadvertently brought with them, germs that caused numerous epidemics of an extent and mortality comparable to the fourteenth-century Black Death in Eurasia and North Africa. Scholars and scientists have carefully assembled various lists of diseases that arrived in the Americas with Europeans and Africans. These lists vary somewhat in length and content, being products of what must be speculation, however well informed. Most contain the following maladies: smallpox, measles, chicken pox, whooping cough, chicken pox, typhus, typhoid fever, bubonic plague, cholera, scarlet fever, malaria, yellow fever, diphtheria, and influenza.[6] Whether a disease should be added or subtracted is relatively unimportant. What is important is that there was undeniably an avalanche of disease that decimated all native American peoples, and even obliterated many, such as the Tainos of the Greater Antilles, who were struck by the microinvaders and the macroinvaders simultaneously.

The World's Greatest Labor Shortage

In 1493 Columbus dropped into the laps of Europeans an unprecedented opportunity for conquest, empire, and fortune. Fertile lands, mines of silver and gold, and myriads of Amerindians to work them were to be had by right of arms. Amerindians, however, did not wear well. The demographic collapse in the highlands of the Aztec and Inca Empires is more fully documented than that of other Amerindians for the simple reason that in central Mesoamerica and Peru lived the populations most coveted by those Spanish monarchs and their subjects who were or aspired to become holders of the *encomiendas*. These highland populations fell by 90 percent or so in the first postconquest century, and vast, sparsely staffed *haciendas* sprawled where the conquistadores had anticipated manors teeming with native laborers.[7] The decline in the number of Amerindians of the hot, wet, coastal lowlands is not so fully recorded, although it was even more extreme. In the comparatively cool highlands the chief killers were the diseases that had been circulating in Europe: pustular infections, such as smallpox and measles, and respiratory infections, such as whooping cough and pneumonia. The peoples of the lowlands were afflicted by the same diseases *plus* diseases from the Old World tropics, including malaria, yellow fever, dengue fever, and amoebic dysentery. These swept into oblivion the small number of West Indians who had survived the initial European onslaught and early epidemics of infections such as smallpox, and eliminated most of the inhabitants of the littoral of the Gulf of Mexico and the Caribbean and, in time, the occupants of lowland Brazil and the hot, humid Pacific coasts. The Maya of Yucatán were the greatest exception to the generality that lowland Amerindians melted away after the Old World peoples arrived. The reason for their survival in large numbers might be that their stony and seasonally arid peninsula was a difficult environment for the anopheles mosquito. Be that as it may, survival of Amerindians of the sultry lowlands was the exception, not the rule. Father José de Anchieta wrote from Bahia, Brazil, in the 1560s that the native population had plunged precipitously during the previous twenty years, and that "one never believed that so many people would ever be used up, let alone in such a short time." A century after Columbus, the historian of the Spanish Empire, Antonio de Herrera, wrote that Spain's lowland Amerindian laborers were "so wasted and condemned, that of thirty parts of the people that inhabit it, there wants twenty-nine; and it is likely the rest of the Indians in a short time will decay."[8]

As their lowland Amerindian subjects died off, Europeans reached out to the Bahamas, Nicaragua, and the backlands of their Brazilian settlements for slaves, but the newly enslaved died off as rapidly as those who were first subjugated.[9] A century and more later, the English in Carolina tried to make do with Amerindian slaves as local labor and an export commodity but also failed.[10]

European conquerors faced the greatest labor shortage of all time. With Amerindians dying so precipitously, who was to do the work of reshaping the Americas in accordance with the schemes of imperial governments and the demands of the European and the world market? Who, for example, was going to do the brute labor of making Jamaica into a giant sugar plantation and Maryland into a giant tobacco plantation? The new masters of the American lowlands tried to persuade Europeans to volunteer for work that would make a mule balk and to live in environments with tropical diseases that killed Europeans about as fast as they killed Amerindians.[11] Convicts were conscripted, and some unfortunates were simply kidnapped, but there were never enough laborers. White laborers rattled around like peas in the bucket-sized vacancy.

Epidemics and Slaves

Epidemics often produce labor shortages, which strengthen the hand of the yeoman in his negotiations with the squire, and also encourage slavery as a way to refill the ranks of laborers. In the sixth century, Justinian's plague swept through the Mediterranean basin, creating a servant shortage that made it profitable to reach beyond the epidemic's farthest ravages to obtain slaves from northern and especially eastern

Europe to supply the Christian and Muslim slave markets. "Slav" is the root for words meaning slave in all western European languages and also the root for *sakaliba*, which is Arabic for both slave and eunuch. The return of plague in the fourteenth century stimulated the slave trade between southern Europe and the Black Sea, and also black Africa. Mediterranean Europe wanted slaves for domestics, artisans, sexual partners, and, in Portugal, for field hands. By 1551 slaves made up 10 percent of the population of Lisbon; there were more slaves in the countryside.[12]

The influx of slaves into western Europe, however, amounted to no more aliens than the resident populations could and did assimilate socially and genetically within a few generations.[13] Population expansion in fifteenth- and sixteenth-century Europe made up for much of the plague losses and presumably would have eventually reduced to naught the Europeans' demand for slaves. Europe's African slaves would have been lost in the footnotes of history books, as were the Tartar and Circassian slaves from an earlier time. But then Europe reached out for the Americas, where its touch quite literally killed.

The history of transatlantic migration divides into two periods. Until the end of the eighteenth century, most migrants were African and slave, about 10 million, as compared with perhaps as few as 2 million European migrants in the same period.[14] After 1800 most migrants (by an enormous margin) were European and free. The first migration was appallingly coercive and brutal; the second was less so but scarcely humane. Mass movements across the face of the earth are not accomplished without human suffering. The horror of the near extinction of Native Americans was echoed in the agony of Africans enslaved to replace them, and faintly in the anxieties of the uprooted Europeans who followed.

European demand for tropical crops such as sugar was the economic force that drove the Atlantic migration in the first period. The Christian effort to seize the Holy Land from the Muslims had failed several centuries before Columbus, but the Crusades did introduce western Europeans to sugar, the cultivation of which spread throughout the Mediterranean from the Levant to Granada, and then to Madeira, the Canaries, and São Tomé in the near Atlantic. Madeira and São Tomé were uninhabited when Europeans landed, and imported disease and brutal invaders quickly destroyed the Aborigines of the Canaries. From Europe the new masters of these islands brought convicts, Jewish children, and recent converts to Christianity from Islam, but there were never enough laborers to work the plantations.[15] The solution to the labor problem lay in the Berber and later in the black African. Before depopulation in the Americas raised the question of where laborers were to be found to cut the cane, chop the cotton, and pick the coffee beans, the plantation masters of the islands of the eastern Atlantic had the answer.[16]

Africa's Millions

The greatest transoceanic migration and probably the greatest long-distance migration by water or land before the nineteenth century was that of African slaves crossing the Atlantic to the New World. Between the first decade of the 1500s, when the Spanish monarchy authorized the shipment of slaves directly from Africa to the Antilles, and 1870, when the last American market for slaves locked its gates, 10 million Africans arrived alive in American ports, most of them to work in plantations raising cash crops for the European market: sugar, tobacco, rice, indigo, cotton, and coffee. Ninety percent went to fill the vacuum left in the hot, wet tropics by the now-extinct aboriginal populations. Brazil alone took 38 percent of the slaves, the Caribbean islands 40 percent. Saint Domingue (the French name for Española) received twice as many African slaves as the thirteen colonies and later the United States.[17]

The classic plantation lands from Brazil through the Guianas and around the West Indies never established self-sustaining slave populations in colonial times, and could not have maintained their exports of cash crops to Europe without continually importing workers from Africa. The birth rate of their black populations fell far short of the death rate. There are many explanations for this: overwork, inadequate diet, the preponderance of males over females (plantation masters found it more practical to replace dying workers than to encourage the birth of American-born replacements), and disease. The pathogens and parasites that had eliminated the Native Americans from most of the lowlands also shortened the lives of those who came to replace them. Africans were, genetically and by childhood exposure, more resistant to malaria, yellow fever, and many of the various tropical parasites than were the whites, but Africans were by no means immune to all strains of invasive species. Although the disease environments of torrid

America were more like those of West Africa than of Europe, they were not identical. In America the Africans were also subject to infections brought overseas by their European masters.[18] In hot, wet America, disease eliminated Amerindians, kept Europeans to a small number, and killed many Africans, stimulating the need for slaves up to the time of José Martí.[19]

Europe's Millions

The greatest century of the transatlantic slave trade in terms of absolute numbers was the eighteenth, when 6 million crossed from Africa. In the next century, after the arrival of 2 million more Africans, slavery was abolished in the Americas.[20] The change was not a comfortable one for the plantation elite. Former slaves tended to avoid work on the old plantations: "They turn out to work when they like," one white Jamaican complained, "do what they choose, take what days they like—in fact, do as they think proper." To replace them in the West Indies, a few Europeans, a greater number of Chinese, and hundreds of thousands of East Indians were brought in as contract laborers. Many East Indians returned home after a few years, but the descendants of those who remained today comprise half of Guyana's population and well over a third of Trinidad's, representing the most ethnically distinctive addition to the New World's tropical population since the first waves of Europeans and Africans.[21]

The last 2 million black slaves and the East Indian influx were ripples in comparison with the wave of Europeans that rolled across the Atlantic in the nineteenth and early twentieth centuries, veered away from the tropics, and broke on the shores of the American temperate zones: Canada, the United States, southern Brazil, Argentina, and Uruguay. The Europeans swept far inland, where the number and morale of Amerindians had been drastically reduced by two centuries and more of European and African-American pressure and imported disease.

Europeans, in contrast with Amerindians, had the advantage of long contact with many of the world's chief infectious diseases, which had thereby become endemic rather than epidemic, that is, something more in the nature of an incubus than a lightning bolt. In addition, public health and prophylactic techniques were at long last having some positive effects, and diet was improving in quantity and quality, enabling Europeans to survive all infections in greater numbers than ever before. Demographically, their story in the late eighteenth and nineteenth centuries was opposite that of Amerindians: Europeans were experiencing a population explosion.

In the seventeenth and early eighteenth centuries, western Europe's population had staggered along, its mortality rates, especially for children, always high and in some years extremely so. Births barely exceeded deaths even in the best of times. War killed soldiers and peasants indiscriminately. Hunger accompanied war and killed on its own behalf.[22] Worse than famine and war on average, and amplified by both in its effects, was disease, particularly bubonic plague, the chief arbiter of demography during the *ancien régime*.

For four hundred years, from the mid-fourteenth to the first years of the eighteenth century, plague epidemics in western Europe never ceased for long, if at all. In eastern Europe they continued for another century. The plague commonly killed 60 to 80 percent of those it infected. There was no known cure, and no one understood its etiology. In the second half of the seventeenth century, it began to retreat. London's last plague epidemic took place during 1665 and 1666, and the disease made its last sweep through the south of France in 1720. The retreat was a truly blessed mystery. Diseases can spontaneously lose their virulence and communicability, and it is possible that subtle changes in western European architecture and general behavior and in the use of quarantine and *cordon sanitaire* might have been effective in battling the disease.[23]

The retreat of plague left Europeans with only war, hunger, and a raft of other diseases to deal with, such as smallpox, measles, tuberculosis, and various dysenteric infections. None of them were singly as deadly as the bubonic scourge, but they were quite enough in their sum to cause, with the help of chronic malnutrition, an extremely high mortality rate. Armies, bit by bit, became professional, murdered fewer civilians, and lived off their own provisions rather than what they ravaged from an impoverished peasantry. The problems of crop failures and peacetime food shortages were harder to solve, but they were solved, and healthier populations resulted. Improved transportation sped the transfer of food from areas of surplus to areas of hunger and turned epidemic diseases into endemic diseases, thus softening their impact on society. When endemic diseases kill, they usually carry off the most expendable and easily replaced members of society, that is, immunologically inexperienced children.[24]

The improvements in agricultural techniques that historians have collectively entitled "the agricultural revolution" were also significant, although not decisive in initially sparking the population explosion. Populations were already increasing before that revolution had proceeded far enough to make much difference in the availability of food supplies. In the beginning, the key factor might have been the cultivation of Amerindian crops in Europe, especially maize and white potatoes, which produced more food per hectare than any traditional European crop. By the eighteenth century, maize was well on its way to becoming the staple of millions of the poorer peasants in a band of territory from northern Portugal to the Black Sea, and the potato was launched as the basic food of the Irish and impoverished farmers and urban lower classes of northern Europe. All of this occurred before the agricultural revolution, before the rise of the sanitationist movement, and certainly before medical science and the practices of variolation and vaccination had much influence on mortality rates.[25]

Europe's population was about 80 million when Columbus sailed. In the period circa 1800, when the United States and the nations of Latin America won their independence and the transatlantic slave trade entered its final decline, the population of Europe was about 180 million. In the same three centuries, the inhabitants of the British Isles—the English, Welsh, Scots, and Irish—the most migratory of all Europeans, leaped from 5 to 16 million.[26] Europe and the British Isles were ready to export people. In fact, they had to. But where?

They went to Australia, New Zealand, southern Brazil, Uruguay, Argentina, Canada, and, above all, to the United States. Aboriginal populations, ravaged by unfamiliar diseases, epidemic and newly endemic, were plunging in all these areas, probably nowhere more steeply than in North America. In 1800 there were probably no more than six hundred thousand Amerindians in the United States, down from an estimated 5 million in 1492; the European and African-American population of the United States was more than 5 million and climbing. In terms of absolute numbers, there were probably as many people in the area of the United States as there had been three hundred years before, but much had changed. Early Europeans had exposed the natives of North America to a score of new infections to which they had not had time to adapt, immunologically or through medical or public health practices. (For example, while the statistics of the 1800 census were being compiled, epidemics were devastating Amerindians in the interior of North America, reducing the Omaha by two-thirds.[27]) Europeans had, in their many centuries of experience with these diseases, adapted to them in one way or another. They had also mastered systems of agriculture and animal husbandry that enabled them to live in North America in numbers several times over the maximum pre-Columbian population.

Many thousands of Europeans emigrated to North America in the first decades of the nineteenth century, but another generation or so passed before they began to leave Europe en masse. It took another epidemic (if that word can be extended to the spread of disease among plants) to give the signal for the exodus of Europeans by the millions. In the mid-1840s, an American fungus *(Phytophthora infestans)* began to spread rapidly through the potato fields of northern Europe, hitting Ireland hardest. In a five-year period, more than a million Irish died of hunger and of jackal diseases, such as typhus and cholera, and hundreds of thousands fled across the Irish Sea and the Atlantic, primarily to the United States.[28] Other Europeans—Germans, Scandinavians, and, by the end of the century, southern Europeans, Ashkenazim, and Slavs—followed the Irish, although not faced with so direct a threat of death. Between 1820 and 1930, about 55 to 60 million people left Europe for the lands across the oceans and Siberia. That figure amounts to about one-fifth of Europe's entire population in 1820. Over half of them went to the United States, swamping the vestigial native population with a Caucasian tidal wave and reducing the proportion of African Americans in the total population from 19 percent in 1800 to 12 percent at the end of the century.[29]

By 1900 the population of the Americas had risen to 145 million, a total equal to that accorded by the most extravagant of the demographic historians to Amerindians in 1492. The great majority of those 145 million were Old World immigrants or their descendants.[30]

An Interim Assessment

Columbus and his blue-water emulators initiated a transoceanic revolution of unprecedented magnitude and significance by carrying Old World microlife across the ocean. The migrant pathogens and parasites obliterated millions of Amerindians, broke the morale of the survivors, and rendered vacant large parts of the New World, or at least reduced the population of the original inhabitants to such small numbers that the invaders could claim that the land was going unused—an offense to God! As a result, some Europeans set aside their ambitions for conquest to become lords of the manor, importing millions of Africans and transforming themselves into masters of plantations.

Europeans who remained at home benefited from improvements, technological and administrative, in their transportation system. Food moved rapidly from areas of surplus to areas of want, as did infections. The former process almost eliminated absolute starvation, and the latter homogenized the disease environment, ameliorating epidemics that had dictated Europe's demography since the coming of the Black Death. In increasing numbers, Europeans turned to the immensely productive Amerindian crops for sustenance. The resulting surplus of people then diffused to areas of lesser population density on the other side of the oceans, almost as if in obedience to laws of physical chemistry.

Notes

1. This thesis has many parents. The two whom I regard most reverentially are Sherburne F. Cook and Woodrow Wilson Borah.

2. For evidence and arguments in favor of a highly controversial hypothesis of a very large Amerindian population circa 1492, see, for instance, Henry F. Dobyns, "Estimating Aboriginal American Population: An Appraisal of Techniques with a New Hemispheric Estimate," *Current Anthropology* 7 (1966): 395–416. For evidence and arguments in favor of not so large yet considerable numbers of Amerindians, see William M. Denevan, ed., *The Native Population of the Americas in 1492* (Madison: University of Wisconsin Press, 1976); and the second chapter of Russell Thornton, *American Indian Holocaust and Survival: A Population History since 1492* (Norman: University of Oklahoma Press, 1987).

3. I dug this chestnut, in a somewhat different form, out of Carolo M. Cipolla, *The Economic History of World Population* (Harmondsworth: Penguin, 1964), 88–89.

4. Thornton, *American Indian Holocaust*, 34–37.

5. Samuel Eliot Morison, ed. and trans., *Journals and Other Documents on the Life and Voyages of Christopher Columbus* (New York: Heritage Press, 1963), 199–200; Samuel Eliot Morison, *Admiral of the Ocean Sea: A Life of Christopher Columbus* (Boston: Little, Brown, 1942), 567–68; James Lockhart and Stuart B. Schwartz, *Early Latin America: A History of Colonial Spanish America and Brazil* (Cambridge: Cambridge University Press, 1983), 68–71, 92–96; Carl Ortwin Sauer, *The Early Spanish Main* (Berkeley: University of California Press, 1969), 101, 200–204.

6. For instance, consult Henry F. Dobyns, *Their Numbers Become Thinned: Native American Population Dynamics in Eastern North America* (Knoxville: University of Tennessee Press, 1983), 34; Thornton, *American Indian Holocaust*, 39, 44. See also Alfred W. Crosby, *Ecological Imperialism: The Biological Ex-*

pansion of Europe, 900–1900 (Cambridge: Cambridge University Press, 1986), 195–216. For the latest consideration of this matter, see *Disease and Demography in the Americas,* ed. John W. Verano and Douglas H. Ubelaker (Washington, D.C.: Smithsonian Institution Press, 1992), passim.

7. James Lockhart, "Encomienda and Hacienda," *Hispanic American Historical Review* 49 (1969): 411–29; Woodrow Borah, *New Spain's Century of Depression* (Berkeley: University of California Press, 1951), passim.

8. Denevan, ed., *The Native Population of the Americas in 1492,* 35–41, 120, 176; Stuart B. Schwartz, "Indian Labor and New World Plantations," *American Historical Review* 83 (1978): 58; Alfred W. Crosby, *The Columbian Exchange: Biological and Cultural Consequences of 1492* (Westport, Conn.: Greenwood Press, 1972), 38.

9. David R. Radell, "The Indian Slave Trade and Population of Nicaragua during the Sixteenth Century," in *The Native Population of the Americas in 1492,* ed. Denevan, 73–75; Lockhart and Schwartz, *Early Latin America,* 197–200; Schwartz, "Indian Labor," 43–83.

10. Charles H. Hudson, *The Southeastern Indians* (Knoxville: University of Tennessee Press, 1976), 435, 437–38.

11. See, for instance, chapter 10 of Kenneth F. Kiple, *The Caribbean Slave: A Biographical History* (Cambridge: Cambridge University Press, 1984).

12. J.-N. Biraben and Jacques LeGoff, "The Plague in the Early Middle Ages," in *Biology of Man in History: Selections from the Annales, Economies, Societies, Civilisations,* ed. Robert Forster and Orest Ranum (Baltimore: Johns Hopkins University Press, 1975), 48–80; William D. Phillips, Jr., *Slavery from Roman Times to the Early Transatlantic Trade* (Minneapolis: University of Minnesota Press, 1985), 47, 57, 69, 105–6; William H. McNeill, *Plagues and Peoples* (Garden City: Doubleday, 1976), 77–148; Robert S. Gottfried, *The Black Death: Natural and Human Disaster in Medieval Europe* (New York: Free Press, 1983); Lockhart and Schwartz, *Early Latin America,* 27–28.

13. Ruth Pike, "Sevillian Society in the Sixteenth Century: Slaves and Freedmen," *Hispanic American Historical Review* 47 (1967): 344–59.

14. Philip D. Curtin, *The Atlantic Slave Trade: A Census* (Madison: University of Wisconsin Press, 1969), 87; William H. McNeill, *The Great Frontier: Freedom and Hierarchy in Modern Times* (Princeton: Princeton University Press, 1983), 18–19.

15. Crosby, *Ecological Imperialism,* 73, 92–99; Baily W. Diffie and George D. Winius, *Foundations of the Portuguese Empire, 1415–1580* (Minneapolis: University of Minnesota Press, 1977), 147; G. Y. Scammell, *The World Encompassed: The First European Empires, c. 800–1650* (Berkeley: University of California Press, 1981), 246.

16. The subject of the plantations and slavery is vast and intimidating. A good place to start is Philip D. Curtin, *The Rise and Fall of the Plantation Complex* (Cambridge: Cambridge University Press, 1990).

17. Curtin, *The Atlantic Slave Trade,* 89, 92.

18. Kiple, *The Caribbean Slave,* 104–19, 172.

19. Philip D. Curtin, *Death by Migration: Europe's Encounter with the Tropical World in the Nineteenth Century* (Cambridge: Cambridge University Press, 1989); Crosby, *Ecological Imperialism,* 140–41.

20. Curtin, *The Atlantic Slave Trade*, 268.

21. David Lowenthal, *West Indian Societies* (London: Oxford University Press, 1972), 57–58, 62; Orlando Patterson, "Migration in Caribbean Societies: Socioeconomic and Symbolic Resource," in *Human Migration, Patterns and Policies*, ed. William H. McNeill and Ruth S. Adams (Bloomington: Indiana University Press, 1978), 110–11; David Watts, *The West Indies: Patterns of Development, Culture and Environmental Change since 1492* (Cambridge: Cambridge University Press, 1987), 472–81; Brinley Thomas, "Migration: Economic Aspects," in *International Encyclopedia of the Social Sciences*, ed. David L. Sills (New York: Macmillan and Free Press, 1968), 10:294; Curtin, *The Rise and Fall of the Plantation Complex*, 175–77.

22. Michael W. Flinn, *The European Demographic System, 1500–1820* (Baltimore: Johns Hopkins University Press, 1981), 47–55; Thomas McKeown, "Food, Infection, and Population," in *Hunger and History: The Impact of Changing Food Production and Consumption Patterns on Society*, ed. Robert I. Rotberg and Theodore K. Rabb (Cambridge: Cambridge University Press, 1983), 29–50; E.A. Wrigley and R.S. Schofield, *The Population History of England, 1541–1871* (Cambridge, Mass.: Harvard University Press, 1981), 207–15, 244.

23. Flinn, *The European Demographic System*, 59–61.

24. McNeill, *Plagues and Peoples*, 225–26; Emmanuel Le Roy Ladurie, "A Concept: The Unification of the Globe by Disease," in *The Mind and Method of the Historian*, trans. Siân Reynolds and Ben Reynolds (Chicago: University of Chicago Press, 1981), 28–83.

25. William Langer, "American Foods and Europe's Population Growth," *Journal of Social History* 8 (1975): 51–66; Gretel H. Pelto and Pertti J. Pelto, "Diet and Delocalization: Dietary Changes since 1750," in *Hunger and History*, ed. Rotberg and Rabb, 314–16. The classic work on this subject is Thomas McKeown, *The Modern Rise of Population* (New York: Academic Press, 1976).

26. Colin McEvedy and Richard Jones, *Atlas of World Population History* (Harmondsworth: Penguin, 1978), 18, 49.

27. Thornton, *American Indian Holocaust*, 90, 94; E. Wayne Stearn and Allen E. Stearn, *The Effect of Smallpox on the Destiny of the Amerindian* (Boston: Bruce Humphries, 1945), 73–76.

28. Redcliffe N. Salaman, *The History of the Social Influence of the Potato*, rev. ed. (Cambridge: Cambridge University Press, 1985), 289–316.

29. McEvedy and Jones, *Atlas of World Population History*, 46; Huw R. Jones, *A Population Geography* (New York: Harper and Row, 1981), 254; William Woodruff, *Impact of Western Man: A Study of Europe's Role in the World Economy, 1750–1960* (New York: St. Martin's Press, 1967), 106–8; Peter M. Bergman, *The Chronological History of the Negro in America* (New York: New American Library, 1969), 82, 327.

30. Thornton, *American Indian Holocaust*, 23; Henry Dobyns, "Reassessing New World Populations at the Time of Contact," paper delivered April 18, 1988, Institute for Early Contact Studies, University of Florida, Gainesville, Florida.

6 VIRGIN SOIL EPIDEMICS AS A FACTOR IN THE ABORIGINAL DEPOPULATION OF AMERICA

During the last few decades historians have demonstrated increasing concern with the influence of disease in history, particularly the history of the New World. For example, the latest generation of Americanists chiefly blames diseases imported from the Old World for the disparity between the number of American Aborigines in 1492—new estimates of which soar as high as 100 million, or approximately one-sixth of the human race at that time—and the few million pure Indians and Eskimos alive at the end of the nineteenth century. There is no doubt that chronic disease was an important factor in the precipitous decline, and it is highly probable that the greatest killer was epidemic disease, especially as manifested in virgin soil epidemics.[1]

Virgin soil epidemics are those in which the populations at risk have had no contact within the lifetime of their oldest members with the diseases that strike them and are therefore immunologically almost defenseless. The importance of virgin soil epidemics in American history is strongly indicated by evidence that a number of dangerous maladies—smallpox, measles, chicken pox, whooping cough, chicken pox, typhus, typhoid fever, bubonic plague, cholera, scarlet fever, malaria, yellow fever, diphtheria, influenza, and undoubtedly several more—were unknown in the pre-Columbian New World.[2] In theory, the initial appearance of these diseases is as certain to have set off deadly epidemics as dropping lighted matches into tinder is certain to cause fires.

The thesis that epidemics have been chiefly responsible for the awesome diminution in the number of Native Americans is based on more than theory. The early chronicles of America are full of reports of horrendous epidemics and steep population declines, confirmed in many cases by recent quantitative analyses of Spanish tribute records and other sources.[3] The evidence provided by the documents of British and French America is not as definitely supportive of the thesis because the conquerors of those areas did not establish permanent settlements and begin to keep continuous records until the seventeenth century, by which time at least some of the worst epidemics of imported diseases had probably already taken place. Furthermore, the British tended to drive the Indians away, rather than ensnaring them as slaves and peons, as the Spaniards did, with the result that many of the most important events of aboriginal history in British America occurred beyond the range of direct observation by literate witnesses.

Even so, the surviving records for North America do contain references—brief, vague, but plentiful—to deadly epidemics among the Indians, of which I shall cite a few of the allegedly worst. In 1616–19 an epidemic, possibly of bubonic or pneumonic plague, swept coastal New England from Cape Cod to Maine, killing as many as nine out of every ten it touched.[4] During the 1630s and into the next decade, smallpox, the most murderous of all the recurrent Indian killers, whipsawed back and forth through the St. Lawrence–Great Lakes region, eliminating half the people of the Huron and Iroquois confederations.[5] In 1738 smallpox destroyed half the Cherokees, and in 1759 nearly half the Catawbas.[6] During the American Revolution it attacked the Piegan tribe and killed half its members.[7] It ravaged the plains tribes shortly before they were taken under United States jurisdiction by the Louisiana Purchase, killing two-thirds of the Omahas and perhaps half the population between the Missouri River and New Mexico.[8] In the 1820s, fever devastated the people of the Columbia River area, erasing perhaps four-fifths of them.[9] In 1837, smallpox returned to the plains and destroyed about half of the Aborigines there.[10]

Unfortunately, the documentation of these epidemics, as that of the many others of the period, is slight, usually hearsay, sometimes dated years after the events described, and often colored by emotion. Skepticism is eminently justified and is unlikely to be dispelled by the discovery of great quantities of firsthand reports on epidemics among the North American Indians. We must depend on analysis of what little we now know, and we must supplement that little by examination of recent epidemics among Native Americans.

Let us begin by asking why the American Aborigines offered so little resistance to imported epidemic diseases. Their susceptibility has long been attributed to special weakness on their part, an explanation that dates from the period of colonization, received the stamp of authority from such natural historians as the Comte de Buffon, and today acquires the color of authenticity from the science of genetics.[11] In its latest version, the hypothesis of genetic weakness holds that during the pre-Columbian millennia the New World Indians had no occasion to build up immunities to such diseases as smallpox and measles. Those Aborigines who were especially lacking in defenses against these maladies were not winnowed out before they passed on their vulnerabilities to their offspring.[12]

The hypothesis might possibly have some validity: the immune systems of people who have lived in isolation from each other for millennia probably would be somewhat different; but whether that difference was enough to be significant in this case is questionable. The death rate among white United States soldiers in the Civil War who contracted smallpox, a disease to which their ancestors had been exposed for many generations, was 38.5 percent, probably about the percentage of Aztecs who died of that disease in 1520.[13] The difference between the Union troops and the Aztec population is, of course, that most of the former had been vaccinated or exposed to the disease as children, while the latter was a completely virgin soil population.

It should also be asked why the decline in numbers of the American Aborigines went on as long as it did, 400 years or so, in contrast to the decline caused by Europe's most famous virgin soil epidemic, the Black Death, which lasted no more than 100 to 200 years.[14] The answer is that the Indians and Eskimos did not experience the onslaught of Old World diseases all at the same time and that other factors were also responsible for depressing their population levels. As far as we can say now, Old World diseases were the chief determinants in the demographic histories of particular tribes for 100 to 150 years after each tribe's first full exposure to them. In addition, the newcomers, whose dire influence on Native Americans must not be underestimated just because it has been overestimated, reduced the aboriginal populations by warfare, murder, dispossession, and interbreeding. Thereafter the Indians began a slow, at first nearly imperceptible, recovery. The greatest exceptions were the peoples of the tropical lowlands and islands who, under the extra heavy burden of insect-borne fevers, mostly of African provenance, held the downward course to oblivion.[15]

The Indians of Mexico's central highlands perfectly fit this pattern of sharp decline for four to six generations followed by gradual recovery. Appalling depopulation began with the nearly simultaneous arrival of Cortés and smallpox; the nadir occurred sometime in the seventeenth century; and then Indian numbers slowly rose. The pattern of European population history was approximately the same in the two centuries following the Black Death.[16] The recovery in numbers of the Indians of the United States in the twentieth century is probably part of a similar phenomenon.

But why did Europeans lose one-third or so to the Black Death, imported from Asia, while the American Aborigines lost perhaps as many as 90 percent to the diseases imported from the Old World? The answers are probably related to the factors that have caused many fatalities in recent virgin soil epidemics among Native Americans, not of such deadly diseases as smallpox and plague, which have been tightly controlled in our era, but of such relatively mild maladies as measles and influenza. In 1952, the Indians and Eskimos of Ungava Bay in Northern Quebec had an epidemic of measles: 99 percent became sick and about 7 percent died, even though some had the benefit of modern medicine. In 1954 an epidemic of measles broke out among the Aborigines of Brazil's remote Xingu National Park: the death rate was 9.6 percent for those of the afflicted who had modern medical treatment and 26.8 percent for those who did not. In 1968, when the Yanomamö settlements of the Brazilian-Venezuelan borderlands were struck by measles, 8 or 9 percent of the villagers died despite the availability of some modern medicines and treatment. The Kreen-Akorores of the Amazon Basin, contacted in the 1970s for the first time by outsiders, lost at least 15 percent of their people in a single brush with common influenza.[17]

The reasons for the massive losses to epidemics in the last four hundred years and the considerable losses to the epidemics just cited can be grouped conveniently in two categories, the first relating to the nature of the disease or diseases, and the second having to do with how individuals and societies react to the threat of epidemic death.

First, we must recognize that the reputations of measles and influenza as mild diseases are not entirely justified. Contemporary Native Americans who contract them are not cured by "miracle drugs," even when modern medical treatment is available, because there are no such drugs. Modern physicians do not *cure* measles, influenza, and such other viral maladies as smallpox, chicken pox, and mumps, but try, usually successfully, to keep off other infections until the normal functioning of undistracted immune systems kills off the invading viruses. If doctors fail in this task or are not available, the death rate will be "abnormally high." Measles killed more than 6 percent of all the white Union soldiers and almost 11 percent of all the black Union soldiers it infected during the Civil War, even though the waves of this disease that swept the army were not virgin soil epidemics.[18]

Virgin soil epidemics are different from others in the age incidence of those they kill, as well as in the quantity of their victims. Evidence from around the world suggests that such epidemics of a number of diseases with reputations as Indian killers—smallpox, measles, influenza, tuberculosis, and others—carry off disproportionately large percentages of people aged about fifteen to forty, men and women in the prime years of life who are largely responsible for the vital functions of food procurement, defense, and procreation.[19] Unfortunately, little evidence exists to support or deny the hypothesis that Native American virgin soil epidemics have been especially lethal to young adults. There is no doubt, however, that they have been extremely deadly for the very young. Infants are normally protected against infectious diseases common in the area of their births by antibodies passed on to them before birth through the bloodstreams of their immunologically experienced mothers and afterward via breast milk, antibodies which remain strong enough to fend off disease during the first precarious months of life. This first line of defense does not exist in virgin soil epidemics. The threat to young children is more than just bacteriological: they are often neglected by ailing adults during such epidemics and often die when their ailing mothers' milk fails. Infants in traditional aboriginal American societies are commonly two years of age or even older before weaning, so the failure of mothers' milk can boost the death rate during epidemics to a greater extent than modern urbanites would estimate on the basis of their own child-care practices.[20]

Mortality rates rise sharply when several virgin soil epidemics strike simultaneously. When the advance of the Alaska Highway in 1943 exposed the Indians of Teslin Lake to fuller contact with the outside world than they had ever had before, they underwent in one year waves of measles, German measles, dysentery, catarrhal jaundice, whooping cough, mumps, tonsillitis, and miningococcic meningitis. This sort of pulverizing experience must have been common among

Epidemics among the Dakota Indians, 1780–1851[23]

1780–81	Smallpox
1801–1802	Smallpox ("all sick winter")
1810	Smallpox
1813–14	Whooping cough
1818–19	Meales ("little smallpox winter")
1837	Smallpox
1845–46	Disease or diseases not identified ("many sick winter")
1849–50	Cholera ("many people had the cramps winter")
1850–51	Smallpox ("all the time sick with the big smallpox winter")

Aborigines in the early post-Columbian generations, although the chroniclers, we may guess, often put the blame on only the most spectacular of the diseases, usually smallpox. A report from Española in 1520 attributed the depopulation there to smallpox, measles, respiratory infection, and other diseases unnamed. Simultaneous epidemics of diseases, including smallpox and at least one other, possibly influenza, occurred in Mesoamerica in the early 1520s.[21] The action of diseases other than the one most apparently in epidemic stage will often cause dangerous complications, even if they have been long in common circulation among the victims. In the Ungava Bay and Yanomamö epidemics cited above, the final executioner was usually bronchopneumonia, which advanced when measles leveled the defenses of Aborigines weakened by diseases already present—malaria and pneumonia among the South Americans, and tuberculosis and influenza among the North Americans.[22]

Successive epidemics may take longer to dismantle societies than simultaneous attacks by several diseases, but they can be as thorough. The documentation of American Indians' experience of successive epidemics is slim and not expressed as statistics, but the records are nonetheless suggestive. The Dakotas kept annual chronicles on leather or cloth, showing by a single picture the most important event of each year. These records indicate that all or some of this people suffered significantly in the epidemics listed above, at least one of which, cholera, was virgin soil in nature, as were possibly several others. It should be noted that the considerable lapses of time between the smallpox epidemics meant that whole new generations of susceptibles were subject to infection upon the return of the disease and that the repeated ordeals must have had much of the deadliness of virgin soil epidemics.

Virgin soil epidemics tend to be especially deadly because no one is immune in the afflicted population and so nearly everyone gets sick at once. During a period of only a few days in the 1960s, every member of the Tchikao tribe of Xingu Park fell ill with influenza, and only the presence of outside medical personnel prevented a general disaster. Witnesses to the Ungava Bay and Yanomamö epidemics noted the murderous effect of nearly universal illness, however brief in duration. The scientists with the Yanomamö found that when both parents and children became sick, "there was a drastic breakdown of both the will and the means for necessary nursing." The observers saw several families in which grandparents, parents, and their children were simultaneously ill.[24]

The fire goes out and the cold creeps in; the sick, whom a bit of food and a cup of water might save, die of hunger and the dehydration of fever; the seed remains above the ground as the best season for planting passes, or there is no one well enough to harvest the crop before the frost. In the 1630s, when smallpox swept through New England, William Bradford wrote of a group of Indians who lived near a Plymouth colony trading post:

> they fell down so generally of this disease as they were in the end not able to help one another, no not to make a fire nor to fetch a little water to drink, nor any to bury the dead. But would strive as long as they could, and when they could procure no other means to make fire, they would burn the wooden trays and dishes they ate their meat in, and their very bows and arrows. And some would crawl out on all fours to get a little water, and sometimes die by the way and not to be able to get in again.[25]

The second category of factors—those that pertain to the ways in which Native Americans reacted to epidemic diseases—often had as decisive an influence on the death rate as did the virulency of the disease. American Aborigines were subjected to an immense barrage of disease, and their customs and religions provided little to help them through the ordeal. Traditional treatments, though perhaps effective against pre-Columbian diseases, were rarely so against acute infections from abroad, and they were often dangerous, as in the swift transfer of a patient from broiling sweathouse to frigid lake.[26] Thus, to take a modern example, when smallpox broke out among the Moqui Indians in Arizona in 1898, 632 fell ill but only 412 accepted treatment from a physician trained in modern medical practice. Although he had no medicines to cure smallpox or even to prevent secondary bacterial infections, only 24 of his patients died. By contrast, 163 of the 220 who refused his help and, presumably, put their faith in traditional Indian therapy, died.[27]

Native Americans had no conception of contagion and did not practice quarantine of the sick in pre-Columbian times, nor did they accept the new theory or practice until taught to do so by successive disasters. The Relation of 1640 of the Jesuit missionaries in New France contains the complaint that during epidemics of the most contagious and deadly maladies the Hurons continued to live among the sick "in the same indifference, and community of all things, as if they were in perfect health." The result, of course, was that nearly everyone contracted the infections; "the evil spread from house to house, from village to village, and finally became scattered throughout the country."[28]

Such ignorance of the danger of infection can be fatal, but so can knowledge when it creates terror, leading to fatalism or to frenzied, destructive behavior.[29] A large proportion of those who fall acutely ill in an epidemic will die, even if the disease is a usually mild one, like influenza or whooping cough, unless they are provided with drink, food, shelter, and competent nursing. These will be provided if their kin and friends fulfill the obligations of kinship and friendship, but will they do so? Will the sense of these obligations be stronger than fear, which can kill by paralyzing all action to help the sick or by galvanizing the healthy into flight?

If we may rely on negative evidence, we may say that aboriginal kin and tribal loyalties remained stronger than the fear of disease for a remarkably long time after the coming of the microorganisms from the Old World. We will never be able to pinpoint chronologically any change as subtle as the failure of these ties, but whenever it happened for a given group in a given epidemic, the death rate almost certainly rose. In most epidemics, contagious disease operating in crowded wigwams and long houses would spread so fast before terror took hold that panicky flight would serve more to spread the infection than to rob it of fresh victims, and any decline in the number of new cases, and consequently of deaths that might result from flight, would at the very least be canceled by the rise in the number of sick who died of neglect. Observers of the Ungava Bay epidemic reported that a fatalistic attitude toward the disease caused the loss of several entire families, whose members would not help each other or themselves. Scientists with the Yanomamö during their battle with measles recorded that fatalism killed some and panic killed more: the healthy abandoned the sick and fled to other villages, carrying the disease with them.[30] When a killing epidemic strikes a society that accepts violence as a way of reacting to crises and believes in life after death—characteristics of many Christian and many Indian societies—the results can be truly hideous. Many fourteenth-century Europeans reacted to the Black Death by joining the Flagellants or by killing Jews. Some Indians similarly turned on the whites, whom they blamed for the epidemics, but most were obliged by their circumstances to direct their fear and rage against themselves. During the epidemic of 1738 many Cherokees killed themselves in horror of permanent disfigurement, according to their contemporary, James Adair. Members of the Lewis and Clark expedition were told that in the 1802 smallpox epidemic the Omahas "carried their franzey to verry extrodinary length, not only burning their Village, but they put their *wives* and children to *Death* with a view of their all going to some better Countrey." In 1837 smallpox killed so many of the Blackfeet and so terrified those left alive after the first days of the epidemic that many committed suicide when they saw the initial signs of the disease in themselves. It is estimated that about six thousand, two-thirds of all the Blackfeet, died during the epidemic.[31]

The story of that same epidemic among the Mandans, as George Catlin received it, cannot be exceeded in its horror:

> It seems that the Mandans were surrounded by several war-parties of their most powerful enemies the Sioux, at that unlucky time, and they could not therefore disperse upon the plains, by which many of them could have been saved; and they were necessarily enclosed within the piquets of their village, where the disease in a few days became so very malignant that death ensued in a few hours after its attacks; and so slight were their hopes when they were attacked, that nearly half of them destroyed themselves with their knives, with their guns, and by dashing their brains out by leaping head-foremost from a thirty foot ledge of rocks in front of their village. The first symptoms of the disease was a rapid swelling of the body, and so very virulent had it become, that very many died in two or three hours after their attack, and in many cases without the appearance of disease upon their skin. Utter dismay seemed to possess all classes and ages and they gave themselves up in despair as entirely lost. There was but one continual crying and howling and praying to the Great Spirit for his protection during the

nights and days; and there being but few living, and those in too appalling despair, nobody thought of burying the dead, whose bodies, whole families together, were left in horrid and loathsome piles in their own wigwams, with a few buffalo robes, etc. thrown over them, there to decay, and be devoured by their own dogs.[32]

During that epidemic, the number of Mandans shrank from about 1,600 to between 125 and 145.[33]

Whether the Europeans and Africans came to the Native Americans in war or peace, they always brought death with them, and the final comment may be left to the Superior of the Jesuit Missions to the Indians of New France, who wrote in confusion and dejection in the 1640s, that "since the Faith has come to dwell among these people, all things that make men die have been found in these countries."[34]

Notes

I wish to thank Dauril Alden, Frederick Dunn, Wilbur Jacobs, and William McNeill for their suggestions.

1. Henry F. Dobyns, "Estimating Aboriginal American Population: An Appraisal of Techniques with a New Hemispheric Estimate," *Current Anthropology* 7 (1966): 395–449, is an excellent place to begin an examination of this theory.

2. Percy M. Ashburn, *The Ranks of Death: A Medical History of the Conquest of America*, ed. Frank D. Ashburn (New York, 1947); Sherburne F. Cook, "The Significance of Disease in the Extinction of the New England Indians," *Human Biology* 45 (1973): 485–508; Alfred W. Crosby, *The Columbian Exchange: Biological and Cultural Consequences of 1492* (Westport, Conn., 1972), 31–63; Henry F. Dobyns, "An Outline of Andean Epidemic History to 1720," *Bulletin of the History of Medicine* 37 (1963): 493–515; Frederick L. Dunn, "On the Antiquity of Malaria in the Western Hemisphere," *Human Biology* 37 (1965), 385–93; Robert F. Fortuine, "The Health of the Eskimos, as Portrayed in the Earliest Written Accounts," *Bulletin of the History of Medicine* 45 (1971): 98–114. For the latest consideration of this matter, see John W. Verano and Douglas H. Ubelaker, eds., *Disease and Demography in the Americas* (Washington, D.C., 1992), passim.

3. Wilbur R. Jacobs, "The Tip of an Iceberg: Pre-Columbian Indian Demography and Some Implications for Revisionism," *William and Mary Quarterly* 3d ser., 31 (1974): 123–32, is a good brief introduction to the subject which cites most of the recent works.

4. Cook, "The Significance of Disease," 487–91, 497.

5. John Duffy, "Smallpox and the Indians of the American Colonies," *Bulletin of the History of Medicine* 25 (1951): 328; Wilcomb E. Washburn, *The Indian in America* (New York, 1975), 105.

6. Duffy, "Smallpox and the Indians of the American Colonies," 335, 338.

7. Washburn, *The Indian in America*, 105.

8. E. Wagner Stearn and Allen E. Stearn, *The Effect of Smallpox on the Destiny of the Amerindian* (Boston, 1945), 74–76.

9. James Mooney, *The Aboriginal Population of America North of Mexico*, Smithsonian Miscellaneous Collections, 80, No. 7 (Washington, D.C., 1928), 14.

10. Stearn and Stearn, *The Effect of Smallpox*, 81–85; Henry R. Schoolcraft, *Information Respecting the History, Condition and Prospects of the Indian Tribes of the United States*, Part 3 (Philadelphia, 1853), 254.

11. Henry Steele Commager and Elmo Giordanetti, eds., *Was America a Mistake: An Eighteenth-Century Controversy* (New York, 1967), passim.

12. John F. Marchand, "Tribal Epidemics in the Yukon," *Journal of the American Medical Association* 123 (1943): 1020; Maurice L. Sievers, "Disease Patterns among Southwestern Indians," *Public Health Reports* 81 (1966): 1075–83; Jacob A. Brody et al., "Measles Vaccine Field Trials in Alaska," *Journal of the American Medical Association* 189 (1964): 339–42; Willard R. Centerwall, "A Recent Experience with Measles in a 'Virgin-Soil' Population," in *Biomedical Challenges Presented by the American Indian*, Pan-American Sanitary Bureau, *Scientific Publication*, No. 165 (Washington, D.C., 1968), 77–79; James V. Neel et al., "Notes on the Effect of Measles and Measles Vaccine in a Virgin-Soil Population of South American Indians," *American Journal of Epidemiology* 91 (1970): 418–29; interviews with Dr. Frederick L. Dunn of the George Williams Hooper Foundation, University of California at San Francisco.

13. Surgeon General, U.S. Army, *The Medical and Surgical History of the War of the Rebellion*, 1, Part 3 (Washington, D.C., 1888), 625; Crosby, *The Columbian Exchange*, 52.

14. William H. McNeill, *Plagues and Peoples* (Garden City, 1976), 149–234.

15. Dobyns, "Estimating Aboriginal American Population," 415; Joseph de Acosta, *The Natural and Moral History of the Indies*, trans. Edward Grimston (New York, n.d.), 1:160.

16. Charles Gibson, *The Aztecs under Spanish Rule: A History of the Indians of the Valley of Mexico, 1519–1810* (Stanford, Calif., 1964), 139, 141. McNeill, *Plagues and Peoples*, 149–234.

17. A.F.W. Peart and F.P. Nagler, "Measles in the Canadian Arctic, 1952," *Canadian Journal of Public Health* 45 (1954): 155; Noel Nutels, "Medical Problems of Newly Contacted Indian Groups," in *Biomedical Challenges Presented by the American Indian*, Pan-American Sanitary Bureau, *Scientific Publication*, No. 165 (1968): 70; Neel et al., "Notes on the Effect of Measles," 426; W. Jesco von Puttkamer, "Brazil's Kreen-Akarores, Requiem for a Tribe," *National Geographic* 147 (1975): 254.

18. Surgeon General, *Medical and Surgical History*, 1, Part 3, 649.

19. Macfarlane Burnet and David O. White, *Natural History of Infectious Disease*, 4th ed. (Cambridge, 1972), 97–100.

20. Frederick W. Hodge, ed., *Handbook of American Indians North of Mexico*, Part 1 (Washington, D.C., 1912), 265.

21. Marchand, "Tribal Epidemics in the Yukon," 1019–20; *Colección de Documentos Inéditos, Relativos al Descubrimiento, Conquista y Organización de las Antiguas Posesiones Españoles de América y Oceania* (Madrid, 1864–1868), 1:397–98, 428–29; Crosby, *The Columbian Exchange*, 49, 58.

22. Peart and Nagler, "Measles in the Canadian Arctic, 1952," 147, 152; Neel et al., "Notes on the Effect of Measles," 422, 425.

23. Garrick Mallery, "Pictographs of the North American Indian: A Preliminary Paper," *Fourth Annual Report of the Bureau of Ethnology: 1882–1883*, 4 (Washington, D.C., 1886), 103–25, 131–42; Alexis A. Praus, *The Sioux, 1798–1922. A Dakota Winter Count*, Cranbrook Institute of Science, Bulletin 44 (Bloomfield Hills, Mich., 1962), 15.

24. Orlando Boas and Claudio Villas Boas, "Saving Brazil's Stone Age Tribes from Extinction," *National Geographic* 134 (1968): 444; Peart and Nagler, "Measles in the Canadian Arctic, 1952," 153; Neel et al., "Notes on the Effects of Measles," 427; Centerwall, "A Recent Experience with Measles," 80–81.

25. William Bradford, *Of Plymouth Plantation*, ed. Samuel Eliot Morison (New York, 1952), 271.

26. Harold E. Driver, *Indians of North America* (Chicago, 1961), 396–430.

27. *Report of the Commissioner of Indian Affairs*, Part 1, in *Annual Reports of the Department of Interior for the Fiscal Year Ended June 30, 1899* (Washington, D.C., 1899), 158–59.

28. Reuben Gold Thwaites, ed., *The Jesuit Relations and Allied Documents: Travels and Explorations of the Jesuit Missionaries in New France, 1610–1791 . . .*, 19 (Cleveland, 1898), 89.

29. The fear of epidemic disease and the psychic stress created by the advance of European and African invaders doubtless had a direct effect on disease and death rates. Extreme anxiety decreases the organism's ability to resist attack. See J. E. Nardini, "Survival Factors in American Prisoners of War of the Japanese," *American Journal of Psychiatry* 190 (1952): 241–48; Henry Krystal and William G. Niederland, *Psychic Traumatization, Aftereffects in Individuals and Communities* (Boston, 1971); Robert Jay Lifton, *Death in Life: Survivors of Hiroshima* (New York, 1967).

30. Peart and Nagler, "Measles in the Canadian Arctic, 1952," 153; Centerwall, "A Recent Experience with Measles," 81. We must not regard such behavior as typical only of Indians and other pre-literate peoples. The classic description of this kind of pathological individualism is contained in the first pages of *The Decameron*, in which Giovanni Boccaccio depicts how medieval Florentines reacted to the Black Death.

31. Samuel Williams, ed., *Adair's History of the American Indians* (Johnson City, Tenn., 1930), 245; Bernard DeVoto, ed., *The Journals of Lewis and Clark* (Boston, 1953), 18–19; John C. Ewers, *The Blackfeet: Raiders on the Northwestern Plains* (Norman, Okla., 1958), 65–66.

32. George Catlin, *Letters and Notes on the Manners, Customs, and Condition of the North American Indians*, 11 (Minneapolis, 1965 [orig. publ. London, 1841]), 257. For corroboration see M. M. Quaife, ed., "The Smallpox Epidemic on the Upper Missouri," *Mississippi Valley Historical Review* 17 (1930): 278–99.

33. Hodge, ed., *Handbook of American Indians*, 797–98.

34. Thwaites, ed., *Jesuit Relations*, 32, 253.

7 "GOD . . . WOULD DESTROY THEM, AND GIVE THEIR COUNTRY TO ANOTHER PEOPLE . . .

In December of 1620, a group of English dissenters who "knew they were pilgrimes," in the words of William Bradford, stepped ashore on the southern coast of Massachusetts at the site of the Wampanoag Indian village of Pawtuxet. The village was empty, abandoned long enough for the grasses and weeds to have taken over the cornfields, but not long enough for the trees to have returned. The Pilgrims occupied the lonely place and called it Plymouth. It was pestilence that had cleared the way for this tiny colony in New England, and the shadow of death would be a major factor in giving the settlement form and substance in the months ahead.

New England Indians and European fishermen and traders had been in intermittent contact for a century, and it was inevitable that more than otter skins, beaver pelts, knives, and kettles would be exchanged. Disease was among the commodities, and in this trade the Indians would come off second-best. Europe, with ancient contacts by land and new ones by sea with the chief disease communities of the world, and with her relatively dense populations of often hungry and always filthy people, had all the advantages of her disadvantages: an arsenal of diseases.

Europe was in the midst of a golden age for infectious disease organisms, an era ushered in by the Black Death in the fourteenth century. To such old regulars as smallpox and consumption were added such new, or newly recognized, diseases as plague, typhus, and syphilis. Bubonic plague, the greatest killer of them all, smoldered continually and broke out periodically in consuming epidemics. Early in 1617 southeast gales drove whales ashore in the Netherlands. The fearful thought them a portent of plague, and sure enough, by August the plague was general throughout the land. London had full-scale epidemics of that killer in 1603 and again in 1625, and the plague—or something very like it—soon made its presence felt among the Indians of the northeast coast of America.

European slavers taught the Indians of the New England coast the necessity of defending themselves against the aliens' raids, but nothing of how to defend themselves against the infections the aliens sometimes brought with them. In the second decade of the seventeenth century, a French ship wrecked on the shores of Massachusetts, and some of the crew escaped alive. Possibly, in retaliation for a recent kidnapping raid by whites, the Indians eventually killed all but three or four, whom they reduced to slavery. According to what the Indians told the Pilgrims, one of these captives, angry and helpless, had struck at his captors with words, telling them that "God was angry with them for their wickedness, and would destroy them, and give their country to another people, that should not live as beasts as they did but should be clothed. . . ." The Indians laughed at him, saying that they were so numerous that the white man's god could not kill them. He answered "that though they were never so many, God had many ways to destroy them that they knew not." Within a year or two an epidemic struck the coast of New England, devastating the tribes like an autumnal nor'easter raking leaves from the trees.

When did this pestilence first appear in New England? Probably no earlier than 1616 and no later than 1617, and it lasted until at least 1619. What vessel brought it? It is improbable that we will ever know. What was the disease? Another difficult question. We know it lasted through winters, which suggests that it was not a mosquito-borne disease, like yellow fever. We know that the few Europeans who actually saw its victims did not identify it as smallpox, measles, mumps, chicken pox, or any of Europe's common diseases, which they certainly would have recognized. We know it spread along the coast no farther southwest than Narragansett Bay, nor farther northeast than the Kennebec River or possibly Penobscot Bay, nor did it penetrate inland more than twenty or thirty miles. The narrow geographical limitations of the epidemic suggest that the disease was not one of the breath-borne maladies, like smallpox or measles, which normally surge across vast areas. A flea- or louse-borne disease like typhus or plague seems more likely.

We know that the disease produced spots on its victims' skins; and we know by hearsay that some Englishmen in New England at the peak of the epidemic slept in huts with dead and dying Indians, but that not one of these whites fell ill or even so much as "felt their heads to ache while they stayed there." Spots certainly suggest typhus. The Europeans' freedom from infection suggests some disease so common in Europe that they all had acquired immunity to it at home, or that they did not stay around long enough to get a proper dose of the disease—or that the account is in part or whole false.

Most of the seventeenth-century chroniclers called the disease "the plague," although "plague" was and is a word often used to mean any pestilence. Captain Thomas Dermer, one of the few Europeans actually to see Indians who were freshly recovering from the experience, called their infection in 1619 "the Plague, for wee might perceive the sores of some that had escaped, who described the spots of such as usually died."

Plague is certainly capable of doing what this pestilence did, and Europeans certainly knew it well enough to recognize it by sight or description. And it is true that plague was well established in western Europe in the early years of the seventeenth century. Like some kinds of typhus, it is a disease carried by rats and their attendant vermin, rats which swarmed in the holds of the sailing vessels of that era. The disease travels readily by ship, as the European colonists in America knew. Many Britons fell ill and died on the vessels of the Third Supply sailing to Virginia in 1609, and the rumor was that one of the vessels had plague on board. In the 1660s, during London's last great siege of plague, Virginians fled from their ports for fear of the disease coming across on the ships from England.

Fear was justified because ship rats were coming across and establishing beachheads in America. Captain John Smith tells us that they already numbered in the thousands in Jamestown in 1609, when the rats almost starved out the colony by eating its stores of food. They were present and prospering in New England by at least the 1660s, and probably a great deal earlier. It is likely that they found living in the layered bark walls of the Indian wigwams warm and comfortable, and the Indian food-storage practices and eating habits conducive to good diet. Once the rats were established, the transfer of their plague-ridden fleas to the Indians would have been almost automatic and perhaps not even noticed by the new hosts. Body lice were even more common among New England Indians than among white settlers, and the natives commonly passed the time by picking lice and killing them between their teeth.

It is puzzling, though, to those who diagnose the pestilence as plague, that Dermer described its chief signs as sores and spots, rather than the terrible buboes or boils of the groin and armpits that are impossible to overlook in typical victims of the plague. And it is even more odd that the plague-infected fleas did not establish themselves and their bacilli permanently among the wild rodents of New England, as they did in those of the western United States at the end of the nineteenth century. A diagnosis of typhus is tempting, but the historian is reluctant to contradict firsthand witnesses.

Whether plague or typhus, the disease went through the Indians like fire. Almost all the seventeenth-century writers say it killed nine of ten and even nineteen of twenty of the Indians it touched—an incredible mortality rate. But if it was, indeed, plague, especially if it changed from bubonic to pneumonic plague, it could well have killed that proportion. In the fourteenth century, plague killed one-third of all the people in Europe and a much higher percentage than that in many towns and districts. Further, the Indians knew nothing of the principle of contagion and had an ancient custom of visiting the sick, jamming into extremely hot little huts with them, assuring maximum dispersal of the illness. Their methods of treating illness, which usually featured a stay in a sweatbox, followed by immersion in the nearest cold pond or river, would have been a dreadful trauma for a person with a high fever, and a fine way to encourage pneumonic complications. Consider, too, that the epidemic could not have failed to disrupt food-procurement patterns, as women lay too ill to tend the corn and men too weak to hunt. Starvation often gleans what epidemic disease has missed. Consider, finally, that after the Indians realized the full extent of the disease, some of them, at least, ran away and left the sick and convalescent to die of neglect. In short, one does not necessarily have to credit a 90 percent death rate to the infection per se in order to accept a 90 percent depopulation rate.

It is undeniable that the pestilence largely emptied the Indian villages of coastal New England by 1619. That year, Thomas Dermer found "ancient plantations, not long since populous, now utterly void; in other places a remnant remains, but not free of sickness." In 1621 a party of Pilgrims went to visit Massasoit, the most powerful

Wampanoag sachem, at his summer quarters on a river about fifteen miles from Plymouth. They saw the remnants of many villages and former Indian cornfields along both sides of the river grown up in weeds higher than a man's head: "Thousands of men have lived there, which died in a great plague not long since: and pity it was and is to see so many goodly fields, and so well seated, without men to dress and manure the same."

Near Boston Bay, Thomas Morton saw even more vivid indications of the plague:

> For in a place where many inhabited, there hath been but one left alive, to tell what became of the rest, the livinge being (as it seemed) not able to bury the dead, they were left for Crowes, kites and vermin to prey upon. And the bones and skulls upon the severall places of their habitations, made such a spectacle after my coming into those partes, that as I travailed in that Forrest, nere the Massachusets, it seemed to mee a new found Golgotha.

What destroyed Indian bodies also undermined Indian religion—the Indians' entire view of the universe and of themselves. Disease was always considered a manifestation of spiritual influences, and the power of the powwows (priests) to direct and cure disease was central to the Indian religion. Later in the century we hear of powwows being hounded, punished, and even killed for failing to produce promised cures. What was the impact when hundreds, even thousands, died in the care of leaders whose chief distinction had been their ability to cure? Many of the powwows themselves, in constant contact with the sick they sought to cure, must have died. What was the impact of this final and irrevocable defeat of these priestly physicians?

What seemed cosmically appalling to the Indians was interpreted as clear proof of God's love by the Pilgrims—a divine intercession that revealed itself from the beginning. They had planned to settle in the Hudson River area or thereabouts, but the master of the *Mayflower* deposited them on the coast of New England. His inability or refusal to take them where they wanted to go proved a bit of luck—"God outshoots Satan oftentimes in his own bow"—for the lands about the Hudson's mouth, though more attractive because more fertile than Plymouth's, were "then abounding with a multitude of pernicious savages. . . ." God had directed the Pilgrims to a coast His plague had cleared of such savages: "whereby he made way for the carrying of his good purpose in promulgating his gospel. . . ." There were no Indians at Plymouth and none for eight or ten miles, and yet it had recently been a village of Wampanoags who had, over the years, removed the tough climax growth of forest to plant maize. When the weak and hungry colonists went out to plant in the following spring, all they had to do was to clear out the weeds. Death, it seemed obvious, was God's handyman and the Pilgrims' friend.

The wind of pestilence did more than merely clear a safe place for the Pilgrim to settle; in the long run, it enabled that settlement not only to survive, but to take root and, in the end, to prosper with a minimum of native resistance. The natives of coastal Massachusetts were fewer in number than in a very long time, possibly than in several thousand years, but there were still quite enough of them to wipe out the few Europeans from the *Mayflower,* and they had reason to hate whites. English visitors, the Indians told Dermer, recently had lured a number of Wampanoags on board their ship and had then "made great slaughter of them with their murderers [small ship's cannon]. . . ." When a party of Pilgrims visited the next tribe to the south, the Nausets, in 1621, they met an old woman who broke "forth into great passion, weeping and crying excessively." She had lost three of her sons to kidnappers, and now was without comfort in her old age. A Wampanoag said that the Nausets had killed three English interlopers in the summer of 1620.

Half the English at Plymouth died of malnutrition, exhaustion, and exposure that first winter. Indian anger and Indian power could have made Plymouth one of the lost colonies, like the one Columbus left behind on Española in 1493 or Sir Walter Raleigh's Roanoke colony of the 1580s. At some time during this low ebb of Pilgrim history the powwows gathered in the fastnesses of a swamp, where, for three days, they "did curse and execrate" the newcomers to destroy them or drive them away. It almost worked: at times the number of English healthy enough to offer any real help to the sick and, if necessary, any real resistance to attackers was as low as six or seven. But in the end the Indians' gods failed, and the English survived, "having borne this affliction with much patience, being upheld by the Lord."

What held the Indians back from physical attack? They had the strength and motive, and bloody precedent had been set by both whites and Indians. The answer must be fear. The coastal Indians may have been second only to the Pilgrims in New England as believers in the power of the white man's god. A visitor to Plymouth in 1621 wrote that the plague had sapped Wampanoag courage, as well as the tribe's numbers: "their countenance is dejected, and they seem as a people affrighted." They were coming to the English settlement in great numbers every day, "and might in one hour have made a dispatch of us, yet such a fear was upon them, as that they never offered us the least injury in word or deed."

Direct relations between the Wampanoags and the Pilgrims began in March of 1621, approximately three months after the English arrival. An Indian walked out of the woods and through the fields and into Plymouth. He was Samoset, who spoke some English, having learned it from English fishermen on the coast of Maine. He asked for beer, and received "strong water," biscuit, butter, cheese, pudding, and a piece of duck. It was he who told the Pilgrims the old Indian name for their village and explained what had happened to its original inhabitants. A few days later he returned with the individual whom the Pilgrims would soon rank as "a special instrument sent of God for their good beyond their expectation." The man was Squanto, a Pawtuxet who had been kidnapped, had escaped in Spain, and had lived in Cornhill, London, before making his way back to America.

An hour later the sachem, Massasoit, walked in with a train of sixty men. If he had come to fight, he could have swept Plymouth out of existence, but he came in peace, and what amounts to a nonaggression and mutual defense pact was soon agreed upon—the Treaty of Plymouth. Massasoit, wrote Edward Winslow in his first-person account of that day in March, "hath a potent adversary, the Narrohigansets [Narragansets], that are at war with him, against whom he thinks we may be some strength to him, for our peeces are terrible unto them."

In the eyes of the native people of New England, the whites possessed a greater potency than any Indian people. Nothing could be more immediately impressive than firearms, which made clouds of smoke and a sound like the nearest of thunderclaps and killed at a distance of many paces. And what could seem more logical but to see a similarity between the muskets and cannon, which reached out invisibly and tore bodies, and the plague, which reached out invisibly and corrupted bodies? In the 1580s, Indians in the vicinity of Roanoke had blamed the epidemic then raging on "invisible bullets" that the whites could shoot any distance desired; and it is quite likely that Massasoit and his followers had a similar interpretation of their experience with epidemic disease. No wonder the mighty sachem literally trembled as he sat beside the governor of Plymouth that day in March of 1621.

The following year, the Pilgrims learned that Squanto, taking advantage of his position as go-between for the Indians and English, had been telling the former that he had such control over the latter that he could persuade them to unleash the plague again, if he wished. He tried to use this claim of immense power to persuade the Wampanoags to shift their allegiance from Massasoit to himself. It was a game which nearly cost the schemer his life, and he had to spend the rest of his days living with the Pilgrims.

He told the Indians that the plague was buried under the storehouse in Plymouth, where, interestingly enough, the Pilgrims did have something buried: their reserve kegs of gunpowder. He told the Wampanoags that the English could send the plague forth to destroy whomever they wished, while not stirring a foot from home. When, in May of 1622, the Pilgrims dug up some of the gunpowder kegs, another Wampanoag, understandably disturbed, asked the English if they did, indeed, have the plague at their beck and call. The answer he got was as honest a one as could be expected from a seventeenth-century Christian: "No; but the God of the English has it in store, and could send it at his pleasure, to the destruction of his or our enemies." Not long after, Massasoit asked Governor William Bradford if "he would let out the plague to destroy the Sachem, and his men, who were his enemies, promising that he himself, and all his posterity, would be their everlasting friends, so great an opinion he had of the English."

Those enemies were the Narragansets, whose presence was the greatest immediate threat to Plymouth, and whose fear of the Englishmen's power was Plymouth's (and the Wampanoags') best shield. In the late fall of 1621, Canonicus, the Narragansets' greatest sachem, sent a bundle of arrows wrapped in a snakeskin to Squanto at Plymouth. Squanto was not present when they arrived, for which the messenger who brought the bundle was visibly thankful, and he departed "with all expedition." When Squanto returned and examined Canonicus's package, he explained that it signified a threat and a challenge to the new colony. The governor, who as a European of the Reformation era knew as much of threat and challenge as any Indian, stuffed the skin with gunpowder and shot, and sent it back to Canonicus. The great and terrible sachem refused to accept it, would not touch the powder and shot, nor suffer the bundle to remain in Narraganset country. The sinister package, "having been posted from place to place a long time, at length came whole back again." The plague perhaps had taught the Indian the principle of contagion.

Disease, real and imagined, remained a crucial element in English–Indian relations for at least the next two years, seemingly always to the advantage of the English. In 1622 and 1623 the Pilgrims were still so incompetent at living in America that only the abundance of shellfish and maize obtained from the Indians saved them from starvation: a dangerous situation, because by then the Indians' fear of and respect for the whites were declining. As one Pilgrim chronicler put it, the Indians "began again to cast forth many insulting speeches, glorying in our weakness, and giving out how easy it would be ere long to cut us off. Now also Massassowat [Massasoit] seemed to frown on us, and neither came or sent to us as formerly." A letter arrived from Jamestown far to the south in Virginia telling of how the Indians had risen there, killing hundreds of the colonists. In the summer of 1622 a band of ne'er-do-well English settled at Wessagusset (Weymouth), not far from Plymouth, and after begging food from the impoverished Pilgrims, set about stealing it from the Indians. That fall, Squanto, the almost indispensable man in the Pilgrims' dealings with the Indians, fell ill on a trip to collect maize from the natives. After fever and nosebleeds he died, asking the governor to pray for him "that he might go to the Englishman's God in heaven. . . ."

The Indians, apparently with the Massachusetts tribe in the lead, began to plot to exterminate the Wessagusset settlement. They were less intolerant of the Plymouth than the Wessagusset people, but their plan was to destroy the Pilgrims, as well, for fear that the latter would take revenge for the murder of any English. The scheme never got beyond the talking stage. Why were the Indians not able to organize themselves and take the action they planned? Pilgrims collecting maize from the Massachusetts in the latter part of 1622 learned of a "great sickness" among them "not unlike the plague, if not the same." Soon after, Wampanoag women bringing corn to Plymouth were struck with a "great sickness," and the English were obliged to carry much of the corn home on their own backs.

Disease or, at least, bodily malfunction most dramatically affected New England history in 1623 when Massasoit developed a massive case of constipation. In March the news arrived in Plymouth that Massasoit was close to death and that a Dutch vessel had grounded on the sands right in front of his current home. The English knew of the Indian custom that any and all friends must visit the ill, especially the very ill, and they also wanted to meet with the stranded Dutch; so a small party set out from Plymouth for the sachem's sickbed. The Pilgrims found the Dutch afloat and gone, and Massasoit's dwelling jammed to bursting with well-wishers and powwows "making such a hellish noise, as it distempered us that were well, and therefore unlike to ease him that was sick."

Edward Winslow undertook the sachem's case and managed to get between his teeth "a confection of many comfortable conserves, on the point of my knife. . . ." He then washed out his patient's mouth, put him on a light diet, and soon his bowels were functioning again. The Englishman had, with the simplest of Hippocratic remedies, apparently saved the life of the most powerful man in the immediate environs of Plymouth. For the next day or so Winslow was kept busy going from one to another of the sachem's sick or allegedly sick followers, doling out smidgens of his confection and receiving "many joyful thanks." In an era that was, for the Indians, one of almost incomprehensible mortality, Winslow had succeeded where all the powwows had failed in thwarting the influences drawing Massasoit toward death. The English could not only persuade a profoundly malevolent god to kill, but also *not* to kill.

The most important immediate product of Massasoit's recovery was his gratitude. He revealed the details of the Indian plot against Wessagusset and Plymouth, a plot involving most of the larger tribes within two or three days' travel of Plymouth, and even the Indians of Capawack (Martha's Vineyard). He said he had been asked to join when he was sick, but had refused for himself and his people. The Pilgrims probably had already heard rumors of the plot, and the sachem's story was confirmed by Phineas Pratt, one of the ne'er-do-wells from Wessagusset, who made his way by fleetness of foot and luck through hostile Indians to Plymouth.

Captain Miles Standish sailed to Boston Bay with a small group of armed men, tiny in number but gigantic in the power the Indians thought they possessed. They killed five or so of the alleged leaders of the plot and returned home with the head of one of them. The remnants of the Wessagusset colony were swept together and brought to Plymouth, where in time most of them made the decision to go back to Europe as hands on the vessels fishing along the Maine coast. The Indian head was set up at Plymouth fort.

The Indian plan to wipe out the white colonies fell to pieces. Members of the several tribes within striking distance of Plymouth "forsook their houses, running to and fro like men distracted, living in swamps and other desert places, and so brought manifold diseases amongst themselves, whereof very many are dead. . . ." Ianough, sachem of the Massachusetts, said "the God of the English was offended with them, and would destroy them in his anger. . . ." The Pilgrims noted smugly that the mortality rate among their opponents was, indeed, high, and "neither is there any likelihood it will easily cease; because through fear they set little or no corn, which is the staff of life, and without which they cannot long preserve health and strength."

By 1622 or so the very last cases of the plague had occurred in New England—if indeed these were examples of plague and not of misdiagnosis—and the only remains of the great pestilence were disarticulating bones lost in fallen walls of rotting bark that had once been homes. But it had done its work. In 1625, the Pilgrims, for the first time, raised enough maize to fill their own stomachs *and* trade with the Indians. They had survived and were getting stronger, thanks more to pathogens than religion, despite Pilgrim preconceptions; but Thomas Morton nevertheless was reminded of a line from Exodus: "By little and little (saith God of old to his people) will I drive them out from before thee; till thou be increased, and inherit the land."

8 HAWAIIAN DEPOPULATION AS A MODEL FOR THE AMERINDIAN EXPERIENCE

We are at the frayed finish of the age of Europe's territorial expansion, which stimulates curiosity about its beginnings. The Social Darwinists were sure that white people were genetically superior to the other strains of humanity, and that was why they were such successful imperialists; at the end of the twentieth century that explanation seems as antiquated as a whalebone corset. Technological and managerial superiority are probably adequate to explain the brief subjugation of such lands as Algeria and Burma, but meager when matched to the Europeans' much more thorough and seemingly permanent takeovers of the temperate regions of the Americas. The new right-off-the-shelf-and-ready-for-instant-use explanation is that the Amerindians, unlike Africans or Asians, died in huge numbers of Old World diseases carried for the first time across the Atlantic by Columbus and his emulators, and therefore were easily displaced and replaced by the invaders.

There is a large body of documentary evidence in support of this theory, but much of the evidence was collected in the pre-scientific and pre-statistical centuries and almost always by soldiers, missionaries, trappers, and traders, rather than by physicians and demographers; that is, it is no better than impressionistic. Furthermore, the enormous extent of the Americas, the number and variety of their aboriginal peoples, and the length of time since the first contacts between the Old World invaders and the New World Aborigines bring into question even the most obvious interpretations of what accounts we do have of the impact of exotic diseases on Amerindians.

Take, for example, the Huron of the eastern corner of Georgian

Bay: they were drastically reduced by smallpox in the 1630s, then ravaged by the Iroquois—and then we hear little of them. What proportion survived the smallpox? How many did the Iroquois kill and how many did they adopt into their tribes, as was their custom? How many fled and joined the Neutral, the Petun, and the Ottowa? What percentage of the Wyandot of the Upper Great Lakes area in the nineteenth century were descendants of Hurons who escaped both smallpox and Iroquois and fled west?[1]

The Hawaiian Model

We need a model, a case study with the same advantages for us as the Galápagos finches provided Charles Darwin. We need a case study narrowly limited in time and space and in the number of factors at work. I nominate the Hawaiian Islands and the Hawaiian Polynesians.

In 1778, when Captain James Cook happened upon the Hawaiian archipelago, its Polynesian population numbered from 242,000 (the lowest contemporary estimate) to 800,000 (a recent assessment: startlingly large, yet the product of exhaustive scholarship and analysis). A hundred years later there were only 48,000 native Hawaiians, including even those of only part Hawaiian parentage.[2] The steepness of the Hawaiians' decline recommends them as a model for the post-Columbian demographic history of the Amerindians, but first let us consider whether they and their islands qualify as a laboratory case.

First, the matter of isolation from unaccountable influences: the Hawaiian Islands are among the most isolated in the world, over two thousand miles from the nearest continent, North America, and hundreds of miles from the nearest islands capable of supporting more than a handful of inhabitants. The archipelago lies north of the latitudes of the most dependable easterly trade winds and to the south of the prevailing westerlies.[3] For two and a half centuries the Manila galleon passed to the south of the islands on its voyage to the Philippines and far to the north on its return to Acapulco. A Spaniard or so may have made a one-way voyage and shipwrecked on Hawaii's shores, but even that is doubtful. Captain Cook came upon Hawaii because he was doing what only an explorer would do intentionally in the eighteenth century: sailing *north* across the Pacific.

The isolation of the Hawaiian Islands was so extreme for so long that about 96 percent of its native flowering plants occur naturally

Population of Hawaii: 1778–1878[a]

Year	Population	Percentage of Annual Change
1778	242,000–800,000	—
1823	134,925	—
1831–32	124,449	−0.9
1835–36	107,954	−3.6
1850	84,165	−1.8
1853[b]	73,138	−3.5
1860	69,800	−0.7
1866	62,959	−1.7
1872	56,897	−1.7
1878[c]	57,985	+0.3

Notes: The 1778 total is, of necessity, the most speculative. The numbers from 1823 through 1835–36 are estimates by well-informed missionaries living in Hawaii. From 1850 onward the numbers are the products of official censuses. Note that the number of Hawaiians of all or part Polynesian ancestry continued to drop for the rest of the nineteenth century, although the total number of people living in the Hawaiian Islands grew after 1872.

[a] Robert C. Schmitt, *Demographic Statistics for Hawaii: 1778–1965 (Honolulu, 1968)*, 10; Robert C. Schmitt, "New Estimates for the Pre-Censal Population of Hawaii," *Journal of the Polynesian Society* 80 (June 1971): 240–42; Eleanor C. Nordyke, *The Peopling of Hawai'i* 2d ed. *(Honolulu, 1977)*, 17–19; David E. Stannard, *Before the Horror: The Population of Hawai'i on the Eve of Western Contact* (Honolulu, 1989), 45, 49, 56, and passim.

[b] 97.5 percent of population born in Hawaii.

[c] Only 83.6 percent of population born in Hawaii.

nowhere else in the world.[4] Its only native land mammal when the Polynesians arrived a thousand years and more before Cook was a species of bat, a *very* distant relative indeed of *Homo sapiens*. When Cook landed, the only land mammals were the bat, plus what had come in the Polynesian canoes: the dog, the pig, the rat (probably a stowaway), and, of course, the Hawaiians themselves.[5] The islands had, we may safely surmise, no micro-organisms or parasites pre-adapted to preying on humans when the Polynesians debarked, and no more than a few when Cook stepped ashore.

The Polynesians arrived 1,500 to 2,000 years ago, after which there may have been contacts with other Polynesian islands but for no more than a few hundred years.[6] It is unlikely that the Polynesians brought many kinds of pathogens with them. They came to these islands by a series of voyages in open-decked vessels, voyages linked backward through several millennia and across the broadest ocean on the planet to the Asian mainland. Acute diseases that kill swiftly or produce long-lasting immunity would have used up their fuel (i.e., the suscepti- ble passengers on said vessels) and burned out during the long voy- ages. People with chronic diseases like tuberculosis would probably not have volunteered and would not have been chosen for such voy- ages, or, if they embarked anyway, would probably have died on the high seas and have been thrown overboard, taking their germs with them. In other words, the founders of the Hawaiian people in all proba- bility deserved a clean bill of health.[7]

The archeological record supports the hypothesis that the pre-Cook Hawaiians had few infectious diseases. Examination of 864 prehistoric skeletons dug out of the sand dunes at Mokapu, Oahu, reveals that the ancient Hawaiians commonly suffered from traumatic arthritis, dental caries, and possibly such diseases as usually affect only soft tissue, such as yaws, but otherwise were, just as Captain Cook described them in 1778, a healthy lot.[8]

Fortunately for historians, the myriad infections of the mainland populations did not arrive in Hawaii until after the spread of scientific and statistical habits of thought in Europe and her colonies. Captains Cook, La Perouse, Vancouver, Krusenstern, and others and their offi- cers were much more apt to describe disease in terms of symptomol- ogy and epidemiology than had been their sixteenth- and seventeenth- century counterparts coasting the shores of America. The estimations of Captain Cook et al. of Hawaiian population size, while sometimes based on no more than a glance at coastal settlements, were the prod- ucts of minds familiar with the techniques of quantification. When an Hernán Cortés said "a hundred thousand," he may have meant nothing more precise than "a whole lot." When a James Cook said "a hundred thousand," he meant just that.

The first consecutive records of the Hawaiian experience we have were written by missionaries, whom the Christian resurgence of the nineteenth century, called the Second Awakening in the United States, dispatched into the Pacific. Many of the earliest to reach Hawaii were New England Protestants of considerable education, some of it in science and mathematics, and of a post-Newtonian frame of mind. They kept good records, and their estimations of the number of Hawaiians, based on firsthand or at worst secondhand observations, between 1823 and the first official census a generation later, are quite respectable. We know more about the demographic history of the

Hawaiians from 1823 on than we do about all but a few peoples in the world.[9]

The charge of direct and conscious genocide often filed against the European invaders of the Americas complicates analysis of the impact of the imported diseases they carried with them. There was some genocide, probably a lot, but just how much? There was no omnipresent census-taker to declare authoritatively that such-and-such a percentage of Amerindians were murdered and such-and-such victims of infection. The role played by disease in the Hawaiian population crash was not so obscure simply because the *haole* (the native Hawaiian word for Caucasians) rarely slaughtered Hawaiians. The haole were not guiltless —in 1790, Captain Simon Metcalfe of the *Eleanora* destroyed more than one hundred unsuspecting Hawaiians with a single broadside[10]— but this massacre was an aberration and quantitatively insignificant compared, for example, to the English slaughter of the Pequots in 1637 or the Argentinian search-and-destroy campaigns against the Amerindians of the pampa and Patagonia in the nineteenth century.[11] We can omit the elusive and volatile factor of direct genocide from our analysis of Hawaiian demographic history.

What about the wars between Hawaiians, wars possibly stimulated by haole influence and certainly made deadlier by imported firearms than the wars of old? When Captain George Vancouver anchored in Hawaiian waters in 1792, he found firearms "solicited with the greatest ardency, by every native of the least consequence. . . ." King Kamehameha I tabooed all trade with the Vancouver expedition "for any commodity whatever than *arms and ammunition*." A number of Kamehameha's subjects were already using these weapons "with an adroitness that would not disgrace the generality of European soldiers." By 1804 he had a quantity of muskets, small guns, swivels, and fifty Europeans competent to utilize them in his service. He used this military power to unite the islands for the first time, and many died in his wars of unification. However, the wars lasted less than a generation, and the population decline went on for a century.[12]

What about murderous exploitation of aboriginal labor, which was certainly a factor in the depopulation of parts of Latin America? Neither Kamehameha I nor any of the Hawaiian monarchs who reigned in the nineteenth century had silver or gold mines where thousands of natives went to their deaths. The islands' plantations were never administered with the disregard for life common in West Indian plantations; and even if it be claimed that they were, plantations only began to figure importantly in the islands' economy *after* the years of steepest decline of the indigenous population.

Hawaii's monarchy and aristocracy were corrupted by contact with the outside world, which had an undeniably dire effect on the native population. The rulers, mad for European-style clothing, firearms, sailing vessels, and what have you (whole houses were broken down, shipped around the Horn, and reconstructed in the islands), fell deeply into debt; and the islands had only one thing of high value per unit of bulk and weight to pay off the haole creditors: sandalwood. North American captains discovered that Hawaiian sandalwood brought high prices at Canton, and by 1817–18 most of the foreign ships dropping anchor in Hawaiian waters were there to take on the sweet-smelling wood and carry it to China. The Hawaiian rulers ordered hundreds, perhaps thousands, of their subjects out of the taro fields and into the rugged highlands to fell and carry down to the shore on their backs ton after ton of the wood. "Many of the poor wretches," wrote one visitor, "died in their harness, while many more of them prematurely sank under the corroding effects of exposure and exhaustion." Can we blame the Hawaiians' population crash on this trade? Probably not, not over the long run, because the trade was over and done with before the 1830s. The Hawaiians' decline was under way before the trade waxed and continued long after it waned.[13]

The Hawaiians' decrease in the century following their first contact with Europeans and North Americans provides us with as good a model as we can expect to find anywhere for testing theories about the connection between aboriginal population crash and contact with the West. The documentation is considerable in quantity and respectable in quality, and the influence and number of tangential factors limited.

The Social and Psychological Causes
of Demographic Collapse

As of the 1840s, Christian missionaries had been living continuously alongside the Hawaiians for two decades and knew a good deal of at least a superficial nature about them. Their guess was that the Hawaiian population had decreased by two-thirds since Cook's first debarkation. The old hands estimated that the decrease in the four years ending in 1836 had been one-twelfth—this while missionary families were averaging between six and seven children each.[14] At the Hawaiians' rate of decrease circa 1840, they would be gone from the face of the earth in a half-century or so. Their plunge, noted the Reverend Bishop, was similar to that of the Aborigines of South and North America, the West Indies, South Africa, and the other islands of the Pacific.[15]

He and other missionaries totted up a list of causes of the plunge: low birthrate, high infant mortality rate, infanticide, sexual licentiousness, venereal disease, alcoholism, inadequate clothing, improvidence, "the rage for horses" and the consequent neglect of agriculture, the ravaging of croplands by imported and newly feral livestock, the declining quality of native housing, corrupt government, the improper use of European-style clothing, the emigration of young men, poor diet, and "genital impotency." The missionaries were especially impressed with the evil effects of the collective ownership of land. Like many other haole, they were sure that the institution of the fee simple system of real estate ownership would provide a sovereign cure for the Hawaiians' problems.[16]

Let us try to make some sense out of the missionary diagnosis of the Hawaiians' demographic nosedive. First let us discard the insignificant. It was true that hundreds of young men were joining the crews of the passing merchantmen and whalers, and that some of them never came back, but their numbers were small relative to the entire population.[17] It was true for a while that Hawaiians would sacrifice nearly anything, including life and limb, to ride the newly imported horses on "the run, trot, or hobble, helter skelter, whooping and shouting, like so many Cossacks." The Hawaiian women insisted on riding astride, in spite of the damage that such a practice was certain to do to their childbearing capabilities, according to the principles of Victorian gynecology.[18] But the equestrian madness only lasted a few years, and made excellent cowboys out of some of the Hawaiians, which probably increased their incomes. It was true that the locust-like herds of feral Old World livestock were a curse to Hawaiian farmers, but there is little in the record to indicate a widespread or long-lasting famine from this or any other cause. Indeed, one might think that the presence of large quantities of free protein-on-the-hoof would have improved, not degraded, the Hawaiian diet. As for who owned the farmland, the traditional system had not prevented the production of plenty of food before the arrival of the aliens.

The other alleged causes were significant. Let us divide them into two categories, anomie and disease. By the word *anomie* I refer to what has sometimes been called "culture crunch," that is, the disorientation —religious, political, culinary, and what have you—that can overtake an individual or people who suddenly confront others of an alien culture. This disorientation can be especially severe if the others are alien in appearance and behavior, and are, in one or more ways, perceived as superior, or at least invincible. Only a few, a very few, people ever die directly of anomie, but it does sap the energies of life; and that may explain the observation of one witness to the Hawaiian condition who remarked in 1848, "The Hawaiians can lie down and die the easiest of any people with which I am acquainted."[19] But let us try to be more specific than that.

Surely we may, in this case, construe narcotic addiction, if widespread and carried to outrageous extremes, as an indicator of anomie. In 1815, Otto von Kotzebue (or Otto E. Kotsbu), an explorer sailing in the service of the tsar, noted that tobacco, an imported plant, was growing in the islands, that children were smoking before they walked, and the adults were using the weed to the point of unconsciousness. He recorded that they, believe it or not, "frequently die of the stupor."[20]

Hawaiians, previously only familiar with one intoxicating beverage, the Polynesian *awa*,[21] swiftly learned and embraced the delights of swift inebriation from the aliens' distilled alcohol. Some time before 1809, William Stevenson, a ex-convict from New South Wales, set up a still in the islands, got drunk on his own product, and stayed that way until Kamehameha seized the still. By 1812 or so every chief had his own still. Kotzebue, a naval officer and, presumably, a man who had seen his share of alcoholism, was appalled at the islanders' drinking habits: "they empty a bottle of rum at one draught, with the greatest ease, and it is inconceivable how much of it they can drink." The missionaries wrote of "periods of general inebriation, when men, women and children are every where met, under all the wild excitement of liquor. . . ." In this matter the Christian men of the cloth were seconded by the clergy of Pele, the Hawaiians' volcano god. When the Reverend Ellis debated a priestess of Pele, she cited names of several dead chiefs and asked, "Who destroyed these? Not Pele, but the rum of the foreigners, whose God you are so fond of." Alcohol, said Henry T. Cheever in 1851, "has been to Polynesians like firewater to the North American Indians."[22]

Abortion and infanticide, again if widespread and carried to outrageous extremes, may also be taken as indicators of anomie. These forms of population control can be very injurious to societies under stress because young humans are in general the most adaptable of their species to new challenges, and they are, after the first few years of life, more resistant to exotic infections than are adults. But there are crises during which the immediate interest of individuals, especially mothers, is at cross-purposes with the creation of new generations. Indeed, there are times so painful and hopeless that racial suicide seems an agreeable alternative to regeneration: Sarah Winnemucca of the Paiutes of the western United States wrote in the 1880s, "My people have been so unhappy for so long they wish to *disincrease,* instead of to multiply."[23]

Many peoples have practiced population control, island peoples plausibly more often than many others. One effective means of population control is celibacy, an abberant behavior of which no one ever accused the Hawaiians. Another is abortion, which tribal peoples as well as the technologically advanced have resorted to frequently, but probably less often than many of us believe. It is likely that tribal peoples realize that the well-being of the mother and baby are intertwined, and that crude attempts to artificially terminate pregnancy often kill both. The one folk method of birth control that is unquestionably effective and safe for the mother is infanticide. (I define infanticide not only as direct killing of babies, but also as the more common form of elimination by semi-intentional neglect in the first days or months of life. By this definition I hope to avoid a lot of semantic quibbling.) [24]

Infanticide is not easy to detect unless the executors are caught *in flagrante delicto.* The number of boys and girls is less than it naturally should be, but how is the investigator to discern that? If, however, more of one gender are eliminated than the other, then the presence of infanticide will stand out sharply in the statistics. Let me explain: It is consistently true across the world that a few more male babies are born than female babies. Among most populations in most years the ratio is something like 103 or 105 boys to 100 girls. The ratio is close to 50/50, and, as a cohort proceeds through life, the male's majority usually narrows and eventually disappears because in most places and times more males than females die by violence and natural causes. Ideally, population records should show a slight majority of boys over girls, a narrower majority in the early decades of adulthood, and then equality and perhaps a majority of women over men in the last part of life.[25] Whenever there is a large majority of males at any age, we can be sure that some abnormal force has eliminated females.

In many societies males are valued more than females. This is particularly true in periods of severe stress, when warriors, hunters, and fishermen may seem more essential than gatherers, farmers, and mothers. In such periods, limiting the birth rate may seem desirable, even necessary; and it is plain that eliminating girls is a more efficient means of doing so than eliminating boys.

Several of the early Christian missionaries in the Hawaiian archipelago were sure that infanticide, especially female infanticide, was widespread despite decrees against the practice and assurances that it had stopped circa 1820. They based their claim on impressions quite probably affected by bigotry, but which were supported by the few contemporary surveys that enable us to compare the ratio of males to females. For instance, a census of the Hawaiians on Oahu taken in 1831 showed nearly 13 percent more males than females, and almost 15 percent more boys than girls. (The precise location of the line between adult and child was, unfortunately, not defined.) There were also some data suggesting a correlation between an abundance of living children, a normal percentage of girls as compared with boys, and geographical remoteness from Honolulu and other areas where Hawaiians were in continual contact with haole.[26]

Hawaii's population statistics after the 1840s were among the most complete in the world, and are very useful in retrospectively assessing the birth and death rates, and birthing and child-care practices of the previous century. In 1850 there were 10 percent more males than females, and Hawaiians under eighteen years of age accounted for less than 30 percent of the population. Among these youngsters there were 25 percent more boys than girls. By the census of 1884 the Hawaiians were turning away from the brink of extinction, and the number of boys under six years was actually fewer than that of girls, 2,450 as compared to 2,488, but the majority of the older cohorts was unequivocally male. Males between the ages of six and fifteen years inclusive exceeded females by 7 percent. The edge for Hawaiian males from sixteen to thirty years of age was 8 percent, for thirty-one years to fifty years 27 percent, and for those over fifty years of age 43 percent.[27] These figures suggest that circa 1880 the Hawaiians, in thousands of individual choices by mothers, midwives, and relatives, voted to survive as a people.

The extreme skewing of the sex ratio among Hawaiians in the nineteenth century is open to many explanations, of course, but few pass examination. The ratio was not carried forward into the twentieth century, and so we can be sure it had little or nothing to do with Polynesian genetics. Female Hawaiians were in the minority from the earliest ages of life, so the sex ratio cannot be blamed on infections or injuries associated with pregnancy or delivery. Adult women might have acquired venereal disease, widespread in the islands, earlier than the men, but soon would have transmitted it to the males, to whom it would have proved no more nor less fatal than to females. Venereal disease certainly affected the organs of reproduction of many women, but there is no sexually transmitted disease that blocks the initiation of female embryos nor kills female fetuses preferentially. There is nothing in the record to suggest that census-takers tended to overlook females, especially older females. There is nothing in the record about the departure of large numbers of women from the islands, voluntarily or involuntarily. Emigration was a male, not a female, behavior. Hundreds, even thousands, of Hawaiian males were at sea or abroad in every year from at least as early as the 1820s onward. If the censuses had covered all Polynesians of Hawaiian birth, no matter where they were, then the male majority would have been even greater.

Some concealed factor or factors were blocking the births of or killing more Hawaiian females than males. The mystery attracted the attention of even Darwin, who could offer no better explanation than a reference to "some unknown law."[28] Overwork and general exploitation may well have erased more adult women than men, but the likeliest candidate as the chief killer of females was infanticide, either by direct intention or, as is much more common, indirectly and semi-intentionally. In 1846, the haole missionaries blamed the deaths of so many Hawaiian children on the lack of proper food, clothing, shelter, medical care, and "unskillful management." I suspect that in Hawaii conventional Christian morality held overt infanticide to a minimum, and, as is true among the poor and desperate across the world today, hunger, dehydration, exposure, and a turning away—a "want of solicitude," as one of the medical missionaries called it—did the actual deed.[29]

Epidemiological Causes

Anomie is an effect as well as a cause. What did the Hawaiians suffer that was so horrible that they fell into such confusion and despair and were driven to behaviors that endangered their very survival? They did find themselves confronted with aliens more powerful than they were, but that is an experience through which, one might guess, all peoples have passed at one time or another, usually without skirting extinction. Radical population declines—50, 75, and 90 percent—do not necessarily follow upon culture shock. But the Hawaiians did suffer a population crash so severe that many haole and at least some of the Hawaiians themselves believed their extinction was inevitable. The chief killer, one who recruited anomie as a lieutenant, was imported disease.

The Hawaiians in 1778 had only a few kinds of communicable disease, as one would expect of an isolated population of less than a million. In contrast, the disease environment of the continental peoples who came to the Hawaiians' home islands in and after 1778 contained numerous kinds of infectious diseases, including many of the most dangerous known to humanity. We can usefully picture the Hawaiian disease environment as a briar patch, and the continental equivalent as a jungle.

Events provided proofs and illustrations of the difference. King Liholiho and Queen Kamamalu of Hawaii sailed for England in November of 1823 "to visit his Majesty the King [George IV], to receive friendly counsel and advice . . . to increase their acquaintance with the world, enlarge their views of human society," and so on. They arrived in mid-May 1824, took up residence in Osborne's Caledonian Hotel, London, were entertained by the secretary of state for Foreign Affairs, Mr. Canning, and visited the theaters, where they occupied the royal boxes. While arrangements were being made for their reception at court, they contracted measles, one of the commoner childhood infections in Europe, but as yet unknown in the Hawaiian Islands. Both died in July 1824.[30]

In the case of King Liholiho and Queen Kamamalu, to coin a phrase, Mohammed went to the mountain, the mountain of disease in this instance. In the case of the majority of Hawaiians, the mountain came to them. After 1778 the Hawaiians were subjected to an influx of alien human beings teeming with dangerous germs, as they, the Hawaiians, realized. In October of 1806 the chief at Anahooroo (Honolulu?) Bay refused to permit a trader to enter the harbor upon hearing there was a sick man on board. The chief feared the introduction of disease, "which calamity had happened on a former occasion, from an American ship." In the 1820s a missionary recorded scornfully that the natives were blaming the foreigners for most diseases.[31] They knew more about the matter than he did.

Let me cite a few of the most salient of the epidemics that swept over Hawaii. The semi-mythic *oku'u,* perhaps the worst single onslaught of disease in the history of the islands, struck in approximately 1804, just as Kamehameha was gathering his forces to invade Kauai. Kamehameha fell ill and recovered, but perhaps two-thirds of his men died, though three humans and four hundred hogs were sacrificed to appease the gods. Nothing much was written down about *oku'u* for many years after the event, and we cannot even be sure whether it was restricted to Oahu or spread throughout the archipelago. It seems to have been some sort of a diarrheal infection, like the approximately contemporary *rewa-rewa* in New Zealand, and may have swept off the majority of Hawaiians. If the epidemiologist's rule of thumb—that an isolated people's earliest epidemics are apt to be their worst—is valid, then *oku'u* may have been as bad as oral tradition claimed.[32]

In 1848–49 three epidemics rolled through the islands at once: measles, whooping cough (both for the first time, apparently), and a strain of influenza. California, where gold had just been discovered and with which contacts were increasing, was identified as the source of the first two. The death rate for the sick was judged as 10 percent, and the total mortality at no less than 10,000.[33]

The infection whose arrival from the mainland was feared the most was smallpox. The missionary doctors vaccinated some Hawaiians in the first half of the nineteenth century, but to what avail we cannot be sure because the vaccine often lost its efficacy during long sea voyages. On February 10, 1853, the *Charles Mallory* arrived from California with a yellow flag flying from her foremast: she had smallpox on board. The disease did not appear among the Hawaiians for four months, a long time for an epidemic of a disease like smallpox to hang fire, and so perhaps the *Mallory*'s arrival was no more than coincidental. Perhaps the infection really came, for instance, in a chest of old clothing from San Francisco. It was certain to have come ashore from some vessel some time. Before this epidemic burned itself out early the next year, there were officially 6,405 cases and 2,485 deaths. The real numbers were probably higher. The deaths, at the lowest estimate, help considerably to account for the decrease of the islands' population from about 84,000 in 1850 to about 73,000 at the end of 1853, a steep decline even by Hawaii's grim standards. The death rate and birth rate were 105 per thousand and 20 per thousand, respectively, in 1853.[34] (I should note here the inappropriateness of Polynesian therapies, and the lethal lack of even minimal care that followed upon the simultaneous prostration of adults and children alike, all defenseless against smallpox as well as the rest of what continental peoples fobbed off as "childhood sicknesses.")[35]

The depressing effect of this disease upon the Hawaiian morale may have been even greater than the number of deaths suggests. Twenty years later Samuel M. Kamakau recalled the look and smell of the victims:

> A person would be full of pimples from the crown of his head to the soles of the feet—no spot had respite. His mouth was full of them; they were in the nostrils, on the face, in the ears—only the teeth and nails had none. The house stank like poison gourds. . . .[36]

No challenge to Hawaiian survival seemed lacking in the middle decades of the century. Hansen's disease (leprosy), according to European tradition the most repugnant of all maladies, arrived some time before mid-century, probably from Asia, and spread more freely among Hawaiians than resident foreigners.[37] Although not a significant factor in the depopulation, it provided one more source of bewilderment for native Hawaiians and one more excuse for haole racism. The Hawaiians had one piece of luck, possibly the only one in the century after Cook. Human malaria did not gain a foothold although Hawaii is tropical and in areas quite humid. Bird malaria did, and may be the chief cause of the extinction of several species of birds endemic to the islands. Anopheles mosquitoes are a prerequisite for the spread of human malaria, and they did not exist in the archipelago.[38]

The epidemics of newly introduced and highly infectious maladies —oku'u, measles, whooping cough, influenza, smallpox—were spectacular in their mortality. We should not, however, let ourselves be hypnotized by them. They were the obvious factor in the depopulation of the islands, but the decisive factor was whatever prevented the

Hawaiians from rebuilding their numbers between these epidemics. What was it that *kept* killing them between epidemics, and what was it that suppressed their birth rate?

We must recognize the importance of the less spectacular diseases, the infections that carried off a constant percentage of babes in arms and toddlers year in and year out, and elbowed adults into the grave ten or twenty years short of their normal span of life. The journal of Francisco de Paula Marin, an early haole resident, which runs from 1809 to 1826, is shot through with references to sickness: "11 Jany. [1820] All the people ill of coughs," "20 May [1824] Many deaths & many coughs," "1 February [1825] There are many sick of fevers & colds, & many dying;" and so on and so on.[39] Nothing bad enough to get itself called an epidemic, mind you, just a steady corrosive flow of infection. A generation later, Drs. Andrews and Chapin judged that half of the native infants died before the age of two, most often of something they vaguely referred to as "fevers." Dr. Chapin noted that these childhood infections were "the seeds of numerous future diseases...."[40]

The scanty medical records of the islands in the first half of the 1800s included a continual refrain of references to such vague ailments as "fevers," "itches," "catarrhs," "eye infections," and "dysenteries."[41] Haole visitors to the Hawaiian villages always remarked about the dirt and blowing dust, which helps account for the eye problems.[42] The influx of new pathogens and unwholesome foods from abroad, plus poor sanitation, provide plausible explanations for the dysenteries. As for most of the "catarrhs," the ships from the mainlands were doubtlessly always bringing to the islands new strains of the rapidly evolving cold and influenza viruses.

One haole wit noted that the standard dress of the Hawaiian was "a smile, a malo [a sort of girdle or sarong], and a cutaneous eruption." Itches, scurf, pustules, and ulcers were ubiquitous. Dr. Chapin attributed the prevalence of skin infections among the Hawaiians to the filth of their clothing and sleeping mats, an explanation which he undermined by also referring to their fondness for water and bathing. Venereal pathogens, which often signal their presence by skin lesions, accounted for some of the examples of "cutaneous eruption." In the category of cutaneous disease, Dr. Chapin also included scrofula, a tubercular infection of the lymphatic system, signs of which often show up in the skin. "Scrofula," he wrote, " is not only frequent but extremely malignant." If the tubercule bacillus was as widespread as Dr. Chapin and others indicated, then that might account for many of the illnesses vaguely diagnosed as "catarrh" and "asthma." It might also provide a partial explanation for Dr. Gerrit P. Judd's statement: "The mortality of the natives does not, however, appear to be owing to the ravages of any particular disease, but they die off suddenly and unexpectedly with any disease that seizes them."[43] Immune systems taxed by smoldering tubercular infections might well collapse under additional stress.

Tuberculosis may have arrived as early as 1778 because it was present among the crew of Captain Cook's command. It unquestionably stepped ashore with the first missionaries, several of whom were tubercular when they arrived. If it were half as deadly among the Hawaiians as among the Amerindians of the Qu-Appelle reservation in western Canada in the 1890s, it was deadly indeed: as many as 9 percent of these Native Americans died in a year of tuberculosis, and in the space of three generations more than half their families died out.[44]

The Hawaiians may have had some venereal infections before 1778, although the liberality of their sexual mores suggests that they were subject to none that were painful, disfiguring, or fatal. These may have first arrived with the Cook expedition when it visited the archipelago at the beginning of 1778.[45] Captain Cook tried to prevent sexual contact between members of his crew with active cases of these infections and the Hawaiians, but when he returned to the islands that same year, some of the Hawaiians already appeared to have lesions of venereal illnesses. When the French explorer La Perouse touched at the islands in 1785, he found the women unattractive: "their dress suffered us to perceive that the syphilis had committed ravages on the greater number." When Captain Urey Lisiansky anchored off the shore of the island of Hawaii in 1804, he made every effort to prevent sexual contact between his men and the Hawaiian women, not for fear that the men would infect the women, but vice versa.[46]

Most of the early haole visitors were men without women, and possessed of items of mainland origin that the Hawaiians quickly learned to covet. The latter were a people with what the anthropologist Marshall Sahlins has called an Aphrodisian culture, which included a tradition of sexual generosity that haole almost universally misinterpreted as prostitution, and soon, by their expectations, made into just that.[47]

Among the few to try to understand were two latter-day pagans, Mark Twain and Robert Louis Stevenson, both of whom spent considerable time in Hawaii, though separately. The American did not condemn Hawaiian sexuality, but instead condemned those who did:

> To refuse the solicitations of a stranger was regarded as a contemptible thing for a girl or a woman to do; but the missionaries have so bitterly fought this thing that they have succeeded at least in driving it out of sight—and now it exists only in reality, not in name.[48]

The Scot pointed to the tradition of sexual generosity as a sadly ironic explanation for the more rapid spread of Hansen's disease among the Hawaiians than other peoples:

> To refuse a male is still considered in most parts of Polynesia a rather unlovely rigor in the female; and if a man be disfigured, I believe it would be held a sort of charity to console his solitude. A kind island girl might thus go to the leper's bed in something of same spirit as we visit the sick at home with tracts and pounds of tea.[49]

The perversion of the Hawaiian tradition of sexual hospitality to important strangers was already under way when Captain George Vancouver, who had first gone to the islands as one of Cook's officers, returned in 1792. On this occasion the licentiousness of the Hawaiians struck him as "a perfectly new acquirement, taught, perhaps, by the different civilised voluptuaries, who, for some years past, have been their constant visitors."[50]

The spread of venereal infection accelerated as more and more strangers found their way to the archipelago. For four decades starting in 1819 the islands were the most important crossroads in the central Pacific for victualling, repairs, and shore leave for the whalers rushing into that ocean in pursuit of sperm whales. In 1855 William Hillebrand, M.D., stated flatly that his opinion was that there was no place on earth where venereal infection was as common as in Hawaii. It is, he said, "no random assertion, but one based on experience and approximative calculation, that in 10 natives 9 have been infected with this disease at one time or another in their life." The archipelago had become "one great brothel," said David Malo, the missionaries' favorite among the Christianized and de-cultured Hawaiians. "For this cause God is angry, and he is diminishing the people, and they are nigh unto desolation."[51] (By "people" he meant, of course, not the haole but the Hawaiians!)

The Hawaiians' low birth rate both appalled and fascinated the haole. Victorian moralists blamed it on "the premature ripening and exhaustion of the reproductive powers"—too much too soon. They believed that sexual generosity per se diminished fertility, "as the history of prostitution shows that it everywhere does,—though *why,* is by no means entirely clear."[52] Sir Paul Edmund Strzelecki, famed explorer of Australia and pillar of the British Empire, had a theory about the low rate of reproduction of the Hawaiians and the other indigenous peoples he had seen on his travels in the Pacific and North and South America. According to the Strzelecki Law (as he modestly called it), once a native woman bears a white man's child, she will ever after be sterile when she mates with a man of her own race. He did not explain how this worked, but claimed that it "follows laws as cogent, though as mysterious, as the rest of those connected with generation."[53]

The Strzelecki Law was an augustly self-serving interpretation of the evidence that white men were spreading venereal diseases among aboriginal women in the New World and Oceania.[54] These infections killed many women, plus children in the womb and others in the first years of life. Mr. Rollins, surgeon-major on board La Perouse's ship in 1786, claimed that he saw Hawaiian children of seven and eight years with the lesions of congenital venereal disease.[55] Endemic venereal infections probably were in part the explanation for the often-cited general debility of the population, and, as well, for the Hawaiians with "eyes rendered blind—noses entirely destroyed—mouths monstrously drawn aside from their natural position" picking their way through the alleys of Honolulu long before Hansen's disease spread in the islands. Most subtly pernicious of all was the damage the venereal infections wreaked on the reproductive systems of the Hawaiian women, preventing the conception and birth of thousands. James J. Jarves, one of Hawaii's very earliest historians, wrote in 1847 that venereal infections were poisoning "the very fountains of life."[56]

Conclusions Applicable to the Amerindian Experience

Captain Cook came to the Hawaiian archipelago in 1778, where he encountered a population in robust health, if we are to trust eyewitness accounts. In the century that followed, that population plunged steeply, almost irreversibly, in number. The decline is a Gothic tale worth studying in and of itself, but that is not my objective. Instead I ask, How useful is it as a model for what happened to the Amerindians?

The Hawaiian model supports the validity of the hundreds of exasperatingly brief and undetailed reports of devastating disease and population crashes on the expanding frontiers of Europe's colonial empires in the New World, from the Greater Antilles in the sixteenth century to the Amazonian hinterlands in the twentieth. We should look for similar events on the frontiers of people of similar pathological and expansionistic characteristics: the Chinese, for instance.

The Hawaiian record also suggests that we need to look at birth rates of the aboriginal casualties of Western expansion more carefully than we have. There is no denying that death rates soared as communicable diseases spread in advance of and along with Western imperialists. But birth rates often plunged, too, and we are not so sure why.

Let us compare the demographic histories of the Hawaiians and Europe's city dwellers. My guess is that in the Renaissance and seventeenth and eighteenth centuries the latter had death rates not tremendously lower than those of the nineteenth-century Hawaiians in all but their worst years. The continental urban populations made up their losses by replacement from two sources: births within the cities and, more important, immigration from the countryside. Children exposed to urban infections from birth were more resistant to them than immigrants from the countryside, but were not numerous. Without the immigrants, the cities would have been no more than large villages, given the nature of the diseases in circulation and the primitive hygiene of the urbanites.[57]

Like Europe's cities, the Hawaiian Islands were rescued from depopulation by immigration. Chinese coolies began arriving in the 1850s, to be followed by waves of laborers from Japan, the Philippines, Portugal, and elsewhere. That influx saved the islands from the kind of demographic and economic decline that afflicted sixteenth-century Mexico, but did the native Hawaiians no good whatsoever. By 1878 the total population of Hawaii had hit bottom and was at last rising, but the number of Hawaiians continued to fall until the next century.[58]

In the cities of Europe of *ancien régime*, spates of new marriages and births between the hard times also helped to compensate for the plunges of the birth rate associated with crises such as epidemics, wars, and famines. Graphs of the birth rate through time have a sawtooth profile—up and down, up and down.[59] A graph of the Hawaiian birth rate in the post-Cook century is similar, *but includes only the downs.*

Sir Paul Edmund Strzelecki asked the right question, though he produced a worthless answer. We must ask the question again: What was wrong with the reproductive capacities of the peoples Strzelecki encountered on the frontiers of European expansion? What we have learned about the Hawaiians suggests that we should look for indications of infanticide by neglect and, possibly of greater importance, venereal disease. Sexually transmitted disease circulated through European populations also, but not to the extent that was common among nearly all classes of Hawaiians, a sexually exploited population with a lethally obsolete set of sexual mores. William F. Blackman, a nineteenth-century historian of Hawaii, found in the annals of North American Indians a story he considered relevant to what had happened to the Hawaiians. An 1895 report from the United States Bureau of Indian Affairs told of two groups of Amerindians: the first consisting of four tribes with limited contact with Euro-Americans, of chaste habits, and no venereal diseases; and the second of seven tribes in continual contact with Euro-Americans, of unchaste habits, and "saturated with venereal disease." The former group was actually increasing in number. The latter was in steep decline, having suffered a diminution of 43 percent in the previous thirteen years.[60]

We need to know more about the sexual mores of the many and various Amerindian peoples.[61] Was there a correlation between the restrictive or liberal attitudes toward sexuality of the various groups and the survival or extinction of said groups? We also need to know more about the sexual attitudes of the white chroniclers through whose sometimes averted eyes we see the Amerindians of the past. How more or less frank about sexuality were, for instance, Columbus's comrades than Anglo-Americans of the nineteenth century? Michele de Cuneo began the letter describing his adventures on Columbus's 1493 voyage to the New World with a dedication to "Jesus and His Glorious Mother Mary, from whom all blessings proceed," but had no compunction about including a vignette about the Carib woman he thrashed with a rope until she submitted "in such a manner that I can tell you that she seemed to have been brought up in a school of harlots." Anglo-Americans were much more restrained than that, but was it in behavior or frankness? Sarah Winnemucca of the Paiutes tells of Amerindian mothers "afraid to have more children, for fear they shall have daughters, who are not safe even in their mother's presence."[62]

How common among a given group of Amerindians was the custom of greeting powerful strangers with sexual hospitality? Were some groups, to use the Sahlins' term again, Aphrodisian? The Chinook who lived around the mouth of Oregon's Columbia River may have been so. When the Lewis and Clark expedition crossed the continent and reached that part of the coast in 1805, the local Amerindian traders welcomed the travelers with sexual satisfactions. "Among these people," wrote Lewis, fumbling to understand a culture not his own,

> as indeed among all Indians, the prostitution of unmarried women is so far from being considered criminal or improper, that females themselves solicit the favors of the other sex, with the entire approbation of their friends and connections. Her person is, in fact, often the only property of a young female, and is therefore the medium of trade, the return for presents, and the reward for services.[63]

Lewis and Clark and their men were by no means the first whites the Chinook women had seen. Whites, come round the Horn, had been frequenting that coast to trade for the sea otter skins ever since Captain Cook obtained such pelts there in 1778 and discovered that the Chinese would pay a fortune for them. For example, a man named J. Bowman had preceded Lewis and Clark, and left his name for the explorers to see tattooed on the arm of one of the women. Several members of the Lewis and Clark expedition contracted venereal disease from the Chinook, rotten with such infections already. In time, Amerindians as far away as Alaska learned to call venereal disease "Chinook." The usual succession of Amerindian troubles, most conspicuously a crushing epidemic of the "cold sick" (probably malaria) in the early 1830s, reduced the once numerous Chinook, already weakened and diseased at the beginning of the century, to a paltry residuum of 112 in 1885.[64]

Lewis's pronouncement that "prostitution" was common "among all Indians" was certainly colored by cultural misunderstanding, and indeed was flat wrong, but we should not reject it totally just because we think it originated in bigotry. People without long experience with venereal disease—the Hawaiians, for instance—perhaps had sexual mores very unlike people of long experience: the ancient Hebrews and the Christians, for instance. We should not be surprised if we find that people unfearful of venereal disease have used sexual favors as a currency in diplomacy and commerce just as they did and we do food and drink. (Indeed, we still use sexual favors to enhance negotiations, but not so openly as Hawaiians and Amerindians.)

What are the implications for the history of early Virginia of Captain John Smith's story of having been received by women of Powhatan's people in the following fashion in 1608? They formed a circle and danced around their visitor for an hour, "oft falling into their infernall passions," and then

> Having reaccommodated themselves, they solemnly invited him [Smith] to their lodgings, where he was no sooner within the house, but all these Nymphes more tormented him than ever, with crowding, pressing, and hanging about him, most tediously crying, Loue you not me? loue you not me?[65]

Was Smith, pen in hand and middle-aged, indulging himself in a lubricious fiction about his swashbuckling prime, or had Powhatan made an extravagantly friendly gesture—a gesture by which he may have innocently poisoned "the very fountains of life" of his people? Europe was in the midst of a pandemic of syphilis in this era, and if Smith did not carry the infection, it is likely that several of his comrades did.[66]

The native peoples of Virginia and bordering colonies suffered epidemics in the next two centuries comparable to those endured by the Hawaiians. These Amerindians, however, were not (according to Euro-American sources) similarly Aphrodisian, which may explain why their numbers *may* not have plunged as steeply as the Hawaiians'. But these Amerindians, too, acquired venereal disease, and were, according to John Heckewelder, a missionary who lived among them in the eighteenth century, "greatly infected with it. . . ."

The Comte de Buffon, author of the immense *L'Histoire Naturelle,* one of the monumental works of the Enlightenment, offered a fanciful explanation for the mysterious plunge in the numbers of the native peoples of the Americas. He announced in 1778 in volume 5 of his *Histoire* that Amerindian males had meager genitalia, lacked sexual drive, fathered few children, and ignored those they did father. Nature had "treated them rather like a stepmother than a parent, by denying them the invigorating sentiment of love and the strong desire of multiplying their species." Thomas Jefferson, an American patriot with firsthand knowledge of the Amerindians of Virginia, countered that in sexual ardor and love for their children they were certainly equal of Europeans. He did grant, however, that the Amerindians had comparatively few children; he blamed this on birth control of some sort, abortion, hunger, and overexertion.[67] An examination of the Hawaiian experience suggests a broader and even grimmer interpretation.

As we examine the histories of the decline of Amerindian peoples, we must, of course, take into account the familiar factors of massacre, alcoholism, extinction of game animals, and expropriation of farm land. In addition, we must attend to the less familiar calamities of exotic water- and breath-borne diseases; and, finally, to the secret blights of abortion, infanticide and infanticidally negligent child care, venereal infection, sterility, and despair.

Notes

I must thank Eleanor C. Nordyke, Robert C. Schmitt, David E. Stannard, and Alan Frost for having given me the benefit of their criticisms. Their advice was invaluable (though not always heeded, so they cannot be blamed for my mistakes and misinterpretations).

1. Conrad E. Heidenreich, "Huron," *Handbook of North American Indians,* vol. 15, Bruce G. Trigger, ed., *Northeast* (Washington, D.C., 1978), 369, 387, 789–92; Elisabeth Tooker, "Wyandot," *Handbook of North American Indians* 15: 398.

2. Robert C. Schmitt, *Demographic Statistics of Hawaii, 1778–1965* (Honolulu, 1968), 10–12; Robert C. Schmitt, "New Estimates of the Pre-Censal Population of Hawaii," *Journal of the Polynesian Society* 80 (June 1971): 240–42; David E. Stannard, *Before the Horror: The Population of Hawai'i on the Eve of Western Contact* (Honolulu, 1989), 45, 49, 56, and passim.

3. R. Warwick Armstrong, ed., *Atlas of Hawaii* (Honolulu, 1973), 9, 48, 59; National Oceanic and Atmospheric Administration, U.S. Department of Commerce, *Climates of the States* (Port Washington, N.Y., 1974), 2:615.

4. Armstrong, ed., *Atlas of Hawaii,* 63.

5. Raymond J. Kramer, *Hawaiian Land Mammals* (Rutland, Vt., 1971), 17.

6. Patrick Vinton Kirch, *Feathered Gods and Fishhooks: An Introduction to Hawaiian Archeology and Prehistory* (Honolulu, 1985), 65–68.

7. A note in Darwin's *Origin of Species* hints at the degree of the Hawaiians' isolation from the disease pool in which most continental humans were immersed. "The surgeon of a whaling ship in the Pacific assured me that when the Peduculi [lice], with which some Sandwich Islanders on board swarmed, strayed on to the bodies of the English sailors, they died in the course of three or four days. These Peduculi were darker coloured, and appeared different from those proper to the natives of Chiloe in South America . . ." Charles Darwin, *The Origin of Species and the Descent of Man* (New York, n.d.), 532.

8. Warner F. Bowers, "Pathological and Functional Changes Found in 864 Pre–Captain Cook Contact Polynesian Burials from the Sand Dunes at Mokapu, Oahu, Hawaii," *International Surgery* 45 (February 1966): 217; Charles E. Snow, *Early Hawaiians: An Initial Study of Skeletal Remains from Mokapu, Oahu* (Lexington, Ky., 1974), 60–75; Peter Pirie, "The Effects of Treponematosis and Gonorrhoea on the Populations of the Pacific Islands," *Human Biology in Oceania* 1 (February 1972): 191, 193–94. See also Stannard, *Before the Horror*, 73–78.

9. Ralph S. Kuykendall, *The Hawaiian Kingdom, 1778–1854: Foundation and Transformation* vol. 1 (Honolulu, 1947), 100–13, 335–36; Eleanor C. Nordyke, *The Peopling of Hawai'i*, 2d ed. (Honolulu, 1977), passim.

10. Kuykendall, *The Hawaiian Kingdom, 1778–1854*, 24.

11. Bert Salwen, "Indians of Southern New England and Long Island: Early Period," *Handbook of North American Indians* 15: 173; Ricardo Levene, *A History of Argentina*, trans. William S. Robertson (New York, 1963), 406–7, 483.

12. Stannard, *Before the Horror*, 62.

13. Theodore Morgan, *Hawaii: A Century of Economic Change, 1778–1876* (Cambridge, 1948), 62–67; Robert C. Schmitt, "Famine Mortality in Hawaii," *Journal of Pacific History* 5 (1970): 113; "The Sandalwood Trade of Early Hawaii," *Hawaiian Almanac and Annual for 1905*, ed. Thos. Thrum, 31:43–74; Harold St. John, "The History, Present Distribution, and Abundance of Sandalwood on Oahu, Hawaiian Islands: Hawaiian Plant Studies 14," *Pacific Science* 1 (January 1947): 5–9; Ross H. Cordy, "The Effects of European Contact on Hawaiian Agricultural Systems—1778–1819," *Ethnohistory* 19 (Fall 1972): 409–10.

14. William F. Blackman, *The Making of Hawaii* (New York, 1899), 213.

15. Artemas Bishop, "An Inquiry into the Causes of Decrease in the Population of the Sandwich Islands," *The Hawaiian Spectator* 1 (January 1838), 52–53.

16. Ibid., 53–61; *Answers to Questions Proposed by His Excellency, R. C. Wyllie, His Hawaiian Minister of Foreign Relations, and Addressed to All the Missionaries in the Hawaiian Islands, May 1846*, 6, 9, 23, 41, 47, 49, 84–85, 92.

17. Nordyke, *The Peopling of Hawai'i*, 22.

18. James J. Jarves, *Scenes and Scenery in the Sandwich Islands* (Boston, 1843), 52; W. Hillebrand, "Report on Labor and Population," *Transactions of the Royal Hawaiian Agricultural Society*, no. 2 (1855): 73–74.

19. Andrew W. Lind, *An Island Community: Ecological Succession in Hawaii* (Chicago, 1938), 97.

20. Otto von Kotzebue, *Voyage of Discovery in the South Sea* (London: Sir Richard Phillips and Co., 1821), Part 1, 87. Alonzo Chapin, M.D., in his "Remarks on the Sandwich Islands; their Situation, Climate, Diseases," *Hawaiian Spectator*, no. 2 (1838): 263, also states that individuals "have been killed" by the effect of tobacco.

21. J.C. Beaglehole, ed., *The Journals of Captain James Cook on His Voyages of Discovery* (Cambridge, 1969), 2:236–37.

22. Kotzebue, *Voyage of Discovery*, 98; Archibald Campbell, *A Voyage around the World from 1806 to 1812* (Edinburgh, 1866), 146, 184–85, 186; C.S. Stewart, *Journal of Residence in the Sandwich Islands during the Years 1823, 1824, and 1825* (New York, 1828), 236; William Ellis, *A Journal of a Tour around Hawaii* (Boston, 1825), 179; Henry T. Cheever, *The Island World of the Pacific* (New York, 1851), 29.

The Census of 1884 . . . Hawaiians

Under 6 years	
Males	2,450
Females	2,488
Between 6 and 15 years	
Males	3,742
Females	3,490
Between 15 and 30 years	
Males	5,552
Females	5,123
Between 30 and 50 years	
Males	6,860
Females	5,387
Over 50 years	
Males	2,900
Females	2,022
Total	40,014

23. Sarah Winnemucca Hopkins, *Life among the Paiutes: Their Wrongs and Claims* (Boston, 1883), 48.

24. This is a subject of enormous importance and great obscurity. We cannot go into it here, but let me recommend William L. Langer, "Infanticide: An Historical View," *History of Childhood Quarterly* 1 (Winter 1974): 353–65; Michael W. Flinn, *The European Demographic System, 1500–1820* (Baltimore, 1981), 39–42; Maria W. Piers, *Infanticide* (New York, 1978); Lionel Rose, *The Massacre of the Innocents: Infanticide in Britain, 1800–1939* (London, 1968); Thomas R. Forbes, "Deadly Parents: Child Homicide in Eighteenth- and Nineteenth-Century England," *Journal of the History of Medicine and Allied Sciences* 41 (April 1986): 175–99.

25. Curt Stern, *Principles of Human Genetics,* 3d ed. (San Francisco, 1973), 528–29, 535–36; Edward Novitski, *Human Genetics* (New York, 1977), 302–3.

26. Robert C. Schmitt, *The Missionary Censuses of Hawaii* (Honolulu: Bernice P. Bishop Museum, Pacific Anthropological Records, no. 20, 1973), 12. See also John H.R. Plews, "Charles Darwin and Hawaiian Sex Ratios, or, Genius is a Capacity for Making Compensating Errors," *Hawaiian Journal of History* 14 (1980): 34–36, 39–41.

27. Hiram Bingham, *A Residence of Twenty-one Years in the Sandwich Islands* (Canandaigua, N.Y., 1855), 368; Ellis, *A Journal of a Tour around Hawaii,* 16; Daniel Tyerman and George Bennet, *Journal of Voyages and Travels* (London, 1831), 1:449; Schmitt, *Demographic Statistics,* 31, 43; Plews, "Charles Darwin," 30–36, 39–41; Thos. G. Thrum, ed., *The Hawaiian Almanac and Annual for 1890,* 9. The latter is the source for my discussion of the 1884 census, which I reproduce in exact copy at the top of this page.

28. Plews, "Charles Darwin," 29.

29. Robert C. Schmitt, *Demographic Statistics of Hawaii, 1778–1965* (Honolulu University of Hawaii Press, 1968), 39; Schmitt, *Missionary Censuses of Hawaii,* 15; Plews, "Charles Darwin," 30–33. I have found Forbes, "Deadly Par-

ents"; and Nancy Scheper-Hughes, "Death without Weeping," *Natural History* 98 (November 1989): 8–16, very helpful. See Scheper-Hughes's, *Death without Weeping: The Violence of Everyday Life in Brazil* (Berkeley, 1989).

30. Kuykendall, *The Hawaiian Kingdom, 1778–1854*, 76–78. Many Hawaiians who shipped out on haole vessels met similar fates. Captain Amasa Delano in *A Narrative of Voyages and Travels* (Boston, 1817), 392, tells the horrific tale of Hawaiian sailors contracting smallpox in Canton, "which most generally proves fatal to them, and the distress and sufferings of the poor creatures have been beyond description; many scenes of which I have been an eye witness to, that would excite the compassion of any man possessed of the least particle of humanity."

31. John Martin, *An Account of the Natives of the Tonga Islands* (London, 1818), 1:36–37; Stewart, *Journal of a Residence in the Sandwich Islands during the Years 1823, 1824, and 1825*, 114.

32. Robert C. Schmitt, "The *Okuu*—Hawaii's Greatest Epidemic," *Hawaiian Medical Journal* 29 (May–June 1970): 359–64; Sheldon Dibble, *A History of the Sandwich Islands* (Honolulu, 1909), 38, 58; James Jackson Jarves, *History of the Hawaiian Islands* (Honolulu, 1847), 97; Tyerman and Bennet, *Journal of Voyages and Travels*, 1:423–24.

33. *The Friend* 7, no. 3 (March 1, 1849): 20; Laura Fish Judd, *Honolulu: Sketches of the Life, Social, Political and Religious, in the Hawaiian Islands from 1828 to 1861* (Honolulu, 1928), 138; Schmitt, *Demographic Statistics*, 10, 37.

34. Richard A. Green, "Oahu's Ordeal—The Smallpox Epidemic of 1853," *Hawaii Historical Review* 1 (July 1965): 221–42; Kuykendall, *The Hawaiian Kingdom, 1778–1854*, 412; Schmitt, *Demographic Statistics*, 10, 12.

35. Laura Judd, *Honolulu*, 138–39; Gerrit P. Judd, "Remarks on the Climate of the Sandwich Islands," *Hawaiian Spectator* 1 (April 1838): 22; Alonzo Chapin, "Remarks on the Sandwich Islands," *Hawaiian Spectator*, no. 2 (1838): 261–62. For further remarks on such matters, see my article, "Virgin Soil Epidemics as a Factor in the Aboriginal Depopulation of America," *William and Mary Quarterly*, 3d Series, 33 (April 1976): 289–99, which is reprinted as chapter 6 in this volume.

36. Samuel M. Kamakau, *Ka Po'e Kahiko, The People of Old*, trans. Mary K. Pukui (Honolulu, 1964), 105.

37. Ralph S. Kuykendall, *The Hawaiian Kingdom, 1854–1874: Twenty Critical Years*, Vol. 2 (Honolulu, 1953), 72–75.

38. Joseph E. Alicata, *Parasites of Man and Animals in Hawaii* (Basel, 1969), 32, 72.

39. Ross H. Gast, *Don Francisco de Paula Marin, A Biography: The Letters and Journal of Francisco de Paula Marin*, ed. Agnes C. Conrad (Honolulu, 1973), 237, 288, 292.

40. Chapin, "Remarks on the Sandwich Islands," 261; Cheever, *The Island World of the Pacific*, 233.

41. Chapin, "Remarks on the Sandwich Islands," 252; Gerrit Judd, "Remarks on the Climate of the Sandwich Islands," 22; Jarves, *History of the Hawaiian Islands*, 13; Cheever, *The Island World of the Pacific*, 224–25.

42. William Shainline Middleton, "Early Medical Experiences in Hawaii," *Bulletin of the History of Medicine* 45 (September–October 1971): 450.

43. Gerrit Judd, "Remarks on the Climate of the Sandwich Islands," 22, 26; Chapin, "Remarks on the Sandwich Islands," 252, 255–56, 258–59; Middleton, "Early Medical Experiences in Hawaii," 445, 450.

44. James Bordley and A. McGehee Harvey, *Two Centuries of American Medicine* (Philadelphia, 1976), 202.

45. The matter of which venereal disease existed where and when in the Pacific is controversial and has a considerable literature. See, for instance, Pirie, "The Effects of Treponematosis and Gonorrhoea on the Populations of the Pacific Islands," 187–206; and Stannard, *Before the Horror*, 69–77.

46. J. C. Beaglehole, *The Life of Captain James Cook* (Stanford, 1974), clix–clxi, 575, 577, 638–39, 709; Jean-François La Pérouse, *The Voyage of La Pérouse Round the World in the Years 1785, 1786, 1787, and 1788* (London, 1798), 1:98; Urey Lisiansky, *A Voyage Round the World in the Years 1803, 4, 5, and 6* (London, 1814), 103; Marshall Sahlins, *Islands of History* (Chicago, 1985), 1–5. This subject is controversial and the evidence ambiguous, as the reader can learn from Pirie, "The Effects of Treponematosis and Gonorrhoea on the Populations of the Pacific Islands," 187–206.

47. Sahlins, *Islands of History*, 9–26.

48. *The Complete Essays of Mark Twain*, ed. Charles Neider (Garden City, 1963), 16–17.

49. Robert Louis Stevenson, *Travels in Hawaii*, ed. A. Grove (Honolulu, 1973), 81.

50. George Vancouver, *A Voyage of Discovery to the North Pacific Ocean and Round the World* (London, 1801), 1:377–78.

51. Kuykendall, *The Hawaiian Kingdom, 1778–1854*, 305–13; W. Hillebrand, "Report on Labor and Population," *Transactions of the Royal Hawaiian Agricultural Society* 2, no. 2 (1855): 75; David Malo, "Decrease of Population," *Hawaiian Spectator* 2 (April 1839): 128. Even Herman Melville, who was present in Hawaii in this period and who cannot be accused of looking at the scene with a missionary's eyes, was appalled: see Herman Melville, *Typee: A Peep at Polynesian Life* (Evanston, 1968), 256–58.

52. William F. Blackman, *The Making of Hawaii* (New York, 1899), 213–14.

53. Blackman, *The Making of Hawaii*, 214; H.M.E. Heney, *In a Dark Glass: The Story of Paul Edmund Strzelecki* (Sydney, 1961), 164.

54. For a candid description of what sexual contacts were like between whites and aboriginal peoples in remote lands as recently as the 1930s, see Bob Connolly and Robin Anderson, *First Contact: New Guinea's Highlanders Encounter the Outside World* (Harmondsworth, 1988), 235–47.

55. *Lapérouse, Voyage of La Pérouse*, 98.

56. Chapin, "Remarks on the Sandwich Islands," 257–58, 263; Hillebrand, "Report on Labor and Population," 73, 75; Jarves, *History of the Hawaiian Islands*, 232.

57. Flinn, *European Demographic System*, 22–23.

58. Kuykendall, *The Hawaiian Kingdom, 1778–1854*, 328–31; Kuykendall, *The Hawaiian Kingdom, 1854–1874*, 178–96; Woodrow W. Borah, *New Spain's Century of Depression* (Berkeley, 1951), passim; Schmitt, *Demographic Statistics*, 10; Nordyke, *The Peopling of Hawaii*, 19.

59. Flinn, *European Demographic System*, 54.

60. Blackman, *The Making of Hawaii*, n. 216.

61. Two places to start the search are John D'Emilio and Estelle B. Freedman, *Intimate Matters: A History of Sexuality in America* (New York, 1988), 6–9, 87–88; and Walter L. Williams, *The Spirit and the Flesh: Sexual Diversity in American Indian Culture* (Boston, 1986), passim.

62. *Journals and Other Documents on the Life and Voyages of Christopher Columbus*, trans. Samuel Eliot Morison (New York, 1963), 212; Hopkins, *Life among the Paiutes*, 48.

63. Meriwether Lewis and William Clark, *The History of the Lewis and Clark Expedition*, ed. Elliott Coues (New York, n.d.), 2:779.

64. Ibid., 778–80; Robert H. Ruby and John A. Brown, *The Chinook Indians: Traders on the Lower Columbia River* (Norman, OK, 1976), 64–65, 127, 156, 188–200, 232–33; John R. Swanton, *The Indian Tribes of North America* (Washington, D.C., 1952), 418–19.

65. Edward Arber, ed., *Travels and Works of Captain John Smith* (New York, 1967), 2:436.

66. Alfred W. Crosby, *The Columbian Exchange: Biological and Cultural Consequences of 1492* (Westport, Conn., 1972), 156–60.

67. Robert Beverley, *The History and Present State of Virginia* (Chapel Hill, N.C., 1947), 170–71; John Heckewelder, *History, Manners, and Customs of the Indian Nations Who Once Inhabited Pennsylvania and the Neighbouring States* (Philadelphia, 1876), 261–62; Henry Steele Commager and Elmo Giordanetti, eds., *Was America a Mistake? An Eighteenth-Century Controversy* (Columbia, S.C., 1967), 60–61, 233; Merrill D. Peterson, ed., *The Portable Thomas Jefferson* (New York, 1975), 93–98.

9 THE DEMOGRAPHIC EFFECT OF AMERICAN CROPS IN EUROPE

François Rabelais, a contemporary of Cortés and Pizarro, mentioned the Canary Islands several times in *Gargantua and Pantagruel,* but ignored North and South America, although Europeans had known of their existence for more than a generation. Few, if any, Europeans in the late fifteenth and early sixteenth centuries were aware that Columbus's 1492 voyage had changed history. They were not equipped to think about the unprecedented, that is to say, a previously undreamed-of world. But the influence of the New World on Columbus's home continent was already considerable, and would presently be immeasurably vast. The gold and silver of Mexico and Peru helped to drive an inflation that did more to disrupt Europe's class structure than anything since the Black Death. The discovery that there were gigantic lands stretching from further north than Norway's most northerly headland to frigid mountains far to the south of Africa's southernmost cape, lands jammed with plants and animals and peoples unmentioned in the Bible, Plato, Aristotle, or Pliny, smashed models of reality that had not been questioned for more than a millennium. In 1590 José de Acosta scoffed at the cartographers and geographers of the ancient world who had been, until his time, unimpeachable authorities. "Ptolomeus and the others," he said, "knewe not the halfe."[1]

Had he known of the ultimate influence of maize and potatoes, humble American crops already growing in European soils, he would have been more impressed with his century. Calories can make as much history as cannons—more in the long run.

For thousands of years we have added nothing of major importance to the domesticated food crops and animals we inherited from our Neolithic predecessors, nothing as important as wheat or rice, cattle or sheep. We have been able to increase the productivity of field and herd, and, more important, we have distributed our Neolithic heritage of plants and animals throughout the world, carrying the sheep of Eurasia to the grasslands of Australia, and the manioc of South America to the hot soils of Uganda. We have shared our crops and livestock, carrying them to lands where their wild ancestors never grew but where they can prosper and so can the humans who grow them.

This sharing has been going on for as long as we have had domesticated plants and animals, but never so extravagantly as in the centuries since 1492. Columbus initiated an exchange of Old and New World domesticates that has had a vast influence on humanity all over the planet, and few places more than in Europe. Europe gained little from the disembarkation of American livestock (the advent of the turkey in the Old World did not trigger vast changes), but the benefit accruing from the acquisition of Amerindian crop plants has been enormous. That benefit is difficult to measure in total because, to give one example, the nutritional significance of the vitamins of American peppers, a condiment, may well be very important, but condiments are not a bulk item in the diet, and historical records usually deal in tons not grams. I will concern myself with the influence on Europe of two Amerindian staples, maize and the potato, foods that millions of Europeans have consumed every day of their lives past weaning. These two are well suited to European soils and climates, maize to the south and potatoes to the north, and they are very productive, much more so per unit of land than, for instance, wheat, the standard cereal of European agriculture.

Both maize and potatoes can be cultivated efficiently with the simplest of hand tools, and in many areas in soils unsuitable for Old World staples. Maize thrives in sandy soils and, in its various strains, prospers with ten to two hundred inches of rain a year. Properly dried, it can be stored safely for years, and makes good fodder, in ear and leaf. Potatoes, which in their productivity are to the temperate zones as rice is to the tropics, produce fat tubers in a variety of loams unsuitable for the small grains. Potatoes have the often handy characteristic of growing their edible parts below ground, where they can survive bad weather and—even worse—armies. Both these Amerindian crops produce food faster than wheat and the other staples of Europe. Maize can be eaten green a few months, even weeks, after planting, long before wheat "heads," and potatoes mature in three to four months, long before wheat produces useful amounts of seed.[2]

Let us turn first to the subject of maize in Europe for the good reason that Europeans saw it decades before the potato, and it was first to be brought to Europe and to spread widely there. In 1498 Columbus wrote that "there is now a lot of it in Castile." According to Gonzalo Fernández de Oviedo, writing a generation later, there were already fields of maize near Ávila and Madrid. Portuguese and Spanish farmers, at least some of them, were quick to adopt the American grain, and it was firmly established as a field crop in sixteenth-century Iberia, particularly in central and northern Portugal and in Galicia in northern Spain. Maize appeared elsewhere in Europe in the same century—for instance, in Spain's Milanese territories as early as 1530—and in North Africa and the Middle East as well, possibly via Muslims fleeing Iberia.[3]

The first strains of maize brought to Europe were probably from the Antilles, where temperatures are not profoundly different from those of Mediterranean Europe, but other conditions are. Europe is entirely outside of the tropics. Indeed, all the chief maize-growing areas of Europe are north of the latitude of New York City and Beijing in areas where day lengths vary markedly with the seasons. The first parts of the Americas touched and settled by the Iberians were entirely within the tropics—that is, in the zone of unvarying day length. It is likely that maize had to undergo a certain amount of adaptation to Mediterranean conditions before it would produce in quantity, and decades must have passed before many farmers found it attractively productive and dependable. Furthermore, I would suggest, the pressure of the population on the land in southern Europe in the sixteenth century was sufficient to force a shift to an exotic food plant in only limited areas.

Before modern times agriculturally and demographically—before 1750, if you would like a benchmark date—the most important limitations on population growth were the Malthusian ones, hunger, pestilence, war, which enforced "moral restraint." We will concern ourselves with hunger alone. One eighteenth-century estimate had it there had been 10 general famines in the tenth century, 26 in the eleventh, 2 in the twelfth, 4 in the fourteenth, 7 in the fifteenth, 13 in the sixteenth, 11 in the seventeenth, and 16 in the eighteenth, not to mention the much greater number of local or regional famines. We can argue about what constitutes a famine, about how many real famines there were, and about the precise effects of varying degrees of malnutrition,[4] but it does seem clear that poor food or no food discourages marriage, and procreation, and encourages a rise in the death rate. When diet improves in quantity and quality, hungry populations grow.[5]

Traditional peoples are very conservative about food, and when Europeans first came upon maize it looked bizarre on the stalk and in the ear, and tasted alien. To this day the great majority of Europeans think of it as fodder and not food for humans. But Europeans have often eaten it, even relished it, when the alternative has been foods of desperation like bark or nothing at all. The seventeenth century was a century of war, severe outbreaks of plague, economic turmoil, and, on the average, worsening food budgets. Food budgets declined in many areas and population dipped at mid-century, nowhere more noticeably than in Mediterranean Europe.[6]

The crisis of the seventeenth century and, afterward, the pressure of a growing population drove an agricultural revolution of sorts in that and the next century: new tools and techniques, new crop rotations, new systems of land holding that stimulated productivity, and, preceding the other changes, the adoption of new crops. In Iberia maize became a common article in the diet after 1650. In Burgundy and southern France maize entered the crop cycle in the same era, and by 1700 it was growing in every district south of a line from Bordeaux to Alsace, and was the chief food of the poor peasant. In Italy the cultivation of maize rose after the plague and famine of the 1630s. In Piedmont the spread of maize cultivation was one of the sequelae of plague and war, disasters that drove diminished numbers of farmers to raise food in quantity rapidly. Similar forces pushed maize adoption in the Balkans, but there the early history of maize is obscure.[7]

In the eighteenth century the population of Europe recovered the numbers it had lost in the seventeenth, and rose to levels previously unknown. Spaniards increased in number from 7.5 million in 1650 to 11.5 million in 1800. Italians, who numbered about 11 million in 1650, jumped to 19 million in 1800. In the same decades the population of England and Wales leaped from 5 million to 9.25 million; that of France from 16 million to 29 million; and so on.[8] More Europeans needed food than ever before, and the landowners and merchants, fixated on the profits to be made in the markets of the growing cities, drove the peasants to produce cash crops, and to restrict themselves to smaller plots per capita from which to produce their own rough fare. The effect was the cultivation of more and more land, greater efficiency, and—in southern Europe—the spread of maize. In the backward southwest of France, where wheat returned five gains for every one sown, maize prospered in the early rains and hot summers, and returned twenty-five and even one hundred. In parts of Languedoc maize reduced the fallow year from one in two to one in three. In northern Italy maize production darted forward, and in time exceeded wheat, rye, and the other anciently familiar grains in Lombardy. In the mid-eighteenth century Tobias Smollett, touring France and Italy, wrote that the nourishment of the poor peasants consisted "of a kind of meal called Polenta, made of Indian corn, which is very nourishing and agreeable." Even where the people could afford food of higher prestige, they valued maize as fodder, both the ears and the leaves. In the expanse of central and eastern Europe drained by the Danube, maize appeared as an important crop in the years around 1700, and became a vital one by the end of the century. By 1800 the peasants of southern Russia were raising this Amerindian crop as well. Its history in the Balkans still under Ottoman rule is not as well known, but we do know that it was raised there in quantity in the eighteenth century. By the nineteenth century, what North Americans call cornmeal mush was a common item of peasant diet, in wide areas the staple, from Galicia to Bessarabia under a variety of names: *millasse, polenta, mamaliga,* and others.[9]

In the nineteenth century the population surge of Europe accelerated into a population explosion—Iberia, Italy, and the Balkans rose from just over 40 million in 1800 to just short of 50 million by 1850, and to 70 million in 1900. For at least the first half of the century the expansion both of maize cultivation and of the number of Mediterranean, Danubian, and Balkan peasants who utilized it as their staple continued.[10]

Now that we have covered maize in the south, the time has come to turn to the north. In southern Europe maize was regionally important west of the Adriatic, and of major national importance to the east, as in Hungary and Rumania. In the north, the potato was of major importance everywhere.

The onset of the European saga of the potato lagged behind that of maize. The potato was not a Caribbean or Mexican crop, and the first European did not see it until Pizarro's invasion of the Incan Empire in the early 1530s. It seems that it was not brought to Spain for another forty years, the explanation for the lack of Spanish interest in it perhaps being that it was not only very different from their current staples, but a cool weather plant unsuitable for Mediterranean Europe except for the high country. The north Europeans, whose climate was suited to the potato, lagged many decades behind the Iberians in their contacts with America.

The northerners were in need of something with the qualities of the American potato because they were still dependent on the crops developed during the Neolithic Period, particularly wheat, barley, rye, and oats. The last three did better in the higher latitudes than wheat, but none of the four was as productive or as dependable as the northerners needed to support population expansion or advances in the complexity and richness of their cultures. Wheat, the classic food of the ancient Mediterranean world, was really at its northern extreme in the lands washed by the English Channel, North Sea, and Baltic.[11] (London, Amsterdam, and Berlin are approximately on a line with southern Siberia and the tip of Kamchatka, with which they share the white nights of summer and the brief days of winter.) Early frost, late spring, a gloomy summer, and hunger would follow. In addition, the small grains, notably rye, were liable to molds and fungus in the cool, wet weather, and those who ate them to ergotism and other disorders— perhaps in greater numbers than we imagine.[12] Irish, Britons, Normans, Netherlanders, Scandinavians, North Germans, Poles, and Russians were in need of a very productive crop that would thrive free of parasites in the northern latitudes and climates.

The answer to their needs, the American white potato, was a long time in coming to Europe, and once ashore, in about 1570, it attracted little interest. It showed up in Belgium in 1587 and in Vienna the following year, where it was apparently regarded as little more than a garden novelty.[13] Europeans were slow to adopt the potato for several reasons. It was, by standards of their agriculture and cookery, bizarre and possibly dangerous. Furthermore, it is likely that the first potatoes brought to Europe were unsuited to the latitudes of northern Europe. These plants were probably collected in the mountain valleys and plateaus of Peru, where temperatures are cool not because of latitude but because of altitude. The lands central to the Incan Empire lay in the tropics, where days are of similar length throughout the year. Peruvian potatoes blossom and produce seed and tubers without signals from the changing day lengths of late summer and autumn. These plants react to the long days of European summers by growing and growing, producing tier after tier of flowers, and when the growing season ends, they have produced only small potatoes, if any at all. Eventually, European farmers obtained potato plants from Chile adapted to fluctuating day lengths like those of northern Europe, but that seems not to have happened until the last half of the 1900s, a century after the potato became a staple for such as the Irish, Scottish, Flemish, and Palatinate peasants.[14]

The adaptation of the Peruvian potato plant to European conditions must have taken place in the seventeenth and eighteenth centuries, but there is no documentation on the matter. Simple farmers, selecting seeds for yield and early maturity of tubers, developed the plant that would revolutionize northern agriculture. (They must have planted the seeds and not pieces of the potatoes containing "eyes," as is usually the practice with this crop, because that is cloning, and would have produced generation after generation of the same tropical plants.) In Viverais in the Rhone Alps, for instance, where the population grew faster than cereal production, the peasants improvised their own humble agricultural revolution in the eighteenth century, utilizing as new food sources the chestnut and their own version of the *truffe blanche* or *pomme de terre*—the white potato.[15]

The Irish people provided a greater and more influential example, the classic story of the effect of the potato on a European population. Ireland's seventeenth-century crisis—the Cromwellian invasion, famine, mass evictions, and the throttling of export trade—forced the peasantry and the native aristocracy, reduced to peasant status, to seek means to extract the greatest amount of nourishment as safely and swiftly as possible from the least amount of land, often land of marginal quality. They discovered that an acre and a half would provide enough potatoes for a family of five, as compared to the five acres needed to produce the equivalent in grain; furthermore, they discovered that they only needed a spade to plant, tend, and harvest the crop. An adult could survive and be healthy on five or so kilograms of potatoes a day and a bit of milk.[16] In 1662 the Royal Society, prompted by no less than Robert Boyle, writing from his Irish estate, recommended the potato as insurance against famine.[17]

Food shortages in the Rhineland and Flanders during the wars of Louis XIV, and harvest failures in Germany in 1740 and 1770–72, convinced many there of the value of the potato. French soldiers returning from imprisonment in Germany during the Seven Years' War brought the news home, and the potato began its sweep across northern France. Poor grain harvests and rising food prices in the last third of the century accelerated the adoption of the potato everywhere on the continent suited to the tuber. Royalty and governments—Frederick the Great, Louis XVI, France's Committee of Public Safety—urged the cultivation of the crop. By the end of the eighteenth century, wherever in northwest Europe the peasants' land holdings were small and getting smaller, as dense populations became denser, and wherever landlords were obliging tenants to raise food for local consumption on smaller plots so as to free land for cash crops, the potato spread. In Ireland, parts of Scotland and the north of England, Flanders, the Rhineland, southwestern Germany, and Switzerland the potato became the peasant staple. In Brandenberg, to cite another example, sowings of potatoes rose from 1,653 *wispel* (a measure of about twenty-four bushels each) in 1765 to 21,188 in 1801.[18] At the beginning of the new century, in the midst of the Napoleonic Wars, an extended crisis that also spurred the cultivation of potatoes, Alexander von Humboldt announced the obvious: the tuber was already indispensable for a large portion of the peoples of northern Europe.[19]

In the nineteenth century the potato became more nearly indispensable in the European diet than ever before or since, with the exception of the years of the two world wars of the succeeding century. In no other country was the dependence on the tuber so nearly total as in Ireland, but in every major northern state cultivation of the potato climbed to unprecedented levels. In 1841 France, one of the major producers, harvested 177 million hectoliters of potatoes. In Sweden production of the tubers increased six times over from 1800–10 to 1820–30. In Prussia the area devoted to potatoes increased tenfold between 1816 and 1861, and in the nation of Germany that grew up around the Prussian core the area under potatoes grew 66 percent between 1850 and 1882.[20] In Russia, where Catherine the Great's attempt to stimulate potato cultivation after the famine of 1765 had come to little, crop failures in 1838–39 turned the trick and in the last half of the century potato production went up more than 400 percent.[21] The years around 1900 mark the peak of the importance of the potato in European history. In the period 1910–14 the annual consumption of potatoes per capita in the United Kingdom was 97 kilograms, 176 in

France, 199 in Germany, and 206.5 in Belgium. Even Italians, for all their fields of maize, accounted for 27.8 kilograms each.[22]

Ironically, the advent of two crops that allowed large numbers of the poor to live on the productivity of small pieces of land did not necessarily improve their lot. The other side of the coin of hearty meals was disease and starvation. The acquisition of a new and richly productive crop could perpetuate inefficient systems of agriculture and exploitative class relationships. In Ireland the productivity of the potato made it possible for landlords to evict the peasantry from vast areas, where livestock and grains for the English market and cash were produced. In southwest France the story was much the same, but there maize was the crop that made it possible for peasants to survive using primitive methods on less land than they had ever needed for the purpose before.[23]

Essential to this exploitation of the peasantry was the reduction of the diets of many peasants to one staple, with all the dangers that entails. Maize provides good nourishment calorically, and in other ways as well, but is far from a perfect food, being deficient in the vitamin B complex constituents, especially niacin. It will serve well for the bulk of a diet, but must be supplemented with foods—meats and greens—that contain what it lacks. In 1755 an article appeared in a French medical journal on a strange malady then endemic in Asturias, where the lower classes were heavily dependent on maize. The symptoms were redness and even crusting of the skin, and in the worst cases feebleness, tremors, depression, mania, and even death. The Italian word for it was *pellagra,* a word in some local dialect meaning rough skin. In 1808 a Professor Bunira reported that he had (doubtlessly in emulation of Dr. Edward Jenner's work with smallpox) collected fluid from the sores of pellagra victims and used it to inoculate animals and even himself, but with no pellagrous result. Without understanding of the cause of pellagra, there was no possibility of controlling the disease. It continued to appear in the provinces of earliest dependence on maize in Iberia, France, and Italy, and was soon reported in the Balkans, southern Russia, and, in time, in the United States, Latin America, Egypt, and South Africa. In 1830 there were 20,282 cases of pellagra in Lombardy, or 1.4 percent of the entire population. In 1856 the number had risen to 37,628 cases, or 1.5 percent of the population. (We may presume that these were severe cases, which otherwise would not have attracted formal recognition. If true, what was the sum of all the cases?)

In the second and third decades of the twentieth century, Dr. Joseph Goldberger of the United States discovered that pellagra was not a disease of infection but one of malnutrition, and that its cause was an unvarying maize diet. That discovery and a rising standard of living enabled North Americans and Europeans to control and cure the disease, and by mid-century pellagra was almost unknown in their parts of the globe (though not in the Third World, where it still ravages the very poor). In the previous two centuries hundreds of thousands had died of the disease, and an uncounted number, no doubt millions, had been devastated by its symptoms. All this because maize was so wondrous a food that the populations of entire provinces slipped into nearly absolute dependence upon it.[24]

On the other hand, a dict of potatoes, with very few inexpensive supplements, will support not only survival, but health. In 1776 Adam Smith praised the potato as healthy food, remarking that:

> The chairmen, porters, and coal-heavers in London, and those unfortunate women who live by prostitution, the strongest men and the most beautiful women perhaps in the British dominions, are said to be, the greater part of them, from the lowest rank of people in Ireland, who are generally fed with this root. No food can afford a more decisive proof of its nourishing quality, or of its being peculiarly suitable to the health of the human constitution.[25]

But Smith also noted that potatoes were not a perfect food in all ways: they tended to rot, and it was impractical to store one year's crop for consumption in another year. Furthermore, he pointed out that if their only or chief effect on their consumers was to enable them to multiply, then the end result would be a rise in land rents and not an improvement in the consumers' lot. Smith's intellectual heir, David Ricardo, wrote to an Anglo-Irish friend in 1822 that the Irish dependence on potatoes worried him: "I think we are not only richer and happier in England than in Ireland and . . . are never so near actual famine than you are. . . ." He asked, "What can you put in the scale against this dreadful evil?" The 3 million Irish of 1750 grew to 5.25 million in 1800, and surged to an all-time peak of over 8 million in 1841. Disraeli declared Ireland the most densely populated country in Europe, and its arable land even more densely populated than China's.[26]

In the 1840s an American parasite of the American potato, left behind when the potato crossed the Atlantic, caught up with its host, destroying crops across a wide breadth of northern Europe. The blight had dire effect, for instance, in Scotland and the Palatinate, but in no country was the effect as catastrophic as in Ireland. The story is one we all know, and there is no need to blaspheme it with repetition. The productivity, ease of cultivation, and wholesome nourishment of the American potato had beguiled the Irish into a Malthusian ambush. One million died in the famine, hundreds of thousands in ensuing epidemics, and hundreds of thousands of others fled across the Irish Sea and Atlantic. Within a generation following the 1841 census, the population of Ireland dropped by half. (Incidentally, of all the foods sent to Ireland to relieve the starving masses, maize, being the cheapest nourishment available, was the most important.)[27]

Norway strayed halfway into the Malthusian cul-de-sac, and it is instructive to examine how that nation avoided disaster. There were a bit fewer than 900,000 Norwegians in 1815, and 1.7 million in 1865, products of one of the very highest annual growth rates in all of Europe. The vital role of potatoes in that growth spurt is certain, although the story is complicated by the spread of smallpox vaccination at the same time as potato cultivation. Informed and careful estimation sets the caloric value of the average Norwegian's daily diet in 1800 at 1,800, and in 1855–56 at 3,300. (The minimum requirement for the average man is 2,000 calories per day.) In that period potatoes spread from the south, where the tuber had first arrived about 1750, throughout the land. In 1809 the potato accounted for only 4 percent of the total food energy provision for Norwegians, and in 1835 for at least 28 percent. In the 1870s the annual per capita consumption of potatoes was 450 pounds, and that of grain only 420 pounds.

Norwegians, it would seem, were nearly as vulnerable to a failure of the potato harvest as the Irish. But they had no catastrophe because they were able to clear new lands, which slowed the subdivision of peasant plots, and they utilized on the new lands new equipment and methods, increasing yields. This saved them from the penalties of dependence on the potato until mid-century, and after that industrialism and mass emigration relieved the population pressure in the rural areas. The Norwegians' chief advantage over the Irish seems to be in having entered the cul-de-sac later and, therefore, not having penetrated quite so deeply before advances in agricultural techniques, industrialism, and the possibilities of transatlantic migration saved them from disaster.[28]

Rising standards of living have allowed Europeans in the twentieth century to make the choices about their diets—first the English working classes a century ago, and in our time the Rumanians—and they have tended to return to their ancient staples, the small grains. There are exceptions, of course: the Finns are too far north to forgo the potato as a staple; and polenta, a constant in rural diet in northern Italy since the seventeenth century, is not going to disappear from dinner tables there. But the era of greatest European dependence on potatoes and maize seems to have passed, and we are now in a position to assess their significance in European history.

First, there is the matter of their influence on the population explosion that carried Europeans from 105 million in 1650 to 390 million in 1900. The two American staples without any doubt whatsoever were elements in that explosion—statistics on food production and consumption prove that—but were they the cause? Causes are perhaps beyond the historian's ken. We can rarely declare with absolute confidence why people did what they did. Moreover, effects usually become causes and all is submerged under a swirl of feedback. Could not the same rise in numbers have been triggered by improvements in yields of traditional crops, from the rise in wealth that came with industrialism, and from such medical advances as the smallpox vaccination?

That I very much doubt, especially for the North, because population increase preceded these developments in many places, but proof is, of course, impossible. I can only refer to what did actually happen, which is that many of the millions of Europeans produced by the population explosion lived on potatoes and maize; and that these extraordinarily productive crops increased the production of other foods by releasing land for small grains and vegetables, and for pasturage. To claim that the population explosion would have taken place without maize and potatoes strikes me as carrying counter-factual history further than it will stretch without breaking.

Europeans industrialized and vastly improved their lives materially in the two or three hundred years of maximum dependence on the Amerindian crops, changing human existence everywhere. Did maize and potatoes play a role in industrialization? The answer must be yes because industrialization drew millions of people out of agriculture, obliging those left behind to raise much more food per person than ever before. They met that obligation by increasing yields of traditional crops, and by resorting to the most productive food crops available to them—maize and potatoes. These became staples in the countryside and necessities for many urban workers. For instance, let us consider the seven-member family of a *skilled and well-paid* worker, Richard Goodwin of 45 Great Wild Street, London, in 1841. In an average week the staples of their diet consisted of twelve loaves of bread, which cost eight shillings, and eighteen pounds of potatoes, which coast only *nine pence.*[29] Friedrich Engels expressed the role of potatoes succinctly in his angriest book, *The Condition of the Working Class in England* (1845):

> The normal diet of the individual worker naturally varies according to his wages. The better-paid workers—particularly when the whole family works in the factories—enjoy good food as long as they are in employment. They have meat every day and bacon and cheese for the evening meal. The lower-paid workers have meat only two or three times a week, and sometimes only on Sundays. The less meat they can afford, the more potatoes and bread they eat. Sometimes the meat consumed is cut down to a little chopped bacon mixed with the potatoes. The poorer workers can afford no meat at all and they eat cheese, bread, porridge and potatoes. The poorest of all are the Irish, for whom potatoes are the staple diet.[30]

Historian Sidney Pollard has called the Irish immigrants of that period "the mobile shock troops of the industrial revolution." They played the dismal role of enabling key areas in the British economy to grow without driving up the price of labor. In 1854 the Reverend A. Campbell of Liverpool wrote that in "the present state of the labour market English labour would be almost unpurchasable if it were not for the competition of Irish labour. . . ."[31] Equivalent groups of poor men, women, and children played similar roles in the industrialization of other European nations, and in more cases than not, they depended on Amerindian foods as the core of their diets. Otherwise, they could not have been as usefully poor as they were, and not starved to death.

In the north of Europe potatoes were important not only in that they enabled the industrial workers to fill their stomachs with substance of rich caloric value and of some protein content, as well, but also of crucially important vitamin content. Potatoes had less vitamin C than fresh vegetables, fruits, and berries, but had the advantage of being available every day throughout the winters. They saved multitudes from scurvy, one of the ancient curses of northern Europe. Even in relatively prosperous Great Britain in 1909–49, potatoes supplied at least forty percent of the mean intake of vitamin C in working-class households. Wherever and whenever potatoes were lacking in Great Britain because of Dickensian meanness, crop failures, or during wars when enemy blockades cut off the supplies, scurvy appeared—or we should say reappeared, because it had been common among rural laborers before potatoes arrived.[32] Similar stories could be told of scurvy following potato shortages elsewhere.

Could there have been an industrial revolution in northern Europe without the potato? Probably, but that is not the way it happened, and all historians really have to deal with is what did happen. The early industrial workers fueled themselves with Amerindian foods, and without these the difficult transition from field to factory would have been slower and for many essential members of the labor pool perhaps fatal. Even with the potato, the urban poor tottered on the brink of intolerable malnutrition in the early decades of the new era. To illustrate, poor boys, fourteen to sixteen years in age, of London in the late eighteenth century and early nineteenth century ranged from about fifty-five to fifty-six inches in height. Of eighty-one ethnic groups for whom modern height data is available, only two, the Lumi and Bundi of New Guinea, have shorter adolescents.[33]

The greatest significance of Amerindian crops in Europe's history is perhaps not merely that they played important roles in the continent's population explosion and the industrial revolution. To appreciate their greatest significance we must pause to consider what is distinctive about Europe over the last six centuries. In that 600 years its people experienced an enormous surge not only of numbers—from 60 million in 1400 to 390 million in 1900—but of economic growth, intellectual achievement, and material power. Other peoples have had similar surges —for instance, the Muslims in the early centuries of what Europeans call the Middle Ages, the Chinese of the Song Dynasty—but their advances ended with general declines, both economic and cultural. Thus far, Europe's surge is unique in its duration and promise of continuation.

Only once before in the last millennium has Europe had a surge comparable to the current one.[34] Between the ninth and fourteenth centuries Europe's population doubled and her people produced the high culture of the Middle Ages: scholastic philosophy, the Gothic cathedral, Dante, the mechanical clock, and the yeasty urban cultures of northern Italy and Flanders. The surge ended in the 1300s when Europe's population exceeded its capacity to feed itself and the Black Death arrived from the East, abruptly reducing the number of Europeans by about one-third.

Europe's medieval surge lasted about three centuries, give or take a half-century or so, before it collapsed. Three hundred years after that collapse, in the middle of the seventeenth century, Europe's population, which had been growing since sometime in the fifteenth century, ceased to grow and even dipped, especially in Mediterranean and northwestern Europe, the most richly innovative regions of the continent. In the same period Europeans suffered what Paul Hazard has called the "crisis of the European consciousness," the kind of failure of nerve that often signals a downturn in a society's arc through time.

Precedent suggests that the seventeenth-century decline in Europe's progress should have been a major one, not to be nullified for generations. Instead it proved to be no more than a hitch in her progress. By the last decades of that century, Europe's numbers were growing again, and in the first decades of the next century economic expansion beyond previous levels was under way. Why? How? Luck played its part, of course. Barbarians did not sweep in from northern forests and eastern steppes to take advantage of Europe's weakness. The Turkish surge did not pass its previous high water mark at the gates of Vienna. The crisis did not include anything so horrendous as the arrival of the Black Death. The plague did take many lives in the seventeenth century, but by then Europeans knew in part how to limit its ravages or at least how to compensate for the lives and treasure it took. It disappeared from western Europe—forever, one hopes—early in the next century. (Carlo M. Cipolla suggests that in Italy maize in a sense replaced the plague, providing food for those whom the disease would normally have carried off, and who, being "extra," would have starved without the new food.)[35] If cholera, Europe's next pestilential import from the East, had arrived in the seventeenth century, generations before sanitationists and scientists learned how to control it, the seventeenth-century crisis might have been more profound.

There were immensely powerful positive factors, as well. By the time of the crisis of the 1700s, Europe was in command in the Americas, and colonial gold and silver, goods, and markets helped to shorten the crisis, as did the profits from trade with West Africa and the Far East. The advance of European science and technology and the improvement of its administrative and financial techniques and institutions helped as well.

Let me also nominate Amerindian crops as a significant element in the recovery. In at least one way the seventeenth-century crisis was similar to the fourteenth-century crisis. Europe could not, with the agriculture it possessed, feed her lower classes and also support the high-flown schemes of her upper classes. Europe was deep into what might have been a major demographic decline when the Amerindian crops, adapted to European conditions and familiar to farmers in scattered areas, were ready for wide dissemination. Europe's farmers would, in time, greatly improve the yields they were able to obtain from their traditional crops and livestock, but what they needed in the seventeenth and early eighteenth centuries was an immediate miracle. That is what maize and potatoes supplied. When the pioneer of the agricultural revolution, Viscount Charles "Turnip" Townshend, was born in 1674 European farming techniques were still primitive, but potatoes were already an essential food to considerable numbers of poor peasants in Ireland and here and there in the British Isles and on the continent; and maize was a staple from Portugal to the Adriatic and becoming so in parts of the Danube Basin and Balkans. In the late seventeenth and eighteenth centuries the Amerindian crops, though often cultivated by distinctly unscientific methods, provided what Folke Dovring has called "nutritional space," a delaying of disaster, a fending off of the Malthusian checks, until those tardy developments that historians have called the agricultural and industrial revolutions were under way.[36]

In the seventeenth century Europeans were able to "skip" a major crisis. In the eighteenth century they were able to launch directly into massive and unprecedented advance from a plateau of capital, knowledge, intact infrastructure, and experience built up since the 1300s, rather than to stagger through additional years of crisis and *then* begin yet more decades of struggle merely to regain what had been lost. For the first time in human history a people were able to break out of the cycle of advance and retreat, of ascent and crash, a cycle that matched every era of success with an era of dismay. We are at least partly in debt to the skills of Amerindian plant breeders for that breakout.

Notes

1. Joseph de Acosta, *The Natural and Moral History of the Indies*, trans. Edward Gimston (New York: Burt Franklin, n.d.), 1:90.

2. William Langer, "American Foods and Europe's Population Growth," *Journal of Social History* 8 (Winter 1975): 52–54, 58; Alfred W. Crosby, *The Columbian Exchange: Biological and Cultural Consequences of 1492* (Westport, Conn.: Greenwood Press, 1972), 171; Barbara Nicholson, *The Oxford Book of Food Plants* (London: Oxford University Press, 1969), 7–8, 177–78. See also Redcliffe Salaman, *The History and Social Influence of the Potato* (Cambridge: Cambridge University Press, 1985), passim; Nicholas P. Hardeman, *Shucks, Shocks, and Hominy Blocks* (Baton Rouge: Louisiana State University Press, 1984), passim.

3. M.M. Postan and H.J. Habakkuk, eds., *Cambridge Economic History of Europe* (Cambridge: Cambridge University Press, 1967), 4:276–77; Antonello Gerbi, *Nature in the New World*, trans. Jeremy Moyle (Pittsburgh: University of Pittsburgh Press, 1985), 32, 189; Carolo M. Cipolla, ed., *The Fontana Economic History of Europe: The Sixteenth and Seventeenth Centuries* (Glasgow: William Collins and Co., 1974), 252, 327–28; Langer, "American Foods," 59.

4. Robert I. Rotberg and Theodore K. Rabb, eds., *Hunger and History: The Impact of Changing Food Production and Consumption Patterns on Society* (Cambridge: Cambridge University Press, 1983), passim.

5. Fernand Braudel, *The Structures of Everyday Life*, trans. Siân Reynolds (New York: Harper and Row, 1981), 74; for a general discussion of the subject, see Rotberg and Rabb, *Hunger and History*.

6. Cipolla, ed., *Fontana Economic History of Europe: The Sixteenth and Seventeenth Centuries*, 117.

7. Cipolla, ed., *Fontana Economic History of Europe: The Sixteenth and Seventeenth Centuries*, 117, 311, 327, 464; Braudel, *The Structures of Everyday Life*, 1:165–66; Langer, "American Foods," 59–60; Giovanni Levi, "Innovazione Tecnica e Resistenza Contadina: Il Mais nel Piemonte del '600," *Quaderni Storici* 14, no. 3, 1092–1100; Troian Stoianovich and Georges C. Haupt, "Le Maïs arrive dans les Balkans," *Annales* 17 (January–February 1962): 84–93.

8. These and the other population numbers not specifically referenced in this article can be easily located in Colin McEvedy and Richard Jones, *Atlas of World Population History* (Harmondsworth: Penguin Books, 1978).

9. Langer, "American Foods," 59–60; Paul M. Hohenberg, "Maize in French Agriculture," *Journal of European Economic History* 7 (Spring 1977): 68–69, 71; Alan S. Milward and S.B. Saul, *The Economic Development of Continental Europe, 1780–1870* (London: George Allen and Unwin, 1973), 78; Gauro Coppola, *Il Mais Nell' economia Agricola Lombarda (dal Secolo XVIII all' Unità)* (Bologna: Società Editrice il Mulino, 1979), 145–47; Stoianovich and Haupt, "Le Maïs arrive dans les Balkans," 84–93.

10. Coppola, *Il Mais*, 154; Langer, "American Foods," 60.

11. Beryl B. Simpson and Molly Conner-Ogorzaly, *Economic Botany: Plants in Our World* (New York: McGraw-Hill, 1986), 156–62; Graeme Barker, *Prehistoric Farming in Europe* (Cambridge: Cambridge University Press, 1985), 43–46.

12. J.G. Hawkes, "The History of the Potato," *Journal of the Royal Horticul-

tural Society 92 (May 1967): 251; Mary Kilbourne Matossian, "Mold Poisoning and Population Growth in England and France, 1750–1850," *Journal of Economic History* 44 (September 1984): 673–74; see also Matossian, "Mold Poisoning: An Unrecognized English Health Problem, 1550–1800," *Medical History* 15 (1981): passim, 73–84; and Matossian, *Poisons of the Past: Molds, Epidemics, and History* (New Haven: Yale University Press, 1989).

13. Hawkes, "The History of the Potato," 251–52, 255.

14. Ibid., 289–93.

15. Ibid., 291–93; Alain Molinier, "En Vivarais au XVIIIc Siècle: Une Croissance Démographique sans Révolution Agricole," *Annales du Midi* 92 (1980): 301–15.

16. Ibid., 124, 225–28; Cecil Woodham-Smith, *The Great Hunger: Ireland 1845–1849* (New York: The New American Library, 1964), 30; Langer, "American Foods," 54.

17. Redcliffe Salaman, *The History and Social Influence of the Potato*, 238, 445–50.

18. Ibid., 54–56; William L. Langer, "Checks on Population Growth: 1750–1850," *Scientific American* 226 (February 1972): 99; Richard J. Evans and W.R. Lee, eds., *The German Peasantry, Conflict and Community in Rural Society from the Eighteenth to the Twentieth Centuries* (London: Croom Helm, 1986), 100 n. 61.

19. Crosby, *The Columbian Exchange*, 184.

20. Langer, "American Foods," 55; Gunnar Fridlizius, "Sweden," in *European Demography and Economic Growth*, ed. W.R. Lee (London: Croom Helm, 1979), 349; Postan and Habakkuk, *Cambridge Economic History of Europe*, Vol. 7, Part 1, 430.

21. Crosby, *The Columbian Exchange*, 184.

22. Carol M. Cipolla, ed., *The Fontana Economic History of Europe: The Industrial Revolution* (Glasgow: William Collins' Sons & Co., 1973), 130.

23. Hohenberg, "Maize," 99; Salaman, *The History and Social Influence of the Potato*, 281–82.

24. Kenneth J. Carpenter, *Pellagra* (Stroudsburg, Pa.: Hutchinson Ross, 1981), xi, 2–3, 7, 31–32, 46, 48, 342; Coppola, *Il Mais*, 127–28; Jacques M. May, *The Ecology of Malnutrition in Central and Southeastern Europe* (New York: Hafner, 1966), 19, 40, 88, 147, 259.

25. Adam Smith, *An Inquiry into the Nature and Causes of the Wealth of Nations* (New York: Modern Library, 1937), 161.

26. Ibid., 160; Langer, "American Foods," 57; Woodham-Smith, *The Great Hunger*, 26.

27. Evans and Lee, eds., *The German Peasantry*, 142; Salaman, *The History and Social Influence of the Potato*, 291, 303–5, 315; Woodham-Smith, *The Great Hunger*, 36, 48–51, 179–80; E.C. Large, *The Advance of the Fungi* (New York: Dover, 1962), 32, 35.

28. Michael Drake, *Population and Society in Norway, 1735–1865* (Cambridge: Cambridge University Press, 1969), 41–74; Drake, "Norway," in *European Demography and Economic Growth*, ed. W.R. Lee (London: Croom Helm, 1979), 293–94.

29. John Burnett, *Plenty and Want, A Social History of Diet in England from 1815 to the Present Day* (London: Scolar Press, 1979), 67.

30. Friedrich Engels, *The Condition of the Working Class in England*, trans. W.O. Henderson and W. H. Chaloner (Oxford: Basil Blackwell, 1958), 85.

31. Sidney Pillard, "Labour in Great Britain," in *The Cambridge Economic History of Europe*, Vol. 7, Part 1, 1978, 113.

32. Kenneth J. Carpenter, *The History of Scurvy and Vitamin C* (Cambridge: Cambridge University Press, 1986), 101-3, 186, 224, 227.

33. Robert W. Fogel et al., "Secular Changes in American and British Stature and Nutrition," in *Hunger and History*, ed. Rotberg and Rabb, 270, 280.

34. Emmanuel Le Roy Ladurie's essay, "The Crisis and the Historian," to be found in the collection of his works entitled *The Mind and Method of the Historian*, trans. Siân Reynolds and Ben Reynolds (Chicago: University of Chicago Press, 1981), was the chief stimulus for the following discussion. Also, see E. J. Hobsbawm, "The General Crisis of the European Economy in the 17th Century," and "The Crisis of the 17th Century—II," *Past and Present*, no. 5 (May 1954): 33–53, and no. 6 (November 1954): 44–65.

35. Carolo M. Cipolla, "Four Centuries of Italian Demographic Development," in *Population in History: Essays in Historical Demography*, ed. D.V. Glass and D.E.C. Eversley (London: Edward Arnold, 1965), 575.

36. Habakkuk and Postan, eds., *Cambridge Economic History of Europe*, Vol. 6, Part 2, 634.

10 DEMOGRAPHY, MAIZE, LAND, AND THE AMERICAN CHARACTER

I recently read in my hometown newspaper, the *Austin American-Statesman,* the following: "We [Americans] are too concerned with Heaven on earth to genuflect to the prophets of other realities."[1] Billy Porterfield, that line's author, a local columnist, is not usually ranked with Alexis de Tocqueville as an acute observer of the American character, but in at least this one sentence he is deserving of our attention. Americans *are* obsessed with the possibilities of Heaven on earth: that is to say, most Americans are chronically materialistic and optimistic, more interested in short-range than long-range prospects, and have been for many generations. Pie on the table today or, at the latest, tomorrow—apple pie, mince pie, pecan pie, apricot pie, coconut cream pie, lemon meringue pie, peach cobbler pie, blueberry, blackberry, huckleberry, and pizza pie—that is what they want, not "pie in the sky," whether the source of that promise be Christianity or Marxism.

It is my supposition that something as central to the American character as this hasty pudding of materialism, optimism, and obsession with immediate satisfaction probably has roots, deep and old, in the positive experience of common Americans, white ones, at least, in meeting life's most basic demands.

The thirteen colonies, with nearly 2.5 million people on the eve of the Revolution, and the United States, with nearly 4 million at the time of the first census in 1790,[2] dominated the eastern third of North America like a spunky colossus, covetous and apt to get what it coveted because it had the numbers to seize what it wanted. It might lose battles and even wars, but demographically it would always win the final decision, with or without immigration. In 1751 a cocky Benjamin Franklin wrote that for every marriage per hundred people in Europe, there were two in British America, and for every four births per marriage in Europe, there were eight in America. He estimated that the population of the American Britons was doubling every twenty years. If it continued to do so at a rate of only once every twenty-five years, it would "in another Century be more than the People of England, and the greatest Number of Englishmen will be on this side of the Water."[3] John Adams, writing in 1780, the gloomy year before Yorktown when the Revolution these American Englishmen were waging against the Mother Country seemed to be languishing, contrived optimism by pointing with genital pride to their fecundity. He estimated that the war had cost them 35,000 men, but that during its six years they had increased by 750,000. They were adding 20,000 men of fighting age every year. "Is this the case with our enemy, Great Britain? Which then can maintain the war the longest?"[4] he asked, sounding a little like Mao Tse-tung in the latter's defiant prime.

Current research supports the claims of the Founding Fathers of the United States of America about their fellow citizens' ability to go forth and multiply. Women tended to marry earlier than in Europe, especially in the first decades of a given settlement; to remarry quickly if widowed; and to have a large number of healthy children. In 1790, half the population of the United States was under sixteen years of age. The birth rate (number of births per 1,000 of population) of the United States in 1800 was much higher than has ever been recorded for any European nation, and remained so for many years; it is equaled in reliably recorded data by only such spectacularly fecund populations as the Hutterites and the people of the Cocos-Keeling Islands in the Indian Ocean. The fertility rate (babies per woman between puberty and menopause) for the white American population in 1800 was about twice the highest rate of the baby boom in the United States in the 1950s.[5]

Perhaps the most astonishing feature of American demography at the end of the eighteenth century is that its rate of natural increase was apparently *in decline,* having been even more spectacular when Adams and Franklin wrote and before.[6] At the beginning of the century John Lawson observed, admittedly not on the basis of statistics but of acute observation, that "women long marry'd, and without

Children, in other Places, have remov'd to Carolina, and become joyful Mothers."[7]

As the decades passed and population density increased in the original colonies, the rate of population growth slowed, but did not halt. Benjamin Rush likened the migration west to "cutting off the suckers of an apple tree," which "increases the size of the tree and the quantity of fruit."[8]

On the frontiers the original fecundity of the colonies continued. Morris Birkbeck, who journeyed from Virginia to the Illinois wilderness in the second decade of the nineteenth century, recorded: "In this land of plenty, young people first marry and then look out for the means of a livelihood. . . ." Big families meant more hands to help on the farm, more men to fight the dispossessed Amerindians; and the open spaces "kindled ambitions for dominion. . . ."[9]

Nearly everyone who has speculated on the cause of the prodigious amount of healthy children produced by the population of English-speaking America in the colonial and early national periods has pointed to the availability of open spaces. Benjamin Franklin stated the theory—we can almost call it the fact—that everyone has embroidered on since, not least among them Frederick Jackson Turner:

> Land being thus plenty in America, and so cheap as that a labouring Man, that understands Husbandry, can in a short Time save Money enough to purchase a Piece of new Land sufficient for a Plantation, whereon he may subsist a Family; such are not afraid to marry; for if they even look far enough forward to consider how their Children when grown up are to be provided for, they see that more Land is to be had at rates equally easy, all Circumstances considered.[10]

Franklin was obviously right, but said nothing about the crucially important choice of what to do with "a Piece of new Land sufficient for a Plantation."

Most of the colonists and pioneers were, except for the African Americans, from northern and northwestern Europe. There the soil and climate were tolerably similar to those of the thirteen colonies and states, but not identical.[11] In northern Europe the soils tended to be heavy and the climate maritime, that is to say, moderate in temperature and usually without such extreme weather as violent downpours and droughts. The heavy soil required deep plowing in order to facilitate drainage and to tap the nutriments carried away from the surface by the soft but persistent rains. Deep plowing required heavy draft animals to pull the plowshare and moldboard through the moist earth. The staple crops were the small grains (wheat, rye, barley, oats), which required clean fields, plowed and harrowed, and lots of skilled laborers for sowing and harvesting.[12]

In North America the Europeans found the loam sometimes shallow and often sandy, and the weather continental—that is, extreme in its deluges and droughts, its frosts and spells of equatorial heat. Captain John Smith compared the winters of Virginia to those of England, and the summers to those of Spain. Peter Kalm, the Finnish traveler and naturalist, found the winters of Pennsylvania and the colonies to the north comparable to those of Sweden, despite their Florentine and Napolitan latitudes. The European immigrants had few plows, and few trained oxen or horses to pull them. Their fields, often overgrown with brush and trees and always undergirded with roots and in the north with rocks as well, defied plowing anyway. They learned, painfully, that European farming wisdom did not necessarily apply in America. Wheat did not do well in Jamestown or Plymouth. The settlers in Carolina tried sowing some barley, but "that Grain requires the Ground to be very well worked with repeated Ploughings, which our general way of breaking the Earth with Hoes, can, by no means, perform. . . ."[13]

In large part the very first Euro-Americans survived because the Amerindians gave or sold them America's native grain, or because the whites stole it. The colonists we now call Pilgrims, looking for a place to spend the winter in November of 1620, found a cache of food on Cape Cod: "divers fair Indian baskets, filled with corn, and some in ears, fair and good, of divers colours, which seemed to them a very good sight (having never seen any such before)." Within four years it would be "more precious than silver" to them, and they would use it as currency.[14]

The food was maize or, as it was often called, Indian corn or just corn, and the Euro-Americans in North America adopted it more enthusiastically and maintained it as their staple for longer than any of their compeers elsewhere in Europe's colonies. It produced far more food per acre than any plant brought from Europe.[15] Naturalist and Linnaeus disciple Peter Kalm observed that near Albany, New York, wheat produced heavy yields—twelve and even twenty bushels for each one sown—but the farmer who planted a bushel of maize on the same land would reap two hundred. Maize, he said, was so very productive that some called it "the lazy man's crop." In Carolina, where the temperatures were warmer and the growing season longer (and the tolerance for hyperbole possibly even greater), Lawson proclaimed that the maize yield was seven or eight hundred times that of the quantity sown.[16]

The prodigality of this plant was a general genetic characteristic, and also the result of its precise adaptation to the climates and soils of the eastern woodlands, where it had been introduced from Mexico as long ago as 300 B.C.[17] For centuries Amerindian farmers had chosen as their seed corn the kernels from the plants best adapted to particular localities, and the plants themselves, by the simple Darwinian process of survival of the fittest, had produced strains fine-tuned to specific environments. European cereal crops were at best suitable for Atlantic North America in only a broad sense, but there were strains of maize for each division of the mosaic of farming environments east of the plains. The strains the Europeans found in the eastern coastal plain did far better than any other food crop in the sandy soils of that area, even in those from which the heavy rains had leached most nutriments. "A sandy ground," wrote Kalm, " could never have been better employed," and he noted as well that maize seedlings could tolerate America's unpredictably late frosts, sometimes even several in a spring, and survive to ripen.[18]

There were two general categories of strains, a southern kind cultivated in the South and middle colonies that grew to eight feet and took a half-year to ripen, and a New England and Canadian kind that rarely exceeded three or four feet in height and matured in a quarter-year.[19] In the 1670s Connecticut's proto-scientist John Winthrop reported to the Royal Society in London that there was a very short strain in the far north, one he seems to have known as "Mohauks Corn," that could be planted as late as June and would still have enough time to ripen. In the eighteenth century Cadwallader Colden, another proto-scientist (this one found time enough while being Tory lieutenant governor of New York to introduce Linnaean taxonomy to America) collected seeds of at least eight different "species" (strains?) of North American maize, planted them in the same soil at the same time, and discovered that "they will come to ripeness at very different seasons in the year & this property they never change unless when sown together that they bastardise." Farmers in the north, he learned, had to be very careful about which strains they planted or risked losing an entire crop.[20]

Maize was suited to American environments and to the Amerindian slash-and-burn style of farming as well. The Aborigines prepared a patch of woods for planting not in the way the Europeans did, by clearing the land of all trees and brush and even grasses, but by stripping a ring of bark all the way around the trees ("girdling") to kill them and open the forest canopy to the sun. They then burned off the undergrowth, leaving the bare trees to rot and fall in their own good time. Then, every few paces, they planted three or four kernels of maize together between the charred trunks, hilling up the dirt up around the maize stalks a few weeks later and planting beans to climb the stalks, and squash and "pompions" to grow in the spaces between the hills. This method often struck European visitors as appallingly messy, but it did not require beasts of burden or expensive tools like plows; it minimized weeding, could be cultivated efficiently with unskilled labor (children could do most of the work); and produced much more food per unit of land than European methods. Not only that, but maize, beans, and squash, eaten together, provided a nutritionally balanced diet. The colonists of British and French North America adopted the Amerindian method of farming,[21] and for two and a half centuries maintained it on the moving frontier, in whole or in part, with hoe or plow (sometimes substituting turnips or rye for squash between the hills, but seldom forsaking maize) until they reached the far edge of the humid eastern third or so of the continent. In the turned sod of the Mississippi Valley's tall grass prairie, as impenetrable as the back of a shag rug, they chopped holes with axes and deposited the maize kernels in the crevices.[22]

Maize was lavishly advantageous: John Lawson called it "the most useful Grain in the World. . . ."[23] If food were needed immediately, the ears could be eaten green. If there were a shortage of labor, the ears could be left on the stalks safely enclosed from storm in their husks, which were resistant (though not forever) to the beaks and claws of hungry birds. Once the ears were picked, shucked, and shelled (all by hand labor), the kernels could be dried and stored almost indefinitely. Maize was as good for livestock as for humans, and as standards of living edged upward it was increasingly used to feed the animals that provided the humans with meat, eggs, milk, leather, fiber, and power. "In a word, without exception," Kalm testified, "I know of no cultivated plant which is so universally and greedily sought by all domestic animals." William Oliver on the Illinois frontier claimed that even the dogs and cats ate maize "in some shape or other." The leaves made good forage and silage, and provided material for thatching and for insulation, too. An effective poultice could be made of corn mush, and corn whiskey made good liniment and provided consolation when all else failed. Corn cobs, of course, were the meerschaums of the frontier.[24]

Maize was part or the whole of every day's meals for the first settlers and pioneers. Four and five-eights inches of the index of *The American Heritage Cookbook* (1964) are devoted to maize recipes.[25] As corn on the cob, mush, hominy, Johnny cake, dodgers, pone, hoecake, ashcake, fritters, cracklin' bread, spoon bread, spider corncake, Indian pudding, hasty pudding, chowder, biscuits, dumplings, hush puppies, beer, mountain dew, white lightning, and bourbon, maize was the American staple for two and a half centuries or more, depending on the area considered. John Winthrop wrote from Connecticut in the 1680s that it had been the usual diet of "first Planters in these Parts," and was still a common food. A half-century later, Peter Kalm recorded that while "traveling in America one sees miles of nothing but maize fields." He himself ate bread of maize or of maize mixed with rye almost exclusively during his first winter in North America. The first "corn belt" in the history of European North America ran from the upper St. Lawrence River to the Florida Straits. The second began extending westward from the frontier of Virginia and the Carolinas into Kentucky and Tennessee in the 1770s and 1780s. In the early 1800s, the third and greatest began its spread from Ohio west through Indiana and Illinois, eventually crossing the Mississippi to encompass all of Iowa and large parts of Missouri, Kansas, Nebraska, South Dakota, Minnesota, and Michigan. According to the 1850 census, maize production in the United States exceeded wheat production by a ratio of six to one in bulk and three to one in value. Where maize was not the most important cash crop, it was usually the most important food crop for local consumption. In 1849 in the South, where cotton was king, 5 million acres were under cotton, and 18 million under maize.

In the first seven to ten generations or so of the European settlements north of the Rio Grande, maize was the primary or at the least the secondary staple in the diet of the great mass of people except for those living in the most northerly latitudes or for the most wealthy and stubbornly European. In Maryland the aristocracy ate "hardly any other bread." Across the Potomac the staples of the weekly diet of George Washington's slaves consisted of about 3 pounds of fish and meat and 11.3 pounds of cornmeal.[26]

The measure of the significance of maize in early North American history was taken more accurately by contemporary observers than we can manage ourselves. John Lawson flatly stated that "had it not been for the Fruitfulness of this Species, it would have proved very difficult to have settled some of the Plantations in America." Peter Kalm said, "If maize were not available for planting, the inhabitants would find it difficult to live in New Jersey. . . ." Count Rumford (Benjamin Thompson), a Yankee loyalist and scientist who emigrated to Europe during the Revolution, maintained his admiration—shall we call it nostalgia?—for maize. He claimed it was more nourishing than rice, called it of all foods "beyond comparison the most nourishing, cheapest, and most wholesome that can be procured for feeding the poor," and wrote a veritable treatise on it, with recipes. William Cobbett ("Peter Porcupine"), the English radical and agricultural expert who fled to America and farmed in New York in the second decade of the nineteenth century, was of the opinion that without Indian corn the settlers of the thirteen colonies would never have been able to raise up "a powerful nation." Maize was, he proclaimed, not only the greatest blessing of the United States, but "the greatest blessing God ever gave to man."[27]

Eaters of wheat and rice might disagree, but there is a good case to be made that Cobbett was right about the United States and maize. Benjamin Franklin rightly advised starry-eyed immigrants that America was not a land "where the fowls fly about already roasted, crying, *Come eat me!*"[28] but it was undeniably a land in which young and fertile people had access to cheap land, and possessed, in the maize plant, a means to secure wholesome nourishment for themselves and their progeny easily and quickly.

The resulting runaway increase in the number of colonists frightened Thomas Malthus, an Englishman, into writing his grim *Essay on the Principle of Population,* the point of which Americans have often been unable to quite comprehend.[29] In the 1790s, Malthus, ensconced in a Europe where land was dear and hunger common, and where the chief crops, the grudgingly productive small grains, required greater inputs of energy and skill than the Amerindian staples, looked across the Atlantic to an amazing country where maize ruled and famine was "almost impossible." That seemingly desirable state of affairs had the paradoxical effect of confirming him in his pessimistic conviction that only a minority of humanity could ever be truly prosperous. He took the rate of natural increase of the people of the thirteen colonies in the middle decades of the eighteenth century, particularly of the northern colonies, as the rate at which any population would expand under conditions of plentiful food and prosperity. Such procreative powers would, he was sure, always and inevitably outstrip the power of humanity to provide itself with nourishment. Therefore, a thousand years would never see lower classes in general attain the material bliss enjoyed by the common folk of the northern half of the thirteen colonies of the generation right before the Revolution.[30]

In contrast, the Americans themselves—who lived in a continent where land was cheap and swayed with maize, its prodigal consort— saw a profoundly optimistic lesson in their demography, one that helped persuade them to seize control of their own destiny (and, soon, the destinies of others). At the beginning of the fateful year of 1775, Edward Wigglesworth of Cambridge, Massachusetts, published "Calculations on American Population," reaffirming Franklin's estimate that British Americans were doubling every quarter-century. He predicted on the basis of the simple mathematics of compound interest that in seventy years British Americans would outnumber the inhabitants of the entire British Isles. ("Happily had it been for America," he noted, "if its present contest with the parent state had been postponed to the middle of the next century! And more happy still had it always slept in silence!" He was not a fire-eating revolutionary, but the Hollis Professor of Divinity at Harvard.)

Like Franklin, Wigglesworth credited the Americans' current rate of natural increase to the availability of cheap land and, as well, to the admirable qualities the settlers, who, "amidst all the difficulties they had to encounter, have been able in so short a period to put a face entirely new on all the country extended from Nova Scotia to Georgia, by changing the forest into a fruitful field."[31] In large part, the period to which he referred was as short as it was because the field to which he referred was in the great mass of its extent planted with American Indian maize.

It was the productivity of the land and maize in both food and people that encouraged John Adams, America's first minister to Great

Britain, to announce in 1786, a gloomy year for his kitten-helpless republic:

> The Americans are, at this day, a great people, and are not to be trifled with. Their numbers have increased fifty percent since 1774. A people that can multiply at this rate, amidst all the calamities of such a war of eight years, will, in twenty years more, be too respectable to want friends. They might sell their friend-ship, at this time, at a very high price to others. . . .[32]

A decade later, the same vigor inspired George Washington to include in his Farewell Address one of those peculiarly American anticipatory boasts: "the period is not far off when we may defy material injury from external annoyance . . . when we may choose peace or war, as our interest, guided by justice, shall counsel."[33] The census of 1800 confirmed Franklin's half-century-old estimation of the doubling rate of Americans, emboldening Jefferson to include in his First Annual Message to Congress a classic statement of American confidence, self-satisfaction, and self-righteousness. "We contemplate," he wrote,

> this rapid growth, and the prospect it holds up to us, not with a view to the injuries it may enable us to do to others in some future day, but to the settlement of the extensive country still remaining vacant within our limits, to the multiplications of men susceptible to happiness, educated in the love of order, habituated to self-government, and valuing its blessings above all price.[34]

You and I live in a different world from that of the Founding Fathers of the first American republic, a world in which commercial hyperbole and political propaganda have dulled our sensitivity to language. We yearn for quantitative measurement—numbers—to fortify the statements of Franklin, Adams, Washington, and Jefferson, however clear their words may once have been in themselves. What was the *magnitude* of the growth these men anticipated so fervently that they could use the future tense as if it were the present tense? In 1775 Professor Edward Wigglesworth bequeathed us such a measurement, his prediction of how many American citizens there would be in the year 2000: "At that time, should their future population [increase] be as rapid as their past, the Americans would amount to ONE THOUSAND TWO-HUNDRED AND EIGHTY MILLIONS!"[35]—that is,

1.28 billion, or about the same as the population of the Peoples' Republic of China, as estimated in 1990, a billion and a quarter Americans presumably well fed, prosperous, materialistic, optimistic, obsessed with the main chance, and, to take us back again to Billy Porterfield and the *Austin American-Statesman,* "too concerned with Heaven on earth to genuflect to the prophets of other realities."

Notes

1. *Austin American-Statesman,* April 13, 1990, B1.
2. Alice H. Jones, *American Colonial Wealth: Documents and Methods* (New York: Arno Press, 1977), 3:1765–66.
3. Leonard W. Labaree, ed., *The Papers of Benjamin Franklin* (New Haven: Yale University Press, 1961), 4:226, 228, 233.
4. Charles Francis Adams, ed., *The Works of John Adams* (Little, Brown, 1852), 7:273.
5. Ansley J. Coale and Melvin Zelnik, *New Estimates of Fertility and Population in the United States* (Princeton: Princeton University Press, 1963), 34–37; Daniel S. Smith, "The Demographic History of Colonial New England," in *Studies in American Historical Demography,* ed. Maris A. Vinovskis (New York: Academic Press, 1979), 27; Robert V. Wells, *Uncle Sam's Family: Issues in and Perspectives on American Demographic History* (Albany: State University of New York Press, 1985), 28–29.
6. Philip J. Greven, Jr., "The Average Size of Families and Households in the Province of Massachusetts in 1764 and in the United States in 1790: An Overview," in *Household and Family in Past Time,* ed. Peter Laslett and Richard Wall (Cambridge: Cambridge University Press, 1972), 556, 559; Smith, "The Demographic History of Colonial New England," 39; John Demos, "Notes on Life in Plymouth Colony," in *Studies in American Historical Demography,* 53–54; Nancy Osterud and John Fulton, "Family Limitation and Age at Marriage: Fertility Decline in Sturbridge, Massachusetts, 1730–1850," in *Studies in American Historical Demography,* 401; Yasukichi Yasuba, *Birth Rates of the White Population in the United States, 1800–1860* (Baltimore: Johns Hopkins Press, 1962), 71.
7. John Lawson, *A New Voyage to Carolina* (Chester, VT: Readex Microprint, 1966), 84.
8. L.H. Butterfield, ed., *Letters of Benjamin Rush* (Princeton: Princeton University Press, 1951), 1:405.
9. John Modell, "Family and Fertility on the Indian Frontier, 1820," in *Studies in American Historical Demography,* 413–14; James E. Davis, *Frontier America, 1800–1840: A Comparative Demographic Analysis of the Settlement Process* (Glendale, Calif.: Arthur H. Clark Co., 1977), 53; Yasukichi Yasuba, *Birth Rates of the White Population,* 50–53, 64–65, 70.
10. Labaree, ed., *The Papers of Benjamin Franklin,* 4:228.
11. Edward B. Espenshade, Jr., and Joel L. Morrison, eds., *Goode's World Atlas,* 14th ed. (Chicago: Rand McNally, 1974), 10, 20.

12. D.B. Grigg, *The Agricultural Systems of the World: An Evolutionary Approach* (Cambridge: Cambridge University Press, 1974), 158–68; Lynn White, Jr., *Medieval Technology and Social Change* (London: Oxford University Press, 1962), 41–78; see also Edward Hyams, *Soil and Civilization* (New York: Harper & Row, 1976), 230–72; Graeme Barker, *Prehistoric Farming in Europe* (Cambridge: Cambridge University Press, 1985), 44–46.

13. Carl O. Sauer, "The Settlement of the Humid East," *Climate and Man: 1941 Yearbook of Agriculture* (Washington, D.C.: United States Department of Agriculture, 1941), 158–59, 161, 163–66, 276–78; Grigg, *Agricultural Systems,* 179–80; Lawson, *A New Voyage to Carolina,* 75.

14. William Bradford, *Of Plymouth Plantation, 1620–1647,* ed. Samuel Eliot Morison (New York: Alfred A. Knopf, 1963), 65, 144–45.

15. Lawson, *New Voyage to Carolina,* 75.

16. Adolph B. Benson, ed., *Peter Kalm's Travels in North America, the English Version of 1770* (New York: Dover Publications, 1987), 335; "Peter Kalm's Description of Maize, How It Is Planted and Cultivated in North America, Together with the Many Uses of this Crop Plant," *Agricultural History* 9 (April 1935): 109; Lawson, *A New Voyage to Carolina,* 75. See also Durand of Dauphiné, *A Huguenot Exile in Virginia,* ed. Gilbert Chinard (New York: The Press of the Pioneers, 1934); William Oliver, *Eight Months in Illinois* (Chester, VT: Readex Microprint Corp., 1966), 39; David Thomas, *Travels through the Western Country in the Summer of 1816* (Darien, Conn.: Hafner Publishing Co., 1970), 229.

17. Stuart J. Fiedel, *Prehistory of the Americas* (Cambridge: Cambridge University Press, 1987), 110.

18. Benson, ed., *Peter Kalm's Travels,* 89.

19. Lawson, *A New Voyage to Carolina,* 75; ibid., 89; John Winthrop, "The Description, Culture, and Use of Maiz," *Philosophical Transactions of the Royal Society of London* 12 (1678): 1065.

20. "Peter Kalm's Description," 102–3; Winthrop, "The Description, Culture, and Use of Maiz," 1065; *Cadwallader Colden Papers, 3, Collections of the New-York Historical Society for the Year 1919,* 52:90; Cadwallader Colden, "Plantae Coldenghamie in Provincia Noveboracensi Americes," *Acta Societatis Regiae Scientiarum Upsaliensis* [Stockholm] 5 (1744–50): 76–77. See also Joseph Nesta Ewan and Nesta Ewan, *John Banister and His Natural History of Virginia, 1678–1692* (Urbana: University of Illinois Press, 1970), 40–41, 357; Luigi Castiglioni Viaggio, *Travels in the United States of North America, 1785–87,* trans. Antonio Pace (Syracuse: Syracuse University Press, 1983), 52.

21. Citations of this can be found in most of the early documents of the English colonies, and of the others in North America, as well. For instance, see P. de Charlevoix, *Journal d'un Voyage Fait par Ordre du Roi dans l'Amerique Septentrionnale* (Paris: Chez Rollin Fils, 1744), 6:45–46.

22. Sauer, "Settlement of the Humid East," 160–61; "Peter Kalm's Description," 104–7; Winthrop, "The Description, Culture, and Use of Maiz," 1066–67; Benson, ed., *Peter Kalm's Travels,* 89; Nicholas P. Hardeman, *Shucks, Shocks, and Hominey Blocks: Corn as a Way of Life in Pioneer America* (Baton Rouge: Louisiana State University Press, 1981), 9, 36, 50, 58, 62; Durand, *A Huguenot in Exile,* 117.

23. Lawson, *New Voyage to Carolina,* 75.

24. "Peter Kalm's Description," 110, 114, 116; Winthrop, "The Description, Culture, and Use of Maiz," 1067; Hardeman, *Shucks, Shocks*, 139, 175, 177, 182; Oliver, *Eight Months*, 39, 40.

25. *The American Heritage Cookbook* (New York: American Heritage Press, 1964), index.

26. "Peter Kalm's Description," 110–14; Winthrop, "The Description, Culture, and Use of Maiz," 1067, 1068; Hardeman, *Shucks, Shocks*, 4, 20–23, 138–39, 143, 160, 168; *Historical Statistics of the United States, Colonial Times to 1970* (Washington, D.C.: U.S. Department of Commerce, 1975), 2:1175. For more on maize and the South, see Sam Bowers Hilliard, *Hog Meat and Hoecake: Food Supply in the Old South, 1840–1860* (Carbondale: Southern Illinois University Press, 1972).

27. Lawson, *A New Voyage to Carolina*, 75; "Peter Kalm's Description," 105; Sanborn C. Brown, ed., *Collected Works of Count Rumford* (Cambridge: Harvard University Press, 1970), 217, 218; Hardeman, *Shucks, Shocks*, 2.

28. Stanley N. Worton, *Population Growth in America* (Rochelle Park, N.J.: Hayden Book Co., 1976), 53.

29. Conway Zirkle, "Benjamin Franklin, Thomas Malthus and the United States Census," *Isis* 42 (March 1957): 58–62. For an example of American obtuseness, see Gaillard Hunt, ed., *The Writings of James Madison* (New York: G.P. Putnam's Sons, 1910), 9:168–71.

30. Thomas Malthus, *An Essay on the Principle of Population and a Summary View of the Principle of Population* (Harmondsworth: Penguin Books, 1982), 74, 105–6, 116, 172.

31. Robert V. Wells, *The Population of the British Colonies in America before 1776* (Princeton: Princeton University Press, 1975), 285; Josiah Quincy, *The History of Harvard* (Cambridge: John Owen, 1840), 2:261–62; "Wigglesworth, Edward," *Dictionary of American Biography*, ed. Dumas Malone (New York: Charles Scribner's Sons, 1936), 10:192–93; Edward Wigglesworth, *Calculations on American Population* (Boston: John Boyle, 1775), passim.

32. Adams, ed., *The Works of John Adams*, 8:385.

33. Henry Steele Commager, ed., *Documents of American History* (New York: Appleton-Century-Crofts, 1949), 1:174.

34. Merrill D. Peterson, ed., *The Portable Thomas Jefferson* (New York: Viking Press, 1975), 300.

35. Wigglesworth, *Calculations on American Population*, 23.

11 REASSESSING 1492

Twenty-odd years ago I finished a book on the impact of the Columbian voyages on the peoples of the world, a book which I hoped would attract enough buyers so that the publisher would at least break even and I would keep my job as a historian.[1] I had a hard time finding a publisher, and almost gave up on the book before Greenwood Press spontaneously wrote me to ask if I had anything publishable on hand. The trouble I had before Greenwood's query clearly indicated that most people who were experienced with what the reading public wanted to read and with what the scholarly community would accept as possibly valid were of the opinion that my book was neither. Greenwood took a chance on me, and to the delight of Greenwood and myself, the book sold and continues to sell, modestly but steadily, for a total of over 80,000 copies so far.

The chief market has been academic. It has been professors of anthropology and American history who have assigned the book to their classes, as one would expect, considering its subject matter; but a few years ago I met someone who was using the book at the University of Wisconsin for a seminar on the history of the concept of progress. I asked him what in the world my book had to do with progress, and he answered, "Oh, I assign it at the end of my course as an illustration of the death of belief in progress."

That shocked me, so I went back and, for the first time in many years, looked at the book—my book!—which, to my knowledge, had nothing to do with progress, pro or con. The last paragraph reads, "The Columbian exchange has left us with not a richer but a more impoverished genetic pool. We, all of the life on this planet, are the less for

Columbus, and the impoverishment will increase." I have to admit that is a bit dreary. I am, as a Euro-American, shocked at the self-laceration implicit in those two sentences, and I am inclined to blame (or credit) some of that to the anger and disillusionment of the 1960s, when they were written. But I am also sure that they are a product of more than ephemeral attitudes because the book keeps selling, though the long-hairs who earned their degrees in that period have long since cut their hair and are at present worrying about their waistlines.

My dour view of the biological side of European imperialism is, of course, not popular with the mass public and certainly does not express what European and Euro-American politicians traditionally proclaim on Columbus Day. Yet as I look around at a rising tide of gloomy articles and books on Amerindian demography, on the rate of suicide among Amerindian adolescents and young adults, and on the rate of New World species extinctions, I am strengthened in my belief that I was, two decades ago, mouthing attitudes characteristic of a rising *zeitgeist,* as the University of Wisconsin professor suggested. (Apropos, the de rigueur scholarly title for the most important event of 1492 is no longer "Columbus-discovered-America." That event is now the "Encounter," with all that word's connotations of equality between the participants, unpredictable results, and, quite possibly, of injurious collision.)

The old Columbian paradigm of purposeful discovery engendering new and healthy societies provided a setting that was satisfactory to most scholars, as well as to the general public, satisfactory all the way from the time of Cortés's secretary, Francisco López de Gómara, to that of Samuel Eliot Morison. López de Gómara ranked the European discovery of the Americas as one of the two best things to happen since Creation, the other being the Incarnation of the Savior.[2] Four hundred years after López de Gómara, Morison ended his magnificent *European Discovery of America* thus: "To the people of the New World, pagans expecting short and brutish lives, void of hope for any future, had come the Christian vision of a merciful God and a glorious Heaven."[3] How did we get from that to our current assessment of the Encounter as, in Francis Jennings's words, *The Invasion of America,* or, as Russell Thornton has entitled his book, *The American Indian Holocaust?* Revision with a vengeance is afoot, and the new historians are not taking prisoners.

What is the source of the new *zeitgeist?* New data? In part, yes, but new questions have had more impact than new information. What inspired the new questions? Many things, of course: Marxism, and the not entirely unfounded claim that the capitalism of the First World survives by exploiting the Third World; the end of the European empires; the revival of China; the rise of what Mexicans call *indigenismo,* with its North American proponents like Russell Means. These are obvious sources, but let me offer the thought that an underrated factor behind our reassessment of the Encounter is a general reassessment of the role of rapid change, even catastrophe, in the history of humanity, the earth, and the universe.

At the beginning of our century, Karl Kautsky achieved one of those annoying Marxist insights, an oversimplification, yes, but a thorn that sinks too deep to ignore:

> While the bourgeoisie were still revolutionary, the catastrophic theory still ruled in natural science (geology and biology). This theory proceeded from the premise that natural development came through great sudden leaps. Once the capitalist revolution was ended, the place of the catastrophic theory was taken by the hypothesis of a gradual imperceptible development, proceeding by the accumulation of countless little advances and adjustments in a competitive struggle. To the revolutionary bourgeoisie the thought of catastrophes in nature was very acceptable, but to the conservative bourgeoisie these ideas appeared irrational and unnatural.[4]

The intellectual leaders of the eighteenth century dabbled heavily in radical theory and even in actual revolution, but for more than a century afterward, from Napoleon to, if you will, Calvin Coolidge, the ideas of most of their successors harmonized with the tempered views of what the most "successful" people in the world—that is to say, the middle and upper classes of western Europe and North America— believed to be normal and natural. Ironically, the successes of these classes were in large part the result of such violent events as the American Revolution, the French Revolution, and—above all—the anomic acceleration of the Industrial Revolution. But abrupt change was not a concept with which they, in the presence of the discontented and dispossessed, were happy. Jacobins, Chartists, Socialists, Molly Maguires, Ghost Dancers—even such moderate types as Populists and trade unionists—struck them as demanding rapid, disconcerting, and therefore unnatural, destructive, and sterile change. No wonder so many of the finest minds of the ruling classes (among the finest any group has ever produced) gloried in slow, slow change. No wonder Charles Lyell and Charles Darwin "discovered" that the present world and its inhabitants were not, as Georges Cuvier and his follower, the retroverse Louis Agassiz of Harvard, claimed, the products of multiple beginnings divided and punctuated by abrupt transformations (a theory called, too sensationally, catastrophism), but of majestically slow and steady change. Lyell, the geologist, called his version of the new paradigm uniformitarianism, according to which changes in the crust of the earth were driven by the stately forces of tectonic uplift and erosion. Darwin's version was biological evolution, driven by what Herbert Spencer, the philosopher par excellence of Victorian capitalism, preceded him in calling "the survival of the fittest," an admittedly nasty but slow and steady business.

"Steady as she goes," the oft repeated command of the sailor who does not want to capsize, was the slogan of most of the best minds of the nineteenth century. Then came the incorrigible twentieth century: the two worst wars in history; the worst depression in history; the instantaneous demise of empires and dynasties that had seemed immortal; the two most enormous revolutions, Russian and Chinese, in history; bombs more destructive than Jules Verne had ever begun to imagine; slaughters so vast that we have been obliged to invent a new word—genocide. Atomic war, followed by nuclear winter, and the extinction of most species became a talk show topic. The thinning ozone layer and the greenhouse effect ride tandem through our nightmares. Rapid, massive, and not necessarily benign change has crashed back into our minds as a crucial factor in our lives, societies, world, and universe.

Catastrophism—that is, large-scale change within narrow time limits—was in its dotage by the time of Cuvier's death 150 years ago, and was supposedly dealt the coup de grace by Darwin's *Origin of Species* in 1859. But it is back, thanks to Stalin, Hitler, Pol Pot, Einstein, Fermi, Oppenheimer, and others of similar views on the possibilities of violence in society and physics. The "Big Bang" has usurped "steady state" among cosmologists. Astronomers commonly talk about galaxies in collision, and astronomers, geologists, and paleontologists gather together to confer about asteroids and comets raining down on earth every 26 million years or so, wiping out most species, and thus providing room for a Cuvieresque surge of speciation.

Abrupt change is back as a respectable concept. Thomas Kuhn and Michel Foucault have recommended looking not for slow and steady growth in the history of science, but for sudden flip-flops in the way scientists view their subject matter. Even the paleontologists, who owe so much to Lyell and Darwin, are assessing catastrophism in a new version called punctuated equilibrium.[5]

The rapidity and magnitude of change in our century has prepared us to ask new questions about history and, specifically, about the Encounter of Amerindians, Europeans, and Africans. I think ours are better questions than were asked a century ago, simply because we are equipped by our twentieth-century lifetimes to see and recognize changes as great as those that the Encounter unquestionably did cause. A century and a half ago William Prescott of Boston, Massachusetts, carefully examined all the sources on the Spanish conquests of Mexico and Peru that he could find. He read the same primary reports as we read on the smallpox pandemic that accompanied Cortés in Mexico and preceded Pizarro into Peru, killing many, many thousands of Amerindians, and yet Prescott granted smallpox oblique mention in only a few paragraphs. He lived in a society troubled with infectious diseases, but not massively endangered by them. The Black Death had disappeared from western Europe more than a century before and, as far as he knew, had never appeared in America. Yellow fever had disappeared from the northern states of his country while he was a young man. The American sanitationists were bewildered by the appearance of cholera in the 1830s, but were still optimistic about controlling future epidemics of whatever kind by means of techniques immediately at hand and easily understood. Smallpox was circulating, but many Bostonians were effectively defending themselves against that infection by means of vaccination, a technique discovered by Dr. Edward Jenner about the same time Prescott was born. Let me propose that Prescott simply was not equipped to "see," so to speak, what the primary sources had to say about smallpox and the conquest of the great Amerindian empires. We, on the other hand, have written and read a great deal of demographic and related epidemiological history in the 140 years since Prescott wrote about Montezuma and Atahualpa, and AIDS has recently snatched away the rose-colored glasses we inherited from our parents and ground them beneath its heel.

Our predecessors among Euro-American scholars believed that

1492 was an extremely important year. Those who lived and wrote north of the Rio Grande tended to believe that representative government, the United States Declaration of Independence, and the British North American Act became probabilities in that year. The Euro-Americans south of the Rio Grande, the Creoles, had similar beliefs pertaining to their several national histories. Amerindians and blacks probably held different views—their lives did not leave them much time for academic opinions—but we know little about their thoughts. The one characteristic shared by all the traditional assessments of 1492 is that they were ethnocentric and speciescentric, and, therefore, far underestimated the true significance of the Encounter.

The significance of the Encounter towers above the origins of this or that kind of government or even the fate of this or that group of humans. The Encounter marks one of the major discontinuities in the course of life on this planet. The measuring of its influence requires reference to a scale of time far greater than historians or archeologists normally consult, that is, reference to the "deep time" discovered by the great geologists, biologists, and thinkers of the eighteenth and nineteenth centuries.[6] To find changes comparable to those wrought by Columbus and friends we have to go back beyond recorded time to the divisions between the periods of geological history. These were characterized by great geological changes—the meeting or separation of continents, the rising up of mountains, the draining or filling of inland seas—and sometimes by large numbers of extinctions and the proliferation of new species.

Of course, Columbus brought about no geological or oceanographic changes de jure, but did he not do so in a de facto sense? He reversed millions of years of continental drift by bringing continents back together again. To illustrate: horses originated in the New World and died out there, but before they did, they migrated to the Old World via a land connection between Alaska and Siberia which the accumulation of water as ice in the great continental glaciers had left bare. Columbus brought horses back from the old to the new not via a land bridge, but on shipboard, and they have propagated in the New World by the tens of millions. How was the latter sailorly transfer different in effect from the transfers of horses and various other creatures via the several land connections of Siberia and Alaska in the deep past?

The rate of extinctions of species in the Americas has speeded up considerably since 1492, and so has the advent in the Americas of new species, that is, the arrival and proliferation here of Eurasian and African species. How do these events, as a practical matter, differ in kind from what happened at the end of the Cretaceous or other geological "moments" of rapid change in the deep past? The driving force of the post-1492 changes happens not to be continental drift or the advance and retreat of glaciers or the impact of comets, but only the actions of one species, *Homo sapiens;* but the actual result is much the same: extinctions and vast changes in the distribution of life forms. In time, providing we have time, there will truly be new species—descendants, in a manner of speaking, of Christopher Columbus.

Let me describe a geological moment of extreme discontinuity in the deep past to which we may want to refer when measuring the full significance of the Encounter. About 220 million years ago, at the end of the Permian Period, there was a great die-off, perhaps the greatest of all time. Nearly one-half of the known families of animals disappeared, including 75 percent of the amphibians and 80 percent of the reptiles. The cause for the die-off was perhaps something like a rain of comets or the arrival of an asteroid, but such deus ex machina devices are still a matter of speculation and research.[7] What did happen, we are certain, was that the several large continents united to form a supercontinent, which the geologists call Pangaea. Paleontologists propose that massive event as the cause, at least in part, of the extinctions: "As the elements of the supercontinent were assembled, these separate biota from each element were forced into competition. The number of sets of niches was drastically reduced and many species must have become extinct from competitive exclusion."[8] Surely we can interpret what Columbus and the sailors of Europe started in the fifteenth century in much the same way. They drew the continents together and their successors are continuing to do so, lately with the assistance of aviators, to produce what is not geographically, but certainly is politically, socially, economically, botanically, zoologically, and bacteriologically a supercontinent. Peru and Chad, for instance, are "closer" together today via human transportation systems than they were when those lands were parts of continents that were actually fused together.

The changes in the biota of our new, cobbled-together Columbian supercontinent have been enormous, despite the brief duration of its existence. It is unlikely that so much of the world's land surface and waters, and its flora and fauna, macro and micro, have ever been altered so abruptly before, unless indeed we have had cataclysmic visitations of asteroids or comets. The effects on human society certainly have been proportionally as vast. The coming together of the continents was a prerequisite for the population explosion of the past two centuries, and certainly played an important role in the Industrial Revolution. The transfer across the oceans of the staple food crops of the Old and New Worlds made possible the former. (Please note that I said "made possible," not "caused.") The enormous accession of capital gained by Midas Europe through its domination of the Americas supplied quantities of capital as fuel for the Industrial Revolution. The relative numbers of the various divisions of the world's human population have drastically altered, with Amerindians plummeting in relation to Euro- and Afro-Americans, and there have been similar changes among other species. To mention just one, in North America there were once 60 million buffalo; there are now 100 million cattle. The frighteningly large number of species extinctions in our era is nothing to compare with the Permian die-off, of course, but before we take comfort from that, we must realize that the full effects of the Encounter have not yet materialized.

Let me anticipate criticism by admitting that tens of thousands of years must pass before the Permian die-off and the Encounter can be usefully compared. My point is not the comparison per se, which is admittedly dizzyingly premature. My primary subject and my argument's point pertain to the Encounter. I propose that its impact has been and is so massive that we should consider it with the same kind of awe and sense of scale as we do events connected with the endings and beginnings of the geological periods and eras, and their influence on the direction of evolution on the planet. We must step back from the specific happenings of 1492 and such trivia as the exact identification of Columbus's first American landfall. We need to look upon the changes that he initiated with the same consciousness of their manifold consequences as we do the changes associated with the end of the Permian. Otherwise, we will lose sight of the forest for the trees, or—following my own advice about scale and utilizing an image proportionate to the subject—we will lose sight of the biosphere for the photo opportunities.

As our ancestors learned more and more about history, filling in gaps, pushing further and further back from the present, they were obliged to expand their concept of time and to "re-periodize" the past. They have needed chronological systems that enable them to estimate with some accuracy how long it took Middle Easterners to invent the alphabet after they invented cuneiform, and to discern what was going on in China when—to choose an obvious example—Columbus first crossed the Atlantic. They have needed chronological systems that enable them to date events that happened eons before the earliest human record.

In the first centuries of the Christian era, Europeans still dated time according to such ephemera as the reigns of kings and magistrates, and such trivia as the founding of Rome. For instance, the Synod of Hatfield (A.D. 680) took place in England "in the tenth year of the reign of our most devout lord Egfrid, King of the Northumbrians; in the sixth year of the King Ethelfrid of the Mercians; in the seventeenth year of King Aldwulf of the East Angles; in the seventh year of King Hlothere of the Kentish people." [9]

As the centuries and events accumulated after God's entry into time, the Incarnation, Christians came to realize that they, as a body of believers, needed a way to count time since and in relation to that event. During the waning of the Roman Empire and the early Middle Ages, Dionysius Exiguus and the Venerable Bede devised a new system of chronology, dating events from the Incarnation, that is, A.D. *(anno domini)*. Their system finally caught on in the eleventh century, and we have been using it ever since. It only applies to A.D., but medieval Europeans knew very little about events before the year 1. During the Renaissance, literary and historical scholarship revived in Europe, and archeology was born. By Columbus's lifetime, the literate classes of Europe knew more about the centuries prior to the Incarnation than Dionysius Exiguus and Bede had known about those after it. An extension backward of the A.D. system was necessary, and, in the early seventeenth century the Jesuit Domenicus Petavius, a contemporary of Galileo and Kepler, brought to its final form the Before Christ or B.C. system.[10] The B.C.–A.D. system is one that devout Christians find very easy to justify, for obvious reasons, and the rest of us all over the world have accepted it for its convenience. We sometimes strip it of its religious elements, substituting B.C.E. and C.E. (Before Common Era and Common Era) for B.C. and A.D., but even so we pay our respects to the ancient Christian problems of coping with time sacralized by the birth of God and growing ever longer and deeper whenever we cite a year numerically.

Let me suggest that the Encounter was as important in the history of material life as Christians claim the Incarnation was for spiritual life. Amerindians had no hesitation in realizing they were the prime victims of the Encounter, and found the experience unprecedented and full of agony. In the seventeenth century the Peruvian Amerindian Felipe Guamán Poma de Ayala called it a *pachacuti,* by which he meant a catastrophe, in spite of his probably sincere Christianity. He referred to the social order and the course of events that followed the catastrophe as *el mundo al revés*—"the world upside down."[11] The benefactors of the Encounter have viewed it approvingly and have been inclined to consider it as perhaps the most important event in the working out of the Manifest Destiny of Western Civilization, but not as a major disjunction in the history of the planet. To that extent they have missed its significance, and their system of periodizing history is inadequate. Historians would be justified by the evidence and the requirements of their craft if they invented a B.C.–A.C. system (Before Columbus, After Columbus) and imposed it on the rest of humanity. That, however, would lead to fighting in the streets, as did the accurate and reasonable calendar offered to Christendom by Pope Gregory XIII a century after the Encounter. But do let me suggest—no, insist—that we should endeavor to *think* in a Before and After Columbus fashion. The Encounter may have been the most influential event on this planet since the retreat of the continental glaciers, and we must pay it its proper due.

Notes

1. Alfred W. Crosby, *The Columbian Exchange: Biological and Cultural Consequences of 1492* (Westport, Conn., 1972). See also Crosby, *Ecological Imperialism: The Biological Expansion of Europe, 900–1900* (Cambridge University Press, 1986).

2. Francisco López de Gómara, *Historia General de las Indias y Vida de Hernán Cortés* (Caracas, n.d.), 1:7.

3. Samuel Eliot Morison, *The European Discovery of America: The Southern Voyages, 1492–1616* (New York, 1974), 737.

4. Karl Kautsky, *The Social Revolution,* trans. A. M. Simons and May Wood Simons (Chicago, 1903), 12. See also Stephen Jay Gould, "Toward the Vindication of Punctuational Change," in *Catastrophism and Earth History: The New Uniformitarianism,* ed. W.A. Berggren and John Van Couvering (Princeton, 1984), 27–29.

5. Gould, "Toward the Vindication," 9–34; Barry Cooper, *Michel Foucault: An Introduction to the Study of his Thought* (New York, 1981), 3.

6. Paolo Rossi, *The Dark Abyss of Time* (Chicago, 1984).

7. Ben Patrusky, "Mass Extinctions: The Biological Side," *Mosaic* 17 (Winter 1986–87): 213.

8. Don L. Eicher, A. Lee McAlester, and Marcia L. Rottman, *The History of the Earth's Crust* (Englewood Cliffs, 1984), 116–17. See also William Lee Stokes, *Essentials of Earth History* (Englewood Cliffs, 1982), 503.

9. Bede, *A History of the English Church and People*, trans. Leo Sherley-Price (Harmondsworth, 1968), 234.

10. Donald J. Wilcox, *The Measure of Times Past: Pre-Newtonian Chronologies and the Rhetoric of Relative Time* (Chicago, 1987), 207.

11. Sabine MacCormack, "*Pachacuti:* Miracles, Punishments, and Last Judgment: Visionary Past and Prophetic Future in Early Colonial Peru," *American Historical Review* 93 (October 1988): 966, 968, 981, 987; see also Rolena Adorno, ed., *From Oral to Written Expression: Native Andean Chronicles of the Early Colonial Period* (Syracuse, 1982); Rolena Adorno, *Guaman Poma: Writing and Resistance in Colonial Peru* (Austin, 1986).

12 LIFE (WITH ALL ITS PROBLEMS) IN SPACE

We have crossed oceans and both benefited and suffered the consequences. Now we stand on the brink of space. What will be the consequences of the next manifestation of humanity's propensity for travel?

The most dangerous enemy of humans beyond Earth's atmosphere and beyond the moon's orbit will be in the long term the implacably hostile environment. It will be a problem for engineers, and their record thus far suggests that although there will be a few awful accidents, there will be very few. The next most dangerous enemy in space in the immediately foreseeable future will be humans themselves and the irrepressible organisms they will carry with them.

Engineers are successful because they apply their skills to quantitatively predictable phenomena. Ecologists, zoologists, botanists, and epidemiologists are not so successful, because they deal with life, which grows, changes, declines, plunges to extinction, scrambles for survival, and rises and plays the phoenix again and again on a merry-go-round that spins in all four dimensions and on a varying number of axles all at the same time. Space engineers are well prepared for their tasks, but not so the space ecologists. In fact, are there any scientists specializing in what will happen to life forms in the hermetic hermitages of space?

Let us begin with kindergarten ecology. An ecosystem is an active collection of interdependent organisms. They depend on one another for food and shelter and much more. Ultimately, all organisms within a given system are in symbiotic relationship. They depend largely on one another even for death, which is so necessary to the continued health of the system.

Species, such as humans, crabgrass, and tobacco mosaic viruses, reproduce many times more than are needed to simply replace the parents numerically. Every ecosystem is in danger of being smothered by the reproductive excesses of its members, but is usually saved from this fate by the appetites of its members—that is, the participating organisms obligingly eat up each other's excessive offspring.

Each ecosystem (and, by extension, each world) is a matter of shifting balances among its participants. Each ecosystem is rather like a tightrope walker: his pole wags up and down, but the walker is stable. He is in a state of what biologists call homeostasis, or what poets, addicted to conceits, might call dynamic stasis. He continually readjusts his balance to stay balanced.

What happens when two tightrope walkers touch or ever so slightly interfere with the serene bobbing of each other's poles? They fall or regain balance only by violent exertion. What will happen when bands of humans and associated life forms, separated in space long enough to establish independent states of homeostasis—perhaps even long enough to start down separate paths of speciation—contact one another?

We are getting too abstract. Let us approach this problem from another angle. An individual organism does not exist in space and time in general, but in a specific place at a specific time. It does not exist in the long run; it exists in the short run. Any period longer than that is simply a series of short runs. Within a specific short run, it works out a specific modus vivendi in a specific environment with specific other organisms, macro and micro. Shift this protagonist—human, bacterium, or what have you—from one short run to another and you may be shifting from a game of chess to a rugby scrum. In fact, you may bring about that appalling transformation simply by the act of arriving unannounced in somebody else's chess tournament.

An example may help. Henry VIII reigned in England in the first half of the sixteenth century, and he worried about Francis I of France and not about kings in general. He married Catherine of Aragon through Catherine Parr, and not (not even Henry) women in general. He ate wheat and beef, not food in general. He was subject to specific variants of specific diseases, plague in particular, and not to disease in general. For instance, his immune system was as unacquainted with— that is, was no more fit to defend him against—yellow fever as he was unqualified to conduct guided tours of the Niger Delta.

Henry VIII was a thorough Renaissance Englishman, as hermetically sealed in his time and space as anyone could be in a spaceship or colony. If he had access to a time machine and if he had had used one to join us here and now, he would find our clothes silly, our English nearly unintelligible, our food weird, our cattle and sheep all giants, the variety of our breeds of dogs nearly infinite, and our women disobedient. He would fall sick with a number of our diseases because his immune system would be no better prepared to protect him from our pathogens than he himself, an excellent musician, would be to play music on instruments tuned according to the system of equal temperament celebrated by Johann Sebastian Bach in the eighteenth-century preludes and fugues of his "Well-Tempered Clavier."

The bacterial flora of Henry's alimentary canal would be different from ours, and as ours invaded his ample gut, he would become the first time traveler to suffer from *turistas*. He would simultaneously or shortly thereafter fall victim to invasions by such constantly altering viruses as those of the common cold and influenza. He would be liable to infection by the bacteria of Legionnaires' disease, which some experts suggest came to its present state of virulence in the special environment of our air conditioners, which, of course, did not exist in the sixteenth century. King Henry, a Renaissance organism (or from the point of view of microlife, a Renaissance ecosystem), would be out of place—in this case out of time—and susceptible to all kinds of alien infections and infestations.

In addition, he would be a threat to us. He could be carrying fleas—the sixteenth century was not fastidious about cleanliness—and the fleas could be carrying the bacteria of plague, one of the chief killers of his age. We have antibiotics to cure plague, but how could we be sure they would be effective against strains of microlife 450 years out of date? Henry might be carrying the spirochetes of syphilis ("the frensshe pockes"), a disease slow to wreak havoc in the individual human body in our time but a kind of galloping leprosy in the sixteenth century, as you might expect of a spanking-new malady that had first been noted in Europe in the 1490s. Henry might bring to our century the organisms that caused the English Sweats, an infection that killed many in his lifetime, organisms for which we probably have no defenses in place because the disease has not appeared—at least not in its virulent form—since.

But this is all fiction. We have resorted to a time machine to assure that our traveler moves from one short-run situation to what would clearly be a very different one. Is there no history, no example from reality, to illustrate the kinds of danger that space dwellers might present to one another? There is: history is full of examples. We have, you see, done all this launching into space before.

Humanity taught itself to live in environments for which it was not and still is not genetically adapted—first by learning how to make tools and then by learning how to make clothing and use fire. However, although this diffusion into new environments spread humanity far and wide, the great majority of human groups were in at least occasional contact with other groups, even though the intervals between contacts might be a matter of generations.

After a long while, *Homo sapiens,* having sifted through Africa and Eurasia, went elsewhere. During the later millennia of the Pleistocene, when much of the world's water was fixed in continental glaciers and the levels of the oceans were lower than they are today, some humans gradually, over a period of generations, migrated from Siberia into Alaska and thence all the way to Tierra del Fuego. Others moved southeast from Asia, skipping over the narrow gaps between the islands of Indonesia, arrived in New Guinea, and from there walked into Australia. By the end of the Pleistocene, humans were by all measures the most widely distributed of all large animals. They had occupied, at least thinly, all the habitable parts of the globe except Madagascar, New Zealand, and smaller islands.

Then the world heated up, the glaciers retreated, the oceans rose, isolating the avant-garde of the human race in the Americas and Australia. A few millennia later the Polynesians, a sort of Johnny-come-lately avant-garde, attained similar isolation by sailing out and settling the atolls and volcanic islands of the pelagic Pacific.

Their isolation and that of the first Americans and Australians would have lasted until oceans fell again or tectonic drift brought continents thumping up against each other—but for human inventiveness. Our teeth and claws are not impressive, but our brains make up for their inadequacies. As of, say, A.D. 1000 there was little if any contact across the Atlantic or Pacific. The various human cultures on opposite sides of those oceans had grown up in isolation, as had the flora and fauna, macro and micro, and the various systems of biological homeostasis.

During the period Europeans call the Middle Ages, peoples of the Old World made important advances in transportation technology. Stirrups, the horse collar, and such may seem minor advances from our perspective, but they were of enormous importance in an age when power was chiefly muscular. Naval transportation technology advanced too. Hull design, sail and rigging design, and navigational instruments and techniques improved more in a few centuries than in the previous two millennia. The results are perhaps the most awesome example of the influence of technology of all time.

The three great naval traditions of the Old World were those of Europe, the Middle East, including the Muslim areas of India, and China. The Muslims were great sailors, coursing back and forth century after century between the Middle East and India at the center and East Africa and Southeast Asia at the periphery. But they rarely sailed outside the Indian Ocean and East Asian seas and did not go on to conquer the Atlantic and Pacific. Why? Possibly because the monsoons, sweeping out of central Asia in winter and back in from the oceans in summer, solved most of their sailing and navigational problems for free, so to speak. After 1000 or 1100, the Chinese and, lagging somewhat behind, the Europeans took over unequivocal leadership in the arts and sciences of nautics.

Chinese navigation right up to the sixteenth century was at least as good as European, and their vessels larger and probably more seaworthy. They had sternpost rudders instead of inefficient steering oars; their hulls slipped through the water with less turbulence and drag and were squarer in cross-section, providing a more stable carrier for more freight than the Occidental equivalent. The Chinese divided their hulls into watertight compartments, giving their vessels the multiple lives Westerners claim for their cats. More important, their bamboo-stiffened sails, capable of turning a nearly rigid edge into the wind, were better than any Western equivalent for beating into the wind.

The Europeans were behind, but making advances too. They adopted the lateen sail from the Arabs, which enabled them also to tack into the wind; the sternpost rudder, possibly taken indirectly from Chinese examples; and schemes of multiple masts and sails, also possibly of Chinese provenance. The compass arrived, probably from the Far East, by the thirteenth century.

The Age of Exploration, of transoceanic voyaging, was about to begin. The first and greatest admiral of the age, in terms of the size of his fleets, was Cheng Ho, chief eunuch to the emperor of China. The eunuch built fleets of scores of ships, many of the vessels among the largest in the world, capable of carrying tens of thousands of officers and men. He personally led or organized and dispatched seven expeditions between 1405 and 1433. They sailed to Siam, the East Indies, and beyond to India, Ormuz, Aden, and East Africa—to Malindi, where a single lifetime later Vasco da Gama would pick up a pilot to guide him across to India. Cheng Ho's last expedition returned to China in 1433, and two years later his emperor died. The conservative Confucianists and rural landlords who dominated the courts of succeeding emperors directed China's attention back to her domestic and dry land affairs. China—on the brink of everything—did an about-face. Europe took over the lead on the high seas.

In 1291, the Vivaldi brothers from Genoa sailed out of the Mediterranean with a plan to circumnavigate Africa and were never heard of again. European naval technologies were not yet up to such a task, but improvements came and with them the kind of successes of which the Vivaldis had dreamed. Italian, Mallorcan, Breton, and Iberian sailors, navigators, and shipbuilders learned the rudiments of oceanic seamanship in the fourteenth and fifteenth centuries and discovered or rediscovered the Canaries, Madeira, and the Azores. In 1488, Dias found the way around Africa, and in 1492 Columbus the way to America. In 1521, the survivors of Magellan's fleet completed the very first circumnavigation of the globe. The continents, which had been connected by land in the Pleistocene, were reunited with a sailmaker's needle.

The ecological facet of this reunification was by far its most spectacular. The first examples of the wild oscillations that commonly follow upon contact between previously isolated ecosystems actually predate the voyages of Columbus. Early in the fifteenth century his future father-in-law innocently brought the first rabbits to Porto Santo, the companion island of Madeira, and in a year or so the colonists had to get out because multitudes of rabbits were eating everything they planted. In the Canary Islands the indigenes, called Guanches, who numbered in the tens of thousands in 1400, were plunging toward extinction by 1492. The cause of their demise was not so much European brutality, of which there was plenty, but alien diseases. *La peste* and *modorra,* whatever they may be precisely, swept through the Guanche populations in the 1480s and 1490s.

These happenings were omens of what was to follow. The European arrival in the Americas set off what are the most awesome ecological events in recorded history. Diseases unknown in the New World—like smallpox, measles, yellow fever, and malaria—rolled through the two continents and, reinforced by the conquerors' penchant for intentional and unintentional genocide, produced the greatest demographic catastrophe in the human record.[1] Demographic historians in general agree that American Indian populations usually declined 50 to 100 percent in the first century after full contact with Europeans and Africans. In central Mexico, where we have the best statistics, this is clearly the case. Smallpox was the chief killer, at least initially, and its impact helps to explain just how and why the conquistadores were so successful. Smallpox accompanied Cortés into the Aztec Empire and preceded Pizarro into the Incan Empire, killing large proportions—no one knows how large—of the peoples of these societies. Death rates of one-third and one-half are often cited and are probably not far from the truth. Other new diseases undoubtedly operated alongside smallpox, as did starvation and war. Similar "virgin soil epidemics" in Polynesia during the last century and in Alaska and the hinterlands of Venezuela and Brazil in our century have produced mortality rates almost as impressive.

While such epidemics transfigured the history of humanity in the Americas, oscillations similar in magnitude were sweeping other species. In 1492 no horses, cattle, sheep, or pigs lived in the New World. Within a hundred years there were millions. Northern Mexico and the pampas of Argentina and Uruguay swarmed with Old World quadrupeds, animals just as wild as their ancestors had been a few thousand years before. The story continues on in our time. In the 1890s a few score European starlings were released in New York's Central Park; today they range from coast to coast and are estimated to number at 100 million.

Similar events mark the histories of Australia and New Zealand. Smallpox slaughtered Australian Aborigines and tuberculosis the New Zealand Maori. In the mid-nineteenth century the first European rabbits were introduced into Australia, and in a hundred years they numbered a half-billion. In New Zealand dozens of Old World species (and Australian ones as well) have become acclimated and have overwhelmed the native creatures over wide areas.

Such biological spectaculars have not been restricted to ecosystems separated by oceans. All that is required is a high degree of isolation and then an abrupt opening of contact. For example, let us turn to Africa in the last years of the nineteenth century. European imperialists had conquered the Americas and Australia with relative ease, but sub-Saharan Africa, populated by peoples with iron weapons and a strong military tradition and defended by yellow fever, malaria, amoebic dysentery, and such, remained independent all the way to 1850 and beyond. Then advances in sanitation and medical science enabled Europeans to penetrate tropical Africa with reasonable safety. Historians call what followed "carving the African melon."

Europe entered Africa, and the ecological disruptions were severe. The most spectacular of these pertain to rinderpest, a commonly fatal viral disease of hooved animals, especially cattle, which apparently was entirely absent from Africa south of the Sahara. It arrived in the 1880s, probably with the cattle brought from Russian and other Black Sea ports to feed the British Army in Sudan and/or with cattle the Italians imported from India and Aden to provide for their invasion of Ethiopia. The disease was first reported in Somaliland in 1889, reached Uganda the next year, Lake Nyasa in 1892, and raced on south and west. "Never before in the memory of man," wrote one witness, "or by the voice of tradition had cattle died in such numbers." Peoples dependent on them, like the Masai, starved in large numbers. Wild game, the usual source of food during famine, was not there to save the Masai this time because the African ungulates fell before the new disease in windrows. Two-thirds of the Masai died, says Oscar Baumann, who was there to see it.

Bringing previously isolated ecosystems together is much like flicking a cigarette lighter near open containers of gasoline. Some of the time nothing will happen. Some of the time the fumes will ignite and blow your head off. Ecological explosions will not always happen if societies and ecosystems that we plant beyond Earth are carelessly brought together after long intervals of separation, but such detonations will take place some of the time, and they will be very difficult to deal with. Measures taken to control the propagation of one or several kinds of organisms will be dangerous to all—especially in situations in which airing out the room will not be a corrective action with much appeal to the rational traveler.

Interstellar migration will maximize the rates of differentiation among the groups of migrants: humans, plants, animals, and microlife. Such groups will develop from small initial stocks, maximizing the founder effect—that is, the inevitable initial differences will magnify over the generations. These stocks will propagate in quite possibly very different environments, and will very probably evolve in hermetic isolation from one another. The moments when they meet will not only be times of extreme opportunity but also of extreme danger for all organisms involved. Humans, who reproduce much more slowly and less often than the other organisms they will intentionally and unintentionally take with them, and whose immune systems react slowly to assaults by unfamiliar enemies, will be hard put to survive the biological chaos that will often follow.

We are sometimes told by optimists that such disasters can be avoided. One, space travelers will all be inoculated against all the standard diseases, and vaccines will be taken along into the void. But effective vaccines do not exist for every disease—AIDS, for instance —and pathogens evolve; the flu vaccine of 1963 gives little protection against the flu virus of 1993. Furthermore, we are now learning that there are infections that take decades to manifest themselves. Providing defenses against them requires miracles of foresight. It may be true that viral DNA can lurk unmanifested within the nuclei of reproductive cells for entire lifetimes, be passed on to descendants, and then declare independence and cause disease and dysfunction. The whole mystery of the relationship between "our" genetic materials and those bits of genetic information we call viruses may contain jolly surprises for humans sealed in tiny quarters whizzing through the interstellar vacuum.

The optimists assure us that extreme care will be taken to restrict space travel to humans plus just those species that humans want as sources of food, oxygen, and companionship and to recycle waste. But such measures will not preclude microstowaways because there is no way to fully sterilize living things inside and out without killing them. Large organisms, like humans, pigs, and cabbages, are gardens of microorganisms, some of which are indeed very likely essential to their health. In addition, we have to consider that a large organism absolutely free of bacterial occupants would be an open invitation to new occupants. Such an organism would be occupied by the first microlife to come along, and the odds are in favor of the occupation being rated by the occupied as a severe infection.

Species, said Charles Darwin in the nineteenth century, are not stable, and they certainly will not be in the twenty-first century. We are assured that space travel will provide plenty of time for genetic change, during which, incidentally, the radiation levels are likely to be higher than on Earth, accelerating that change. Preparing for mutations—what will that be like? Surely, nourishing, fast-growing, tasty molds, likely candidates for space travel, can under certain conditions produce off-spring that will take happily to growing on and in the organic plastics that compose or enclose much of our electronic and other gear.

Humans over time can take measures to bring such threats under control, but when space societies meet, such threats will sometimes rise up meteorically. Your staphylococci is for you a cause of pimples; for me and my comrades it is a cause of confluent rashes, massive loss of fluids, and pioneers for dangerous secondary infections.

We can prepare for the predictable threats of the void—the vacuum, the cold, the heat, the radiation. We will find it very difficult to prepare for the threats that arise from the organic nature of ourselves and of the forms of life we will take with us. Put as simply as possible, the problem is this: we can shake loose from our home planet, but we most assuredly cannot leave DNA behind us.

Note

1. For the latest consideration of this matter, see John W. Verano and Douglas H. Ubelaker, eds., *Disease and Demography in the Americas* (Washington, D.C.: Smithsonian Institution Press, 1992), passim.

INDEX

Alfred W. Crosby is professor of American studies at the University of Texas, Austin. He was educated at Harvard and Boston universities. Professor Crosby specializes in environmental and ecological history and in historical epidemiology. Among his many publications are the books *America's Forgotten Pandemic: The Influenza of 1918* (1989); *Ecological Imperialism: The Biological Expansion of Europe, 900–1900* (1986); and *The Columbian Exchange: Biological and Cultural Consequences of 1492* (1972).